Dialogism

Bakhtin and his world

MICHAEL HOLQUIST

London and New York

First published 1990

Reprinted in 1991

by Routledge
11 New Fetter Lane, London EC4P 4EE
29 West 35th Street, New York, NY 10001

© 1990 Michael Holquist

Typeset by Megaron, Cardiff, Wales
Printed in Great Britain by
TJ Press (Padstow) Ltd, Padstow, Cornwall

British Library Cataloguing in Publication Data
Holquist, Michael
    Dialogism : Bakhtin and his world.
    1. Literature. Theories of Bakhtin, M.
    I. Title
    801

    ISBN 0-415-01179-5
    ISBN 0-415-01180-9 pbk

Library of Congress Cataloging in Publication Data
also available

This book is dedicated to
Nicko and Bas

Contents

General editor's preface

It is easy to see that we are living in a time of rapid and radical social change. It is much less easy to grasp the fact that such change will inevitably affect the nature of those academic disciplines that both reflect our society and help to shape it.

Yet this is nowhere more apparent than in the central field of what may, in general terms, be called literary studies. Here, among large numbers of students at all levels of education, the erosion of the assumptions and presuppositions that support the literary disciplines in their conventional form has proved fundamental. Modes and categories inherited from the past no longer seem to fit the reality experienced by a new generation.

New Accents is intended as a positive response to the initiative offered by such a situation. Each volume in the series will seek to encourage rather than resist the process of change, to stretch rather than reinforce the boundaries that currently define literature and its academic study.

Some important areas of interest immediately present themselves. In various parts of the world, new methods of analysis have been developed whose conclusions reveal the limitations of Anglo-American outlook we inherit. New concepts of literary forms and modes have been proposed; new notions of the nature of literature itself, and of how it communicates, are current; new views of literature's role in relation to society flourish. *New Accents* will aim to expound and comment upon the most notable of these.

In the broad field of the study of human communication, more and more emphasis has been placed upon the nature and function of the new electronic media. *New Accents* will try to identify and discuss the challenge these offer to our traditional modes of critical response.

The same interest in communication suggests that the series should also concern itself with those wider anthropological and sociological areas of investigation which have begun to involve scrutiny of the nature of art itself and of its relation to our whole way of life. And this will ultimately require attention to be focused on some of those activities which in our society have hitherto been excluded from the prestigious realms of Culture. The disturbing realignment of values involved and the disconcerting nature of the pressures that work to bring it about both constitute areas that *New Accents* will seek to explore.

Finally, as its title suggests, one aspect of *New Accents*, will be firmly located in contemporary approaches to language, and a continuing concern of the series will be to examine the extent to which relevant branches of linguistic studies can illuminate specific literary areas. The volumes with this particular interest will nevertheless presume no prior technical knowledge on the part of their readers, and will aim to rehearse the linguistics appropriate to the matter in hand, rather than to embark on general theoretical matters.

Each volume in the series will attempt an objective exposition of significant developments in its field up to the present as well as an account of its author's own views of the matter. Each will culminate in an informative bibliography as a guide to further study. And while each will be primarily concerned with matters relevant to its own specific interests, we can hope that a kind of conversation will be heard to develop between them: one whose accents may perhaps suggest the distinctive discourse of the future.

TERENCE HAWKES

Introduction

In an earlier book, *Mikhail Bakhtin* (by Katerina Clark and Michael Holquist, and published by Harvard University Press in 1984), an attempt was made to present Bakhtin's life and thought in as neutral a manner as possible. Of course, the impossibility of being neutral is one of the founding assumptions of dialogism; I invoke the word merely to suggest that every attempt was made to give the facts as we knew them, without knowingly interpreting them to conform to our own views, even when what we were reporting was at odds with our own values. For instance, I am a non-believer (*neveruyushchiĭ*, неверующий, with all the cultural baggage that term carries in Russian), and yet no attempt was made to downplay the fact that throughout his life Bakhtin was a deeply religious (if also highly eccentric) man, for whom certain Russian Orthodox traditions were of paramount importance.

This book differs from the earlier study in a number of respects, largely because – although drawing on all Bakhtin's texts known to exist – it does not seek to give equal treatment to all of them. Certain works are highlighted, while others are mentioned only in passing. The attempt here is to be as economical as possible, without ceasing to be responsible, in the dialogic sense of that word. Dialogism is a phenomenon that is still very much an open event. Any attempt to be "comprehensive" or "authoritative" would be misguided. This book provides nothing more – or less – than a personal view of what one reasonably intelligent reader has deduced to be significant about dialogism after having spent some years reading, translating, editing, and teaching Bakhtin's work.

I
Bakhtin's life

Mikhail Mikhailovich Bakhtin was born on November 16, 1895
(November 4, old style) in Orel, a medium-sized town south of
Moscow.[1] His father was a bank executive who came of an old
but not particularly distinguished family of the minor nobility.
As a child, Bakhtin was educated at home; his governess was a
German woman of unusual gifts, and from an early age Bakhtin
was bilingual in German and Russian. His life up to 1918, when
he left Petersburg (or, as it then was, Petrograd) University,
could not have been more in character for a man who was to
become a student of heteroglossia (many-languagedness). Since
his father's job required frequent transfers, the adolescent
Bakhtin spent his *gymnasium* years in Vilnius and Odessa, two
cities that stood out even in the patchwork Russian empire as
unusually heterogeneous in their mix of cultures and languages.
Vilnius was part of the ancient Lithuanian kingdom that had
been ceded to the Romanovs after the third partition of Poland
in 1795; thus the "official language" was Russian, but the
majority of citizens spoke Lithuanian or Polish. Vilnius was also
the intellectual center of East European Jewry, the "Jerusalem of
the North" famous for its Talmudic exegetes, so Yiddish and
Hebrew were also in the air. Odessa, a busy port on the Black
Sea, was another of East Europe's large Jewish enclaves, and a
city in whose streets mingled several different cultures, each with
its own language.

In 1913, Bakhtin entered the local university in Odessa, but transferred the following year to St Petersburg University; in his *gymnasium* years he had passionately studied Latin and (especially) Greek, so he registered in the classics department of the historico-philological faculty, following in the steps of his older brother Nikolai, who was two years ahead of him at the university. Nikolai, an extraordinary figure in his own right, inspired Mikhail's lifelong love affair with the Hellenistic age. Indeed, he was in general the greatest influence on the youthful Bakhtin until the two were separated in 1918, never to see each other again. Nikolai joined the White Guards and, after many adventures, ended up as professor of linguistics in Birmingham University, England, where he died in 1950.

In the spring of 1918, Bakhtin, like many others, sought relief from the chaos that followed in the immediate wake of the revolution by going into the country districts where food and fuel were more abundant. He ended up first in Nevel, and then in nearby Vitebsk. In both places, he quickly became a member of a small group of intellectuals who feverishly threw themselves into the debates, lectures, demonstrations, and manifesto writing that characterized life at that extraordinary time. It was in this atmosphere of immense intellectual and political intensity that Bakhtin sought to think through for himself some of the problems then of most concern to philosophers, such as (to name only a few) the status of the knowing subject, the relation of art to lived experience, the existence of other persons, and the complexities of responsibility in the area of discourse as well as in the area of ethics.

Bakhtin had already immersed himself in philosophy from a very early age, particularly in ancient Greek, Hellenistic, and modern European philosophy. He read the German systematic philosophers, as well as Buber and Kierkegaard, while still a *gymnasium* student in Vilnius and Odessa. At university, he trained as a scholar in the Greek and Latin classics as they were taught in the old German philological tradition, in which the study of literature and language were inextricably bound up with each other. In addition, Tadeusz Zielinski, his eminent professor of classics, emphasized the need to know the complete spectrum of classical civilization, including philosophy.

Thus Bakhtin's interests were broad, but no more so than those of the group of young people he joined in 1918, although it was the latest work in philosophy that attracted their most passionate attention. It was here, in the study and disputation of texts by contemporary German philosophers, that the nucleus of an ongoing "Bakhtin circle" was formed. It included the then musicologist Valentin Voloshinov, and the then journalist and organizer of literary events Pavel Medvedev, both of whose names would later become intertwined with Bakhtin's in disputes over the authorship of several texts written in the 1920s.

Until 1924 at least, then, Bakhtin was surrounded by intense philosophical debates. These took place not only in his friends' study circle (of which he very soon became the intellectually dominant member), but in public forums organized by the local Communist Party committee.

The particular school which dominated the academic study of philosophy in Europe during these years, and which was of great importance to the young Bakhtin, was Neo-Kantianism. Since this school has now fallen into some obscurity, a few words will perhaps be helpful on at least those aspects of it that are germane to Bakhtin. By 1918, Neo-Kantianism had been the dominant school of philosophy in Germany for almost fifty years. From roughly the 1870s until the 1920s, most professors of philosophy in Germany defined themselves by taking a position *vis-à-vis* Kant. This period corresponds to a time when Germany was considered by most Russians to be the home of true philosophical thought. Chairs at the leading universities not only in Germany but in Russia as well were held by Neo-Kantians of one kind or another. They were particularly well entrenched at Petersburg University during the years when Bakhtin was a student there.[2]

Although Neo-Kantianism was a widespread phenomenon embracing several philosophies that were highly varied in their concerns, the one feature of Kant's thought they all had to confront was his formulation of the mind's relation to the world, the insistence on a constructive epistemology at the heart of his "Copernican revolution."

In Kant's view, his predecessors had either, like Leibniz, overemphasized the role of ideas, thus diminishing the role of the world outside the mind; or, like Locke, they had gone too far in the opposite direction and by sensualizing concepts had made the mind merely a receptor of information provided by sensations from the world. Kant's breakthrough was to insist on the necessary interaction – the *dialogue* as Bakhtin would come to interpret it – between mind and world.

Kant argued that what we call thought is really a synthesis of two forms of knowledge: sensibility and understanding. "Sensibility" may be taken roughly to mean what empiricists such as Locke or Hume assumed to be the sole basis of knowledge, the realm of physical sensation. And Kant's use of "understanding" is roughly what rationalists, such as Leibniz, assumed to be the sole basis of knowledge, the realm of concepts in the mind.

The ability to think, which Kant assumed to mean the ability to make judgments, requires *both* forms of knowledge, which he triumphantly brought together in his "transcendental synthesis": a priori concepts exist *in* the mind, but they can be used to actively organize sensations from the world *outside* the mind. The world, the realm of things-in-themselves, really exists, but so does the mind, the realm of concepts. Thought is the give and take between the two.

Those who came after Kant interpreted this synthesis in various ways. The Marburg School, the particular Neo-Kantianism in which the young Bakhtin steeped himself, was founded at the University of Marburg by Hermann Cohen.[3] Cohen radically revised the mind/world relation as Kant had defined it. He emphasized the transcendental aspects of Kant's synthesis, pursuing the quest for a oneness so immaculate that it made him a hero to other seekers after metaphysical purity, such as the young Pasternak who in 1912 travelled to Marburg to sit at the feet of the great man. And it was the same lust for unity in Cohen that inspired another Russian, Lenin, to attack him as a particularly virulent idealist.[4] What attracted Pasternak and repelled Lenin was the same quality in Cohen: his opposition to the potential dualism in Kant's account of how internal thought relates to the external world. Cohen had a remarkably precise mind, and his philosophy is a model of the kind of systematic thought that sought to unify all operations of consciousness. Roughly stated, his method for doing so was to abandon Kant's notion of the thing-in-itself in order to declare a "logic of pure knowing"[5] in which there is only a realm of concepts: the world exists as the subject of thought, and the subject of thought, no matter how material it might appear, is still always a subject that is *thought*.

Bakhtin's connection with the Marburg School was relatively direct, in that his closest friend during the years he was in Nevel' and Vitebsk was Matvei Isaevich Kagan, who returned to Nevel' from Germany almost simultaneously with Bakhtin's arrival there from Petrograd. Kagan was a man of remarkable intellect who commanded the respect of all who came into contact with him. Originally fleeing from Russia's Jewish Pale to Germany to escape persecution, and intending to pursue study in mathematics and physics, he had instead taken up the study of philosophy with Cohen in Marburg. Kagan's move from the exact sciences to philosophy was not unusual in the years before the First World War, when scientists such as von Helmholtz sought to reinterpret Kant through the logic of mathematics and the workings of the human nervous system, or when physicists such as Ernst Mach applied what they had learned about the nature of matter and energy in the laboratory to the great questions of metaphysics. The Marburg School was the version of academic Neo-Kantianism most concerned to unite new discoveries in the sciences with the study of philosophy; so Kagan, the erstwhile mathematician, felt quite at home in the old German university on the heights above the river Lahn. But Kagan's budding career as a philosopher in Germany was interrupted by the outbreak of the war in 1914. For the next four years he was held as an enemy alien (although Cohen himself had intervened on his behalf), being released for repatriation to Russia only after the signing of the treaty of Brest-Litovsk in 1918. The enthusiasm of Bakhtin and his other friends for German philosophy was given new depth and impetus by Kagan's return.

Two general aspects of Marburg Neo-Kantianism that played an important role in the composition of Bakhtin's early work should be emphasized. The first of these is the Neo-Kantian desire to relate traditional problems in philosophy to the great new discoveries about the world and nature being made in the exact and biological sciences on the cusp of the nineteenth and twentieth centuries. Bakhtin himself was greatly interested in science, particularly the new physics of Planck, Einstein, and Bohr, as well as in current developments in physiology, or more precisely the study of the central nervous system, an area in which Petersburg was one of the world centers. His closest friends were either lapsed mathematicians such as Kagan or, in later years, the biologist (and historian of science) Ivan Kanaev. This aspect of his activity will perhaps explain the attention paid to questions of perception and materiality in Bakhtin. Dialogism shares in the general effort of thinkers after Einstein and Bohr to come to grips with new problems raised by relativity and quantum theory for anyone concerned with the traditional issues of how mind relates to body, and how physical matter connects with such apparently immaterial entities as relations between things. There is a certain ambiguity about these issues in Bakhtin's philosophy, deriving in some measure from ambiguities inherent in the treatment of the same topics in contemporary science. Einstein was arguing that physical objects were not static matter, but forms of volatile energy. It is perhaps not surprising, then, that matter – while still being a basic category for philosophers and physicists alike – should have lost the kind of certainty that had previously made it seem so convincing when materialists confounded their more idealistic colleagues by merely kicking a stone. In Bakhtin's youth, the clear-cut distinctions that had so unproblematically been assumed in traditional (binary) distinctions between matter and mind, or body and soul were fast being eroded.

A second aspect of the Marburg School's activity that proved to be important in Bakhtin's development was the emphasis of its founder on unity and oneness. Bakhtin was not merely a passive receptor of Neo-Kantian ideas. One of the most important ways he demonstrates his independence from Cohen, even at this early stage, is in his resistance to the idea of an all-encompassing oneness, or *Allheit*. In this, Bakhtin is perhaps best understood as a figure who is trying to get back to the other side of Kant's synthesis, the world, rather than the mind (and in particular the rational mind), the extreme to which Cohen tended. The original Kantian concept of the heterogeneity of ends is much closer to Bakhtin's work than the later Neo-Kantian lust for unity.

During his years in Nevel' and Vitebsk, from 1918 to 1924, Bakhtin pursued a number of different writing projects, all of which, in one form or another, may be seen as an attempt to rethink the possibility of constructing a wholeness in terms more complex than those provided by the Marburg School. Kant's version of how mind and world related to each other defined the knowing subject as one who made sense out of the otherwise inchoate matter of the world. In such early essays as "Author and hero in aesthetic activity" or "Toward a philosophy of the deed," Bakhtin's understanding of perception as an act of *authoring* brings him closer to Kant himself than to Cohen, in so far as he rethinks the problem of wholeness in terms of what is an essentially *aesthetic* operation. In those essays, the individual subject is conceived as similar to the artist who seeks to render brute matter, a thing that is *not* an art work in itself (independent of the artist's activity), into something that *is* the kind of conceptual whole we can recognize as a painting or a text. Cohen's lust for unity, with its attendant rationalism, was not what drew Bakhtin to the sage of Marburg. It was rather his emphasis on *process*, the radical "*un*-givenness" of experience, with its openness and energy – the loopholes in existence – that attracted him.

With the exception of one small piece that was published in a short-lived provincial newspaper, none of what Bakhtin was writing during these years was published. But the philosophical underpinnings of the work he would do for the rest of his life were established during these crucial years.

In 1924, Bakhtin returned to Petrograd, on the eve of its transformation into Leningrad. Although a time of great hardship, during which he lived on the earnings his wife eked out by making stuffed animals from old rags, the next six years were the most active of his life. Bakhtin was unable to take a normal job, because he was both politically suspect (for participating in several discussion circles which had connections with banned groups of Orthodox believers in the "catacomb church") and an invalid (in Nevel' he had contracted the severe osteomyelitis which would necessitate amputation of his right leg in 1938). Although there was hardly money for the endless tea and cigarettes Bakhtin required to work, life was not bad: not working meant there was more time to read and talk to friends, some of whom went back to the Nevel'/Vitebsk discussion circle, and others of whom were newly made, such as the eminent biologist Ivan Kanaev, who permitted the Bakhtins to live in his relatively spacious quarters just off Nevsky Prospekt, the city's main thoroughfare.

But most of all, there was time to write, and during the years from 1924 to 1929 Bakhtin wrote several of the books that would later bring him fame. He abandoned his earlier, rather technical philosophical style for one that was more popular – or at least easier for most people to read. He (and others) would later claim that he published some work from this period under the names of his friends Medvedev ("The formal method in literary study," 1928), Voloshinov ("Freudianism: a critical sketch," 1927; "Marxism and the philosophy of language," 1929), and Kanaev (a two-part article, "Contemporary vitalism", 1926).[6] The claim has struck many subsequent scholars as questionable, and a whole literature has developed on the topic of these texts' disputed authorship.[7] This is not the place to go into the arcana of the dispute, but the reader of this book should be aware that I hold to the opinion that Bakhtin is, in his own charged sense of the word, primarily responsible for the texts in question and that I have treated them accordingly in this book.

One consequence of doing so is to see a shift in the conversation Bakhtin conducted throughout his life. During the late 1920s and early 1930s Bakhtin switched from participation in debates about aesthetics, the status of the subject, and the philosophy of religion (which is not the same as religion itself) – topics heavily influenced by contemporary events in German intellectual life – to the great issues of the day in the Soviet Union. These included controversy in several different disciplines about the relation their traditional methodologies bore to Communist doctrine: how would psychology, linguistics, and literary theory look when inter-illuminated by Marxist theory and Bolshevik practice?

Bakhtin participated (under his own name or that of one of his friends) in all these methodological and political struggles. In the 1928 Medvedev book he took exception to work done by the Russian Formalists, while also pointing out limitations in the still very poorly developed area of Marxist literary theory. In the Voloshinov books, he attacked Freud for his inability to imagine a collective subject for psychoanalysis, and Saussure for failing to recognize the importance of history and everyday speech in his theory of language. And under his own name, he published a book (*Problems in the work of Dostoevsky*, 1929) that argued against the hegemony of absolute authorial control. Thus all of the work that can be associated with his name during this period

– while continuing to extend his attacks on the transcendental ego, continuing further to underline the need always to take others and otherness into account, and continuing to emphasize plurality and variety – also lent itself to the *new* conditions as arguments against the increasing homogenization of cultural and political life in the Soviet Union that would culminate in the long night of Stalinism.

A sign of how things were going was Bakhtin's arrest in 1929; although he was never told exactly why he had been picked up, it can reasonably be surmised that it was in connection with a sweep of intellectuals associated with the underground church. After a brief period when it looked as if he was going to be sent to certain death in the dreaded hard labor camp in the Solovetsky islands of the far north, Bakhtin was sentenced to an easier exile in Kazakhstan. He was saved from this camp by his patently bad health, but only after intervention by (among others) the wife of Maxim Gorky, who had been approached by Bakhtin's wife, Elena Alexandrovna, and his old friend Kagan, who had become a rising star as a mathematician in the prestigious governmental commission on Soviet energy reserves. Bakhtin was sent to Kustenai, where he worked during the day teaching the almost illiterate former partisans who now ran Kazakhstan how to do bookkeeping, while at night continuing his studies on the history of the novel. Supplied with crates of books by Kagan and Kanaev, Bakhtin finished a number of monographs in the general area of the theory of the novel, including the very important "Discourse in the novel" (1934–5) and the long essay on the chronotope (1937–8).

Bakhtin's term of exile came to an end in 1934, but he stayed on in Kazakhstan for another two years, for although the area was particularly hard hit by the horrors of collectivization (it has been estimated that over 1.5 million Kazakhs lost their lives at this time, either through execution or starvation), he was able to make a better life in Kustenai than if he returned to Leningrad or Moscow, where many released political prisoners were being rearrested. In the years leading up to the Second World War, Bakhtin moved about a great deal; he worked for a year in Saransk, at the Mordovian Pedagogical Institute, where he was virtually a one-man literature department, but escaped possible rearrest in the great purge of 1937 by fleeing to Savelovo, a small town on the Volga, where he was able to work fairly undisturbed. During this period he finished two more long manuscripts. The first, called "The novel of education and its significance in the history of realism," was completed in 1938, but was mostly lost because the publishing house that was to bring it out was destroyed by the Germans in the early months of the war; the second was to be submitted to the Gorky Institute of World Literature for a postgraduate degree. It was completed in 1941, but was not published until twenty-five years later as a book on Rabelais. Both books were directed in subtle (and some not so subtle) ways against the official doctrine of Socialist Realism, further indications of Bakhtin's peculiarly decentered way of acting out his responsibility in the historical events of his time.

After the German invasion, restrictions were loosened all over the Soviet Union, and Bakhtin, who had previously been banned from teaching in the high schools for fear he would corrupt the young, was permitted to teach German (using captured Nazi propaganda leaflets that were dropped on the town in both languages) and Russian in the Savelovo *gymnasium*. When the war ended, Bakhtin was recalled to Saransk, where the former teachers' college had been declared a university, and he was made chair of the faculty of "Russian and world literature." In 1947, his dissertation on Rabelais was accepted, but, after great controversy, he was given not the degree of Doctor but the lower one of Candidate. For several years Bakhtin was an enormously successful teacher in Saransk, and became something of a local legend. Through a combination of luck and circumspection (he gave lectures on such delicate topics as "Stalin and the English bourgeoisie"), he escaped rearrest during the insane xenophobia of the anti-cosmopolitan campaigns of the 1950s.

In the early 1960s, a group of young scholars at the Gorky Institute who admired Bakhtin's writings (they knew the Dostoevsky book and had read the Rabelais dissertation in the Institute library) discovered, contrary to their expectations, that Bakhtin had not perished with most of his generation of literary intellectuals. The group, composed of Vadim Kozhinov, Sergei Bocharov, and Georgy Gachev, all of whom would go on to become eminent literary scholars in their own right, dedicated themselves to rescuing Bakhtin from the obscurity into which he had fallen.

There was a dramatic change in Bakhtin's fortunes after 1963, when a second edition of the Dostoevsky book appeared, followed in 1965 by publication of the Rabelais book. Both created a sensation in the Soviet Union. Bakhtin was brought to the Moscow area, but in spite of his new fame, had difficulty getting the necessary permission to live in the city (where residence is very tightly restricted to this day). Through the good offices of one of his young admirers, the daughter of Andropov, the then head of the KGB, he and his wife were put for a time into the state hospital reserved for only the very highest party officials. In 1971, Elena Alexandrovna died, and Bakhtin was distraught for months. He was finally permitted to move into a Moscow apartment in 1972, where he led a quiet life, seeing people, reading proofs for new editions of his earlier works, and writing new essays (largely based on earlier versions of texts he had worked on in the Saransk period). After the death of his wife, Bakhtin revealed to Kozhinov (who, with Bocharov, had by this time become his executor) that there were some unpublished manuscripts in Saransk from his very earliest period of activity. Bakhtin in his last phase turned again to the philosophical questions that had preoccupied him in the early 1920s, and his last activity was to help prepare his earliest texts for republication, which occurred only after his death. Early in the morning of March 7, 1975, Bakhtin finally succumbed to the emphysema that had plagued him (but had not kept him from smoking) in his last years.

In the intervening period almost all his works have been completely translated into several languages, including English. Some stock-taking is now in order. This book is "synoptic" because it treats all the texts of Bakhtin's different styles, periods, and even names (the disputed texts of Kanaev, Medvedev, and Voloshinov) as a single body of work, a position now possible because something like a complete canon has emerged. At the beginning and again at the end of his career, Bakhtin meditated on the different meanings that "consummation" or finishing off might have; he concluded that if done with care and with the constant awareness that the other, too, was an active consciousness, "consummation" could be a kind of gift that one participant in the ongoing dialogue of history could bestow on the other. This book is an attempt to achieve the transgredience necessary at this time to initiate another step in Bakhtin's own consummation.

Bakhtin lived a long life: he was born in 1895 and he died in 1975. His longevity is in itself not so unusual, but in his thought nothing is ever "in itself." If, then, we put his life into the context of the wars, revolutions, famines, exiles, and purges which he managed to live through, the fact that he reached the age of 80 years becomes more remarkable. Given such massive displacements, it is less surprising that for almost sixty of those years he never ceased to think about the mysteries of locating a self. He argued early and late that what a person said was meaningful to the degree his or her utterance answered a question, and the particular set of questions he himself addressed may be understood as growing out of problems that confront anyone seeking to heed Socrates' injunction to "Know thyself!" How could one "know"? And, assuming for the moment that one might somehow be able to know, how could one then know something called a "self" – especially in an age when every sector of knowing raised new challenges to existence of the "self" as anything but the delusion of a discredited metaphysics?

Bakhtin went out of his way to search for the most powerful attacks on the notion of selfhood. Dostoevsky once complained that the atheists of his day were not really very good at inventing arguments against the existence of God, so that in the service of testing his own faith, he had been forced to invent a few of his own. And the more one knows about the life of Bakhtin, the more it seems he found himself in the same dilemma: his meditation on the possibility of selfhood makes its way through the most powerful doubts about its existence that have been raised across the spectrum of the human, social, and even the so-called precise sciences. He was a particularly keen student of questions about individual subjectivity that arose in biology and in physics (which is why some time will be spent in the following pages on parallels between certain turns in the work of Bakhtin and Einstein).

Bakhtin's pondering of such questions is hardly unique in the modern period, of course. More distinctive is his project's radical emphasis on *particularity* and *situatedness*, the degree to which it insists that apparently abstract questions about selfhood are pursuable only when treated as specific questions about *location*.

Given this way of looking at things, it is not surprising that Bakhtin devotes so much attention to questions of time and space, and relations between them. This preoccupation resulted over the years in a reformulation of the question "How can I know myself?" into another question with quite different implications: "How can I know if it is I or another who is talking?" Bakhtin's search for an answer to this last question led him to explore parallels between the conditions at work when any of us speaks in the most common everyday situation on the one hand, and on the other, conditions that obtain when an author writes what we call a literary work. In both cases, utterance is understood as an act of authorship, or, as we shall see in greater detail later on, of *co*-authorship. These two parameters of authorship – utterance as it activates apparently simple address in everyday speech and as it animates complex works of art – constitute the poles between which the following synoptic account of Bakhtin's total *oeuvre* will take its course.

2

Existence as dialogue

Mikhail Bakhtin made important contributions to several different areas of thought, each with its own history, its own language, and its own shared assumptions. As a result, literary scholars have perceived him as doing one sort of thing, linguists another, and anthropologists yet another. We lack a comprehensive term that is able to encompass Bakhtin's activity in all its variety, a shortcoming he himself remarked when as an old man he sought to bring together the various strands of his life's work. At that time he wrote:

> our analysis must be called philosophical mainly because of what it is not: it is not a linguistic, philological, literary or any other particular kind of analysis. . . . On the other hand, a positive feature of our study is this: [it moves] in spheres that are liminal, i.e., on the borders of all the aforementioned disciplines, at their junctures and points of intersection.
>
> (*Estetika*, p. 281)[1]

But if we accept even so privative a sense of "philosophy" as a way to describe the sort of thing Bakhtin does, the question remains: what kind of philosophy is it?

Dialogism as an Epistemology

Stated at the highest level of (quite hair-raising) abstraction, what can only uneasily be called "Bakhtin's philosophy" is a pragmatically oriented theory of knowledge; more particularly, it is one of several modern epistemologies that seek to grasp human behavior through the use humans make of language. Bakhtin's distinctive place among these is specified by the dialogic concept of language he proposes as fundamental. For this reason, the term used in this book to refer to the inter-connected set of concerns that dominate Bakhtin's thinking is "dialogism," a term, I hasten to add, never used by Bakhtin himself. There can be no theoretical excuse for spawning yet another "ism," but the history of Bakhtin's reception seems to suggest that if we are to continue to think about his work in a way that is useful, some synthetic means must be found for categorizing the different ways he meditated on dialogue. That is, some way must be found to conceive his varied activity as a unity, without losing sight of the dynamic heterogeneity of his achievement. Before looking at any of Bakhtin's particular works, it will be useful to have some sense of the ideas that permeate them all. This chapter will seek, then, to lay out in a general way some of the ideas considered by Bakhtin at the beginning of his career, and which – with different shifts of emphasis and new accretions of significance – he never ceased to hold.

Dialogue is an obvious master key to the assumptions that guided Bakhtin's work throughout his whole career: dialogue is present in one way or another throughout the notebooks he kept from his youth to his death at the age of 80. Most of these are lost, some remain in the form of communications so self-directed they are now almost impossible to decipher or understand, while others eventually took on the more public and comprehensible form of published books. But early or late, no matter what the topic of the moment, regardless of the name under which he wrote or the degree of shared communication he presumed, all Bakhtin's writings are animated and controlled by the principle of dialogue. It is becoming increasingly evident that Bakhtin's lifelong meditation on dialogue does not have a place solely in the history of literary theory, capacious as the borders of that subject have recently become. It is now clear that dialogism is also implicated in the history of modern thinking about thinking.

In this it is far from unique: the work of many other recent thinkers, especially in France, combines literary criticism, even literary production, with concerns that are essentially philosophical. But the *kind* of literature and the *kind* of philosophy that are woven together in the writings of a Sartre or a Derrida constitute genres significantly different from those that characterize dialogism. Rousseau, Hegel, Nietzsche, and Heidegger, the philosophers recently "discovered" by students of literature, represent, not surprisingly, the *literary* aspect of philosophy. They are lyrical thinkers, some of whom set out consciously to poeticize metaphysics.

Bakhtin is working out of a very different philosophical tradition, one that is little known, even among many Anglo-American professors of philosophy. The men who constitute a dialogizing background for Bakhtin differ from most thinkers now in fashion in so far as they were, in their own day, very much in the mainstream of academic philosophy. They held chairs in the important German universities and sought to make metaphysics even more systematic than had Hegel (most were, in fact, militantly *anti*-Hegelian, as was Bakhtin himself). Systematic metaphysics is now out of fashion and the names by which philosophy was defined in the latter half of the nineteenth century are for the most part forgotten. It is difficult for most of us now to conceive the passion excited in their time by such men as Hermann Cohen or Richard Avenarius. And if we take the trouble to look into their books, it becomes even harder, for they are written in the forbidding language of German technical philosophy in one of its more complex phases. And there are very few translations. I mention this tradition (emphatically) not to scare anyone away from a deeper involvement in Bakhtin's philosophical roots, but only to make it clear that such an involvement requires the extra effort always required to go beyond the categories and concepts (and translations) currently in fashion.

Dialogism, let it be clear from the outset, is itself not a systematic philosophy. But the specific way in which it refuses to be systematic can only be gauged against the failure of all nineteenth-century metaphysical systems to cope with new challenges raised by the natural and mathematical sciences. The most spectacular of these failures was the increasingly obvious irrelevance of Hegelianism (right *or* left) to the new scientific discoveries. As a result, from the 1860s on, more and more attention was paid to Kant: by the 1890s Neo-Kantianism in one form or another had become the dominant school of philosophy in Germany – and Russia.

Dialogism in the context of neo-Kantianism

There are many reasons why the rallying cry "Back to Kant!" proved so successful, but chief among them was a compatibility between Kant's work and developments in the realm of science outside philosophy. Kant himself had taught scientific subjects for many years before he published his first critique and became known as a philosopher. And the first critique was aimed precisely at the kind of pure reason divorced from experience that would bring Hegel's Absolute Spirit into disrepute in the later nineteenth century, an age when empiricism and experiment were yielding such obvious scientific benefits. In the fields of physics, mathematics, and physiology, such men as Ernst Mach and Wilhelm von Helmholtz were explicitly committed to working out the larger implications of Kant's speculative epistemology not in the philosopher's study, but in the scientist's laboratory, as they charted new paths in physics and physiology.

Dialogism's immediate philosophical antecedents are to be found in attempts made by various Neo-Kantians to overcome the gap between "matter" and "spirit." After the death of Hegel, this gap became increasingly apparent in the growing hostility between science and philosophy. Dialogism, then, is part of a major tendency in European thought to reconceptualize epistemology the better to accord with the new versions of mind and the revolutionary models of the world that began to emerge in the natural sciences in the nineteenth century. It is an attempt to frame a theory of knowledge for an age when relativity dominates physics and cosmology and thus when *non-coincidence* of one kind or another – of sign to its referent, of the subject to itself – raises troubling new questions about the very existence of mind.

Bakhtin begins by accepting Kant's argument that there is an unbridgeable gap between mind and world (but as we shall see, he differs from Kant in assuming that therefore there are things *in themselves*; there may be things outside mind, but they are nevertheless not in themselves). The non-identity of mind and world is the conceptual rock on which dialogism is founded and the source of all the other levels of non-concurring identity which Bakhtin sees shaping the world and our place in it. Bakhtin's thought is a meditation on how we know, a meditation based on *dialogue* precisely because, unlike many other theories of knowing, the site of knowledge it posits is never unitary. I use the admittedly cumbersome term "meditation on knowledge" here, because from his very earliest work Bakhtin is highly critical of what he calls "epistemologism," a tendency pervading all nineteenth- and early twentieth-century philosophy. A theory of knowledge devolves into mere epistemologism when there is posited "a unitary and unique consciousness . . . any determinateness must be derived from itself [thus it] cannot have another consciousness outside itself . . . any unity is its own unity" (*Estetika*, p. 79).

In dialogism, the very capacity to have consciousness is based on *otherness*. This otherness is not merely a dialectical alienation on its way to a sublation that will endow it with a unifying identity in higher consciousness. On the contrary: in dialogism consciousness *is* otherness. More accurately, it is the differential relation between a center and all that is not that center. Now, a caution is in order here. Serious questions have recently been raised about the validity of any discourse that invokes the concept of center, as in various versions of what has come to be called "logocentrism." "Center" has often been used as a name for the unreflective assumption of ontological privilege, the sort of mystification sometimes attacked as the "illusion of presence." It is important from the outset, then, that "center" in Bakhtin's thought be understood for what it is: a *relative* rather than an absolute term, and, as such, one with no claim to absolute privilege, least of all one with transcendent ambitions.

This last point is particularly important, for certain of the terms crucial to Bakhtin's thought, such as "self" and "other," have so often been used as masked claims to privilege. Before we further specify the roles played by these protagonists in Bakhtinian scenarios, the simple yet all-important fact should be stressed again that they always enact a drama *containing more than one actor*.

The fundamental role of simultaneity

Self and other are terms that sound vaguely atavistic in an age remarkable for its celebration of all that is extra- and impersonal.

We are frequently told that not only God has died, but so has the subject. And perhaps no subject is quite so moribund as the particular kind that once was honored as author. It has even been argued with self-immolating eloquence that man (or at least Man) himself has died in history. All these deaths are melodramatic ways of formulating an end to the same thing: the old conviction that the individual subject is the seat of certainty, whether the subject so conceived was named God, the soul, the author, or – my self. Bakhtin, too, is suspicious of untrammeled subjectivity's claims; he perhaps least of all is mystified by them. And he attacks such claims at their root, in the self itself, which is why for him "self" can never be a self-sufficient construct.

It cannot be stressed enough that for him "self" is dialogic, a *relation*. And because it is so fundamental a relation, dialogue can help us understand how other relationships work, even (or especially) those that preoccupy the sometimes stern, sometimes playful new Stoics who most dwell on the death of the subject: relationships such as signifier/signified, text/context, system/history, rhetoric/language, and speaking/writing. We shall explore some of these further in later chapters, not as binary oppositions, but as asymmetric dualisms. But we must begin by recognizing that for Bakhtin the key to understanding all such artificially isolated dualisms is the dialogue between self and other.

Whatever else it is, self/other is a relation of simultaneity. No matter how conceived, simultaneity deals with ratios of same and different in space and time, which is why Bakhtin was always so concerned with space/time. Bakhtin's thought was greatly influenced by the new concepts of time and space that were being proposed by revolutionary physicists after the collapse of the old Newtonian cosmos. In Newton's mechanics it was possible for physical processes to propagate at *infinite* velocity through space. This meant that if one and the same action emanates from one body and reaches another body at the same instant, the process is purely spatial for it has occupied zero time. In Newton's universe, the sum of instants occurring simultaneously over all of space add up to a time that is absolute in the sense that it is a flux of simultaneous instants embracing the whole of the universe. It was, in other words, a dream of unity in *physics* that could serve as the proper setting for a dream of unity in Newton's *theology*, and which could later underwrite in *philosophy* the absolute oneness of consciousness in Hegelian dialectic. Dialogue, by contrast, knows no sublation. Bakhtin insists on differences that cannot be overcome: separateness and simultaneity are basic conditions of existence. Thus the physics proper to such a universe are post-Newtonian. Bakhtin grew up amidst battles that raged over the concepts of space and time among such "empiriocritics" as Mach, his Russian followers (primarily Bogdanov) and his Russian opponents (such as Lenin). Of these scientists and philosophers, the most helpful in grasping Bakhtin's thought is Einstein. Although there can be no question of immediate influence, dialogism is a version of relativity.

Relativity theory and dialogism

Einstein invented a number of just-so stories, or "thought experiments," as a way to elide physical limits on experimentation. Although not directly related, these experiments in some ways correspond to Bakhtin's attempts to use the situation of dialogue as a means for getting around traditional limitations of ideas of the subject. Both resort to what might be called a "philosophical optics," a conceptual means for seeing processes invisible to any other lens. More particularly, both resort to experiments with *seeing* in order to meditate on the necessity of the other. Einstein invented several situations (typically involving people looking at moving objects such as trains) that involve problems in perception raised by the speed of light. For instance, if light travels at a certain velocity in one system and at the same velocity in another system moving without acceleration relative to the first, it is impossible to detect the first system's movement by optical means, no matter how refined: the observer's ability to see motion depends on one body changing its position *vis-à-vis* other bodies. Motion, we have come to accept, has only a relative meaning. Stated differently, one body's motion has meaning only in relation to another body; or – since it is a relation that is mutual – has meaning only in *dialogue* with another body.

Dialogism argues that all meaning is relative in the sense that it comes about only as a result of the relation between two bodies occupying *simultaneous but different* space, where bodies may be thought of as ranging from the immediacy of our physical bodies, to political bodies and to bodies of ideas in general (ideologies). In Bakhtin's thought experiments, as in Einstein's, the position of the observer is fundamental. If motion is to have meaning, not only must there be two different bodies in a relation with each other, but there must as well be someone to grasp the nature of such a relation: the non-centeredness of the bodies themselves requires the center constituted by an observer. But unlike the passive stick figures who are positioned at a point equidistant between two railway trains in the cartoons often used to illustrate Einsteinian motion, Bakhtin's observer is also, simultaneously, an *active participant* in the relation of simultaneity. Conceiving being dialogically means that reality is always experienced, not just perceived, and further that it is experienced from a particular position. Bakhtin conceives that position in kinetic terms as a situation, an event, the event of being a self.

The time and space of self and other

The self, moreover, is an event with a structure. Perhaps predictably for so attentive a student of Kant and post-Newtonian mechanics as Bakhtin, that structure is organized around the categories of space and time. They articulate what has been called the "law of placement" in dialogism, which says everything is perceived from a unique position in existence; its corollary is that the meaning of whatever is observed is shaped by the place from which it is perceived. Bakhtin explicates this law with a just-so story that uses seeing as a means for grasping what is essentially a non-visual situation. He begins with a simple datum from experience; not an observer looking at trains, but an observer looking at another observer. You can see things behind my back that I cannot see, and I can see things behind your back that are denied to your vision. We are both doing essentially the same thing, but from different places: although we are in the same event, that event is different for each of us. Our places are different not only because our bodies occupy different positions in exterior, physical space, but also because we regard the world and each other from different centers in cognitive time/space.

What is cognitive time/space? It is the arena in which all perception unfolds. Dialogism, like relativity, takes it for granted that nothing can be perceived except against the perspective of something else: dialogism's master assumption is that there is no figure without a ground. The mind is structured so that the world is always perceived according to this contrast. More specifically, what sets a figure off from its dialogizing background is the opposition between a time and a space that one consciousness uses to model its own limits (the I-for-myself) and the quite different temporal and spatial categories employed by the same consciousness to model the limits of other persons and things (the not-I-in-me) – and (this is crucial) vice versa.

At a very basic level, then, dialogism is the name not just for a dualism, but for a necessary *multiplicity* in human perception. This multiplicity manifests itself as a series of distinctions between categories appropriate to the perceiver on the one hand and categories appropriate to whatever is being perceived on the other. This way of conceiving things is not, as it might first appear to be, one more binarism, for in addition to these poles dialogism enlists the additional factors of situation and relation that make any specific instance of them more than a mere opposition of categories.

For the perceivers, their own time is forever open and unfinished; their own space is always the center of perception, the point around which things arrange themselves as a horizon whose meaning is determined by wherever they have their place in it. By contrast, the time in which we model others is perceived as closed and finished. Moreover, the space in which others are seen is never a significance-charged surrounding, but a neutral environment, i.e. the homogenizing context of the rest of the world. From the perspective of a self, the other is simply *in* the world, along with everyone and everything else. The contrast between spatial and temporal categories that are appropriate to me and the very different categories I employ to give shape to the other must not be misinterpreted as yet another Romantic claim for primacy of the absolute subject: self for Bakhtin is a cognitive necessity, not a mystified privilege.

We will see this – and the intimate relation dialogism bears to language – if we understand that cognitive time/space is ordered very much as time and space categories are deployed in speech. It has long been recognized that the formal means for expressing subjectivity occupy a unique place in any language. "I" is a word that has no referent in the way "tree," for instance, nominates a class of flora; if "I" is to perform its task as a *pro-noun*, must not be a noun, i.e. it must not refer to anything as other words do. For its task is to indicate the person uttering the present instance of the discourse containing "I," a person who is always changing and different. "I" must not refer to anything in particular if it is to be able to mean everybody in general. In Jakobson's suggestive phrase, "I" is a "shifter" because it moves the center of discourse from one speaking subject to another: its emptiness is the no man's land in which subjects can exchange the lease they hold on all of language by virtue of saying "I." When a particular person utters that word, he or she fills "I" with meaning by providing the central point needed to calibrate all further time and space discriminations: "I" is the invisible ground of all other indices in language, the benchmark to which all its spatial operations are referred, and the Greenwich mean by which all its time distinctions are calibrated. "I" marks the point between "now" and "then," as well as between "here" and "there." The difference between all these markers is manifested by the relation each of them bears either to the proximity of the speaker's horizon (here and now), or to the distance of the other's environment (there and then). As the linguist Émile Benveniste has remarked, "Language itself reveals the profound difference between these two planes."[2] The gate of the "I" is located at the center not only of one's own existence, but of language as well.

The problem of unity

This is so because there is an intimate connection between the project of language and the project of selfhood: they both exist in order to mean. The word Bakhtin uses for "project," (*zadanie*, задание), is another twist on the central distinction between something that is "given" (*dan*, дан) and something that presents itself in the nature of a task, as something that must be "conceived" (*zadan*, задан). The situatedness of the self is a multiple phenomenon: it has been given the task of *not* being merely given. It must stand out in existence because it is dominated by a "drive to meaning," where meaning is understood as something still in the process of creation, something still bending toward the future as opposed to that which is already completed.

It should be added in passing that brute chronological indicators are no guarantee of whether a thing has meaning in this sense or not, for events initiated in the most distant past, as measured by the clock, may still be fresh and unfinished in cognitive time/space. Dialogism's drive to meaning should not be confused with the Hegelian impulse toward a single state of higher consciousness in the future. In Bakhtin there is no *one* meaning being striven for: the world is a vast congeries of contesting meanings, a heteroglossia so varied that no single term capable of unifying its diversifying energies is possible.

Since Bakhtin sees the world as activity, it will come as no surprise that he defines existence as an event. But it will perhaps seem contradictory that his term for existence is "the unique and unified event of being" (*edinstvennoe i edinoe sobytie bytija*, единственное и единое событие бытия), a phrase that recurs with obsessive regularity in Bakhtin's early work, and a formulation so important for understanding Bakhtin that each word requires some glossing.

The activity of the world comes to each of us as a series of events that uniquely occur in the site I, and only I, occupy in the world. If I slash my finger with a knife, an "other" may be intellectually aware that I am in pain, and may even deeply empathize with me. But the pain itself happens to me; it is addressed to where "I" am, not to the other (pre-positions, like pro-nouns, grammatically instance the unique placedness of subjects). One way in which the uniqueness of my place in life may be judged is by the uniqueness of the death that will be mine. However, this uniqueness – in what only appears to be a paradox – is *shared*. We shall all die, but you cannot die in my place, any more than you can live from that site. And of course the reverse is also true: I cannot be in the unique place you occupy in the event of existence.

Nevertheless, the event of existence is "unified"; for although it occurs in sites that are unique, those sites are never complete in themselves. They are never in any sense of the word *alone*. They need others to provide the stability demanded by the structure of perception if what occurs is to have meaning. In order that the event of existence be more than a random happening, it must have meaning, and to do that it must be perceptible as a stable figure against the ground of the flux and indeterminacy of everything else. This unification occurs as the result of an *event*, the action of me fulfilling my task (*zadanie*), i.e. by making the slice of existence that is merely given (*dan*) to me something that is conceived (*zadan*). I perform this transformation by imposing time/space categories appropriate to the other on what is happening. Remember that those categories differ from self-categories precisely in their ability to consummate, to finish off, what is being perceived, to complete it in time and to assign it a space.

The word "event" as it occurs in the formulation above is particularly complex. The Russian word used, *sobytie*, is the normal word Russians would use in most contexts to mean what we call in English an "event." But as Bakhtin uses it, certain aspects of the word long-forgotten in its everyday usage, are brought to the fore. The most important of these emerges from the fact that in Bakhtin's philosophical writings the word is almost never used alone, but always in conjunction with the word "being." He insists on being as an *event*.

The obligatory grouping of these two words in this way is a syntactic doubling that points to the mutuality of their meaning. It points as well to the etymological relations of the two words. In Russian, "event" is a word having both a root and a stem; it is formed from the word for being – *bytie* (бытие) – with the addition of the prefix implying sharedness, "so-, co-, (or, as we should say in English, "co-" as in co-operate or co-habit), giving *sobytie*, event as co-being. "Being" for Bakhtin then is, not just an event, but an event that is shared. Being is a simultaneity; it is always *co*-being.

The self as a sign

Karcevskij, too, meditates on simultaneity: "the simultaneous presence of these two possibilities is indispensable for any act of comprehension."[3] Like Bakhtin – and in marked contrast to the French reading of the asymmetry of the sign that finds its most radical extreme in Derrida's differ*a*nce – Karcevskij recognized that "opposition pure and simple necessarily leads to chaos and cannot serve as the basis of a *system*. True differentiation presupposes a simultaneous resemblance and difference."[4] In other words, it presupposes a center and a non-center.

What Karcevskij is saying about language is essentially what Bakhtin is saying about reality as such: the self (the perceiver) and the other (the perceived) exist not as separate entities, but as "relations between two coordinates . . . each serving to differentiate the other."[5] The coordinates proposed by Bakhtin for modeling this simultaneity are the two sets of time/space categories inherent in each of its poles: self and other (Bakhtin speaks of them as two interacting legal codes). The interaction of the binaries resemblance/difference, and figure/ground, both have at their heart the master distinction of self/other. In cognition, even more than in the physical world, two bodies cannot occupy the same space at the same time. As subject, I must not share the time/space of an object. Using self and other as basic categories does not obliterate the split between subject and object, but it complicates that distinction in ways that make it productive.

The other is in the realm of completedness, whereas I experience time as open and always as yet *un*-completed, and I am always at the *center* of space. This condition has certain virtues; in a world filled with the determining energies of impersonal social force, it is a potential source of freedom, the ground of other liberties from constraint of the sort Bakhtin celebrates in carnival (but as we shall see in greater detail in later chapters, this openness is far less absolute than is sometimes thought by those who know Bakhtin only as the author of *Rabelais and his World*). In common with everything else, however, this openness exists in tension with its dialogic partner, closure. The unfinished nature of self is not mere subjective license: like any border, it is also a limit. The very immediacy which defines my being as a self is the same condition that insures I cannot *perceive* my self: one way to grasp how far removed the self is from any privilege is to be aware that *like anything else*, its perception requires temporal categories that are less fluid and spatial categories that are more comprehensive than are provided by the manner in which my "I" is fated to live the event of being. For all their comparative openness, indeed *because* of it, self-categories cannot do what categories of the other can. Seeing requires a certain outsideness to what is seen, a certain stasis. "In the realm of culture, outsideness is the most powerful factor in understanding," precisely because it permits the finalized quality needed for the whole of a culture to be seen ("Response to a question from *Novy Mir*," *Speech Genres*, p. 7).[6] But as the primal activity that marks being as an *ongoing* event, the self "itself" cannot abide even the most minimal degree of fixity.

When I look at you, I see your whole body, and I see it as having a definite place in the total configuration of a whole landscape. I see you as occupying a certain position *vis-à-vis* other persons and objects in the landscape (you are *one* other among *many* others). Moreover, you not only have definite physical characteristics, specific social standing, and so on, but I see you as having a definite character as well. I imagine you as being good or bad at your trade, a good or bad husband, wife, parent, as being more or less close to dying, and a number of other things that sum you up as a (more or less definitely) consummated whole. If we imagine self and other in painterly terms, the former would be non-figurative and the latter extremely hard-edged. And yet I must have some way of forming myself into a subject having something like the particularity of the other. My "I" must have contours that are specific enough to provide a meaningful addressee: for if existence is shared, it will manifest itself as the condition of being addressed (*obrashchënnost'*, (обращенность, or *addressivnost'* аддрессивность). Existence is not only an event, it is an utterance. The event of existence has the nature of dialogue in this sense; there is no word directed to no one.

Selfhood as authorship

It is here we approach the ineluctable association of dialogism and authorship. In order to see this connection, let us go back for a moment to the peculiarity of the first person pronoun. Remember other nouns are signs in so far as their material sound, such as the locution "tree" when we actually pronounce it, evokes the fixed notion of a particular sort of object (some kind of natural growth, let us say). In the signifier "tree" we see a signified tree. Most nouns work something like this, but not the pronoun for the self, for what "I" refers to cannot be seen, at least in the same way that the word "tree" enables us to see a tree.

In order for my specific subjectivity to fill the general slot of the first person pronoun, that word must be empty: "I" is a word that can mean nothing in general, for the reference it names can never be visualized in its consummated wholeness. But this invisibility (which, as we shall see, is akin to the invisibility of the unconscious) is not mysterious. It is a general token of absence that can be filled in any *particular* utterance. It is invisible only at the level of *system*. At the level of performance, in the event of an utterance, the meaning of "I" can always be seen. It can be said, then, that the pronoun "I" marks the point of articulation between the pre-existing, repeatable system of language and my unique, unrepeatable existence as a particular person in a specific social and historical situation.

Existence, like language, is a shared event. It is always a border incident on the gradient both joining and separating the immediate reality of my own living particularity (a uniqueness that presents itself as only for me) with the reality of the system that precedes me in existence (that is always-already-there) and which is intertwined with everyone and everything else. Through the medium of the first person pronoun each speaker appropriates a whole language to himself. Much as Peter Pan's shadow is sewn to his body, "I" is the needle that stitches the abstraction of language to the particularity of lived experience. And much the same structure insures that in all aspects of life dialogue can take place between the chaotic and particular centrifugal forces of subjectivity and the rule-driven, generalizing centripetal forces of extra-personal system.

The single word "I" is exploited in language very much as the single eye of the fates is used in Greek mythology. The three old women all pass around the same organ. If they did not share their eye they could not see. In order to have her own vision, each must use the means by which the others see. In dialogism this sharedness is indeed the nature of fate for us all. For in order to see our selves, we must appropriate the vision of others. Restated in its crudest version, the Bakhtinian just-so story of subjectivity is the tale of how I get my self from the other: it is only the other's categories that will let me be an object for my own perception. I see my self as I conceive others might see it. In order to forge a self, I must do so from *outside*. In other words, *I author myself*.[7]

Even in this brutalized rendition it will be apparent that things cannot be so simple, and in the event (of being) they are not. First, because the act of creating a self is not free: we *must*, we *all* must, create ourselves, for the self is not given (*dan*) to any one of us. Or, as Bakhtin puts it, "we have no alibi in existence."[8] This lack of choice extends to the materials available for creation, for they are always provided by the other. I cannot choose to model my self as, let us say, a Martian might see me if I have not had experience of Martians. I may, of course, *imagine* what Martians might be like, and then seek to appropriate their image of me as my own. But even an imaginary Martian will be made up of details provided from previous experience, for in existence that is shared, there can be nothing absolute, including nothing absolutely new.

Ratios of otherness

The self, then, may be conceived as a multiple phenomenon of essentially three elements (it is – at least – a triad, not a duality): a center, a not-center, and the relation between them. Until now we have been discussing the first two elements, the center (or I-for-itself) and the not-center (the-not-I-in-me) in terms of the time/space categories appropriate to each. In taking up the third item, the relation that center and not-center bear to each other, we will have to keep in mind one or two new terms that are crucial to Bakhtin's undertaking. Dialogism is a form of architectonics, the general science of ordering parts into a whole. In other words, architectonics is the science of relations. A relation is something that always entails ratio and proportion. In addition, Bakhtin emphasizes that a relation is never static, but always in the process of being made or unmade.

In so far as a relation involves the *construction of ratios*, it is aesthetic in much the same way that a statue or a building may be judged in terms of how its parts have been constructed with respect to each other. Relation, it will be helpful to remember, is also a *telling*, a narrative, an aspect of the word's meaning that Bakhtin will not ignore as he takes the somewhat unusual step of treating the relation of the self to the other as a problem in *aesthetics*.

By choosing aesthetic categories to discuss questions in epistemology, Bakhtin is drawing attention to the importance in dialogism of authoring. Sharing existence as an event means among other things that we are – we cannot choose *not* to be – in dialogue, not only with other human beings, but also with the natural and cultural configurations we lump together as "the world." The world addresses us and we are alive and human to the degree that we are answerable, i.e. to the degree that we can respond to addressivity. We are responsible in the sense that we are *compelled* to respond, we cannot choose but give the world an answer. Each one of us occupies a place in existence that is uniquely ours; but far from being a privilege, far from having what Bakhtin calls an *alibi* in existence, the uniqueness of the place I occupy in existence is, in the deepest sense of the word, an answerability: in that place only am I addressed by the world, since only I am in it. Moreover, we must keep on forming responses as long as we are alive.

I am always answerable *for* the response that is generated *from* the unique place I occupy in existence. My responses begin to have a pattern; the dialogue I have with existence begins to assume the form of a text, a kind of book. A book, moreover, that belongs to a genre. In antiquity, too, the world was often conceived as a book, the text of *libri naturae*.[9] Bakhtin conceives existence as the kind of book we call a novel, or more accurately as many novels (the radically manifold world proposed by Bakhtin looks much like Borges' Library of Babel), for all of us write our own such text, a text that is then called our life. Bakhtin uses the literary genre of the novel as an allegory for representing existence as the condition of authoring.

Outsideness and values

The author of a novel may unfold several different plots, but each will be merely one version of a more encompassing story: the narrative of how an author (as a dialogic, non-psychological self) constructs a relation with his heroes (as others). Authors are somehow both inside and outside their work. In literary texts, interaction between author and heroes is what constructs the relation that gives deepest coherence to the other meanings of relation, not least relation understood as a telling.

The particular corner (really an angle of refraction) in apperception where such authoring can take place – the self's workshop, as it were – Bakhtin calls *vnenakhodimost'* (вненаходимость), or "outsideness" (sometimes rendered into English – from French rather than from Russian – as "exotopy"). The term, as always in dialogism, is not only spatial, but temporal: it is only from a position outside something that it can be perceived in categories that complete it in time and fix it in space. In order to be perceived as a whole, as something finished, a person or object must be shaped in the time/space categories of the other, and that is possible only when the person or object is perceived from the position of outsideness. An event cannot be wholly known, cannot be seen, from inside its own unfolding as an event. As Bergson, an important source of ideas for Bakhtin, puts it: "in so far as my body is the center of *action* [or what Bakhtin calls a deed], it cannot give birth to a representation."[10]

In a dialogue that takes place between two different persons (one self/other constellation to another self/other constellation) in physical space, the medium of exchange is, of course, natural language. In such exchanges it is words that fix (if only very fleetingly) meanings. They can do so because syntax, grammar, and the sound laws governing phonology provide a relatively stable armature for marking distinctions in the unstable flux of life outside language. Words can segment experience into meaningful patterns because their essence is so radically differential: they exist only to register differences. As Saussure, summing up his argument at a crucial point, says: "Everything that has been said up to this point boils down to this: in language there are only differences."[11] Bakhtin insists that language is *also a matter of sameness*, but he would certainly agree that "language is only a system of pure values."[12]

And so, argues Bakhtin, is *the self*. Once again quoting Saussure to gloss Bakhtin, we may say that for the units of existence we call "selves," as for the units of language we call "words," "Their most precise characteristic is in being what the others are not."[13] While the self/other distinction does not operate as a complete algorithm of natural language, it does share with language the three fundamental features of function, means, and purpose. The function of each is to provide a mechanism for differentiating; each uses values to distinguish particular differences, and the purpose of doing so in each case is to give order to (what otherwise would be) the chaos of lived experience.

Let us return, then, to the example of two people regarding each other, each attempting to make sense out of the existence each shares with the other. We may now describe the dialogue of radical self/other distinctions unfolding within their cognitive space in linguistic terms. This dialogue takes place much as dialogues in natural language do: by using particular values to specify otherwise unmarked differences.

In our imagined encounter, the first person will see the second, the "other," through the relation of difference that divides all phenomena either into categories of self or categories of the other, never both. But once the distinction is made that defines the second person as one who must be perceived through the lens of the other, distinctions of a secondary order will follow that fill in the other's general outline with shades of particular differences (the progression from primary to secondary differentiation is, of course, logical, not chronological). These shadings will be made with colors drawn from the palette of specific values that obtain in the event of existence as it manifests itself in a particular time and a particular place. The first person will see the second, then, in terms much too detailed to be frozen into the sort of abstract account that a hapless expositor is condemned to provide as an example. But the terms could reasonably be expected to include such things as how physical appearance is judged (is long hair, or curly hair, or blonde hair, or perhaps no hair a good or bad thing? is being round in the tummy to be "portly" or is it to be "fat"?), also manner of speaking ("common," "stilted," "natural"), politics, relation to the major theory dominating a particular discipline at the moment, and so on. The other is always perceived in terms that are specified socially and historically, and for all the abstraction of our discussion so far, dialogism's primary thrust is always in the direction of historical and social specificity.

The only perspective from which values of such specificity and completeness may be brought to bear on the other is from the position of "outsideness." The first person succeeds in attaining the position needed to perceive the second from outside. But will he or she be able to achieve that extreme degree of outsideness toward the second which Bakhtin calls "transgredience"? Transgredience (*transgradientsvo*, трансградиенцво) is reached when the *whole* existence of others is seen from outside not only their own knowledge that they are being perceived by somebody else, but from beyond their awareness that such an other even exists. It is a cardinal assumption of dialogism that every human subject is not only highly conscious, but that his or her cognitive space is coordinated by the same I/other distinctions that organize my own: there is in fact no way "I" can be completely transgredient to another *living* subject, nor can he or she be completely transgredient to me.

Authoring and authority

We touch here on two other important concerns of dialogism: authority as authorship; and authority as power. Transgredience is a topic that bears on the specificity of art within a general aesthetic (see chapter 3); and it also bears on the question of power in the state (see chapter 5). As we shall see, transgredience, when it is used well, results in art; when used badly, it results in totalitarianism.

Although, then, dialogism is primarily an epistemology, it is not just a theory of knowledge. Rather, it is in its essence a hybrid: dialogism exploits the nature of language as a modeling system for the nature of existence, and thus is deeply involved with linguistics; dialogism sees social and ethical values as the means by which the fundamental I/other split articulates itself in specific situations and is thus a version of axiology; and in so far as the act of perception is understood as the patterning of a relation, it is a general aesthetic, or it is an architectonics, a science of building.

Use of the term architectonics betrays once again Bakhtin's debt to Kant, who used it not only in its technical sense (as a way to refer to any systematization of knowledge), but to emphasize the active, constructive role of mind in perception.[14] By using the same word, Bakhtin also seeks to foreground these aspects; but in addition he wants to draw a line between the kind of authoring we all must do all the time, and the kind of authoring some persons do some of the time, the results of which we then call art. Architectonics involves us all; but the branch of architectonics involving artists is aesthetics proper.

What is the difference between the two? It is the ability of the artist in his or her text to treat other human subjects from the vantage point of transgredience, a privilege denied the rest of us who author only in lived experience (and denied to artists too, when they are not being artists). The author of a novel, for instance, can manipulate the other not only as an other, but as a *self*. This is, in fact, what the very greatest writers have always done, but the paradigmatic example is provided by Dostoevsky, who so successfully permits his characters to have the status of an "I" standing over against the claims of his own authorial other that Bakhtin felt compelled to coin the special term "polyphony" to describe it. Lesser authors treat their heroes as mere others, a relation that can be crafted in architectonics, and which does not therefore require the aesthetic privilege of art for its achievement: it is what we all do anyway. And then there are those authors who treat their characters not only as others, but as having the otherness of mere things, lacking any subjectivity. They exploit their transgredience of their characters much as scientists exploit theirs toward laboratory rats. This is formulaic pseudo-art, in which all possible initiative within the text is sacrificed to a formula pre-existing the text. If in western movies of a certain kind the "hero" ends up kissing a horse instead of a girl, or if in Stalinist fiction the boy always gets a tractor instead of a girl, we feel no violation, because we understand that neither the cowboy nor the collective farmer has any reserve of subjectivity: they are, themselves, effectively, only horses or tractors anyway.

This formulaic art makes explicit the connection of transgredience to power. For not only is snuffing out the "I" of other subjects bad aesthetics, it is bad politics. Dialogically conceived, authorship is a form of governance, for both are implicated in the architectonics of responsibility, each is a way to adjudicate center/non-center relations between subjects. Totalitarian government always seeks the (utopian) condition of absolute monologue: the *Gleichschaltung* which was attempted in Germany during the 1930s to "Nazify" trade unions, universities, publishing houses, professional associations, and so on had as its aim the suppression of all otherness in the state so that its creator alone might flourish. Dialogism has rightly been perceived by certain thinkers on the left as a useful correlative to Marxism, for it argues that sharing is not only an ethical or economic mandate, but a condition built into the structure of human perception, and thus a condition inherent in the very fact of being human. But by the same token dialogism differs from the pseudo-Marxism of regimes that use

"Communism" as a license for totalitarian government. For as the ultimate critique of any claim to monologue, it is intransigently pluralist.

The surplus of seeing

We have looked at several versions of self/other relations. In so doing certain fundamentals have emerged, not least of which is that dialogism is able to make claims in many different areas because it is basically a theory of knowledge, an architectonics of perception. Dialogism argues that we make sense of existence by defining our specific place in it, an operation performed in cognitive time and space, the basic categories of perception. Important as these categories are, they themselves are shaped by the even more fundamental set of self and other. We perceive the world through the time/space of the self *and* through the time/ space of the other. The difference between the two is a relation of otherness that can be gauged by differing positions of outsideness that are enacted as varying degrees of transgredience. Up until this point we have discussed such relations almost exclusively in terms of the other. We must now address the difficult question of how the self achieves the outsideness it needs to perceive itself.

So as always to be an open site where the event of existence can have its occurrence, the self must never stop in time or be fixed in space. Since, however, being finished in time and being specifically located in space are conditions necessary for being "seen" in perception, the self is by definition invisible to itself. In the wake of a still-potent Romanticism, it is necessary to repeat that there is nothing mysterious about this invisibility, for it is merely structural. The self's non-referentiality can be understood by analogy with the non-referentiality of "I" as the first person pronoun in natural language. If each is to perform its function of indicating a unique place that must be shared by *everybody* (which is what the self marks in existence, and what the "I" marks in language), then they must both refer to nothing – or at least not refer to anything in the same manner other signs refer.

But the self is like a sign in so far as it has no absolute meaning in itself: it, too (or rather, it most of all), is relative, dependent for its existence on the other. A conventional sign is not a unitary thing, but rather a differential relation between two aspects, a signifier and a signified. In this triad it is the relation that is absolute, not the elements it yokes together, for neither of the two elements exists in itself; neither has any meaning on its own, without the simultaneous presence of the other. Nor is the "self" a unitary thing; rather, it consists in a relation, the relation between self and other. A traditional metaphor representing the unity of the linguistic sign's two elements is the unity shared by the recto and verso sides of the same sheet of paper. But in so far as the self is an *activity*, such a static means of conceiving it will not do: Bakhtin's metaphor for the unity of the two elements constituting the relation of self and other is *dialogue*, the simultaneous unity of differences in the event of utterance.

One of Bakhtin's simple illustrations will help us overcome the complexity of this last formulation. If we return for a moment to the situation of two people facing each other, we remember that although they share an external space and time (they are physically simultaneous), inside his or her own head each sees something the other does not. Let us envisage you and me confronting each other. There are certain things we both perceive, such as the table between us. But there are other things in the same encounter we do not both perceive. The simplest way to state the difference between us is to say that you see things about me (such as, at the most elementary level, my forehead) and the world (such as the wall behind my back) which are out of my sight. The fact that I cannot see such things does not mean they do not exist; we are so arranged that I simply cannot see them. But it is equally the case that I see things you are unable to see, such as your forehead, and the wall behind your back. In addition to the things we see jointly, there are aspects of our situation each of us can see only on our own, i.e. only from the unique place each of us occupies in the situation.

The aspect of the situation that you see, but I do not, is what Bakhtin calls your "surplus of seeing"; those things I see but you cannot constitute my "surplus of seeing." You know I have a surplus, and I know you have one as well. By adding the surplus that has been "given" to you to the surplus that has been "given" to me I can build up an image that includes the whole of me and the room, including those things I cannot physically see: in other words, I am able to "conceive" or construct a whole out of the

different situations we are in together. I author a unified version
of the event of our joint existence from my unique place in it by
means of combining the things I see which are different from (in
addition to) those you see, and the things you see which are
different from (in addition to) that difference.

The self as a story

Such acts of combination are a rudimentary form of "narrativity," or the ability to put myself into scenarios of the kind I see
others enacting. I never see others as frozen in the immediacy of
the isolated present moment. The present is not a static moment,
but a mass of different combinations of past and present relations.
To say I perceive them as a whole means that I see them
surrounded by their whole lives, within the context of a complete
narrative having a beginning that precedes our encounter and
an end that follows it. I see others as bathed in the light of their
whole biography.

My "I-for-itself" lacks such a consummated biography:
because the self's own time is constantly open, it resists such
framing limits. Within my own consciousness my "I" has no
beginning and no end. The only way I know of my birth is
through accounts I have of it from others; and I shall never know
my death, because my "self" will be alive only so long as I have
consciousness – what is called "my" death will not be known by
me, but once again only by others. In order to remain a
constantly potential site of being, my self must be able to conduct
its work as sheer capability, a flux of sheer becoming. If this
energy is to be given specific contours, it must be shaped not only
in values, but in story. Stories are the means by which values are
made coherent in particular situations. And this narrativity, this
possibility of conceiving my beginning and end as a whole life, is
always enacted in the time/space of the other: I may see my
death, but not in the category of my "I." For my "I," death
occurs only for others, even when the death in question is my
own.

Since Bakhtin places so much emphasis on otherness, and on
otherness defined precisely as other *values*, community plays an
enormous role in his thought. Dialogism is, among other things,
an exercise in social theory. Although frequently overlooked by

those who tear "carnival" out of its larger Bakhtinian context, extrapersonal social force is accorded so much weight in dialogism that it almost (but not quite) begins to verge on determinism. If my "I" is so ineluctably a product of the particular values dominating my community at the particular point in its history when I coexist with it, the question must arise, "Where is there any space, and what would the time be like, in which I might define myself against an otherness that is other from that which has been 'given' to me?"

In answering this question it will be helpful to remember that dialogue is not, as is sometimes thought, a dyadic, much less a binary, phenomenon. Dialogue is a manifold phenomenon, but for schematic purposes it can be reduced to a minimum of three elements having a structure very much like the triadic construction of the linguistic sign: a dialogue is composed of an utterance, a reply, and a relation between the two. It is the relation that is most important of the three, for without it the other two would have no meaning. They would be isolated, and the most primary of Bakhtinian a prioris is that nothing is anything in itself.

The tripartite nature of dialogue bears within it the seeds of hope: in so far as my "I" is dialogic, it insures that my existence is not a lonely event but part of a larger whole. The thirdness of dialogue frees my existence from the very circumscribed meaning it has in the limited configuration of self/other relations available in the immediate time and particular place of my life. For in later times, and in other places, there will always be other configurations of such relations, and in conjunction with *that* other, my self will be differently understood. This degree of thirdness outside the present event insures the possibility of whatever transgredience I can achieve toward myself.

At the heart of any dialogue is the conviction that what is exchanged has meaning. Poets who feel misunderstood in their lifetimes, martyrs for lost political causes, quite ordinary people caught in lives of quiet desperation – all have been correct to hope that outside the tyranny of the present there is a possible addressee who will understand them. This version of the significant other, this "super-addressee," is conceived in different ways at different times and by different persons: as God, as the future triumph of my version of the state, as a future reader.

As the need to posit a category such as "super-addressee" outside the present moment makes clear, conditions for creating meaning in the present moment are not always the best. A dialogic world is one in which I can never have my own way completely, and therefore I find myself plunged into constant interaction with others – and with myself. In sum, dialogism is based on the primacy of the social, and the assumption that all meaning is achieved by struggle. It is thus a stern philosophy. This fact should surprise no one, given dialogism's immediate sources in revolution, civil war, the terror of the purges, and exile. But the very otherness that makes it at times a version of Stoicism is also what insures that we are not alone. Dialogism is ultimately an epistemology founded on a loophole, for

> there is neither a first word nor a last word. The contexts of dialogue are without limit. They extend into the deepest past and the most distant future. Even meanings born in dialogues of the remotest past will never be finally grasped once and for all, for they will always be renewed in later dialogue. At any present moment of the dialogue there are great masses of forgotten meanings, but these will be recalled again at a given moment in the dialogue's later course when it will be given new life. For nothing is absolutely dead: every meaning will someday have its homecoming festival.
>
> (*Estetika*, p. 373)

3
Language as dialogue

Dialogism is unthinkable outside its relation to language. But that relation is complex. It is, not surprisingly, a dialogic relation, and before going any further it will be useful to consider what that means. Bakhtin is not the first, and far from the only, thinker to ponder the potential importance of dialogue in human interaction. In everyday usage, dialogue is a synonym for conversation; the word suggests two people talking to each other. This general sense of the word can obscure its special significance in the thought of Bakhtin. *Speaking* and *exchange* are aspects of dialogue that play an important role in both usages. But what gives dialogue its central place in dialogism is precisely the kind of *relation* conversations manifest, the conditions that must be met if any exchange between different speakers is to occur at all. That relation is most economically defined as one in which differences – while still remaining different – serve as the building blocks of simultaneity. In a conversation, both speakers are different from each other and the utterance each makes is always different from the other's (even when one appears to repeat the "same" word as the other); and yet all these differences – and many more – are held together in the relation of dialogue.

Remembering that dialogue is ultimately a differential relation will help us avoid the confusion that has sometimes attended discussions of how dialogue is connected to language. A frequent question in such discussions is that of primacy: is dialogue a metaphor Bakhtin extracts from language's communicative aspect and then applies to other categories outside the limits of language? Or is it the other way around, is dialogue a master principle governing existence that then finds a particularly paradigmatic expression in the language of conversation? To put the question this way is to pose it as a dialectical either/or. And it is, therefore, already not to be thinking dialogically, for the question so framed precludes the solution "both/and," which is, in the event, Bakhtin's answer. "Both/and" is not a mere wavering between two mutually exclusive possibilities, each of which is *in itself* logical and consistent, thus insuring the further possibility of truth, since a logic of this restrictive sort is so limiting that only one of the two options can be correct. Dialogic has its own logic, but not of this exclusive kind.

Bakhtin's answer to the question of primacy is a reasoned consequence of dialogism's fundamental a priori that nothing *is* in itself. Existence is *sobytie sobytiya*, the event of co-being; it is a vast web of interconnections each and all of which are linked as participants in an event whose totality is so immense that no single one of us can ever know it. That event manifests itself in the form of a constant, ceaseless creation and exchange of meaning. The mutuality of differences makes dialogue Bakhtin's master concept, for it is present in exchanges at all levels – between words in language, people in society, organisms in ecosystems, and even between processes in the natural world. What keeps so comprehensive a view from being reductive is its simultaneous recognition that dialogue is carried on at each level *by different means*. One of these means is natural language, others are analogous to natural language, and others have only the most tenuous relation to the way natural language works. Although it is the most powerful, natural language is only one of several ways that dialogic relations manifest themselves in the larger dialogue that is the event of existence.

But in dialogism there is always more than one meaning, and in another important sense it is clear that language cannot avoid playing a special role in a universe conceived as endless semiosis. Because of the epistemological claims it makes, dialogism is, perforce, a philosophy of language. And since it places so much stress on connections between differences, it will come as no surprise that, in its technical linguistic aspect, dialogism's whole emphasis is on the syntagmatic, rather than paradigmatic, features of language. Although the distinction is not absolute between these two levels, dialogism is a philosophy more of the *sentence* than it is of the *sign*. As such, dialogism's account of language differs in significant ways from that of Ferdinand de Saussure, in whose work the paradigmatic aspects of language, and especially of the sign, reign supreme.

Much has been made of the differences between Saussure and Bakhtin, and these are indeed significant. Contrasts between the two provide a useful heuristic device for any potted exposition of their thought (and will be so used in the present account); but the sheer utility of such a move has also served to conceal certain important points of similarity between Bakhtin and Saussure, which we shall want to examine as well.

For polemical reasons, Bakhtin himself stresses the negative aspects of Saussure's achievement. He invokes Saussure as leading spokesman for "abstract objectivism, a linguistic tendency that dialogism most strenuously opposes. Abstract objectivism treats language as a pure system of laws governing all phonetic, grammatical, and lexical forms that confront individual speakers as inviolable norms over which they have no control. Another tendency opposed by dialogism, "individualistic subjectivism," is the polar opposite of the first (at least in Bakhtin's account of them): it denies pre-existing norms and holds that all aspects of language can be explained in terms of each individual speaker's voluntarist intentions. Notice that each of these tendencies is characterized in terms of self/other relations: in the first, the ground of meaning is a system so dominant that its otherness obliterates all possibility of subjectivity, whereas in the second, it is precisely the individual, the "I" of the self, who controls meaning. The first (abstract objectivism) sees language as happening entirely outside the person, while the second (individualistic subjectivism) treats language as completely inside the person.

In order to specify what "language" means in dialogism, it will be useful to remember the history of its appropriation in Bakhtin's own development. Bakhtin (as Voloshinov) formulated the antinomy between "abstract objectivism" and "individualistic subjectivism" in the 1920s, at a time when he was rearticulating the self/other modality that runs throughout his thought. He had originally treated self/other relations as a contribution to such classical philosophical subjects as aesthetics, ethics, and epistemology. After 1924, however, the same problematic is conceived as a contribution to the philosophy of language, and to the implications of that philosophy for understanding the peculiar status of the novel in intellectual (not just literary) history. This new direction of his concerns is motivated by several factors, two of which are particularly important: the Sovietization of intellectual life that began after 1917, and the excited response of Russian linguists to the theories of Saussure when they first began to appear.

The response to Saussure began very early when Karcevskij, who had worked with the master himself in Geneva, joined Jakobson in Moscow in 1917. But it was really only after 1923, when there appeared a flood of Russian publications explicating, attacking, or defending him, that Saussure's great importance became apparent. In those early years Saussure's impact in the Soviet Union was greater than in any other country. This fact can be explained not only by the intrinsic power of his ideas, but by the particular relevance those ideas possessed in a country that had just experienced a Marxist revolution, for one result of Saussure's radical emphasis on an impersonal system was to provide a new and sophisticated argument for the importance of collective as opposed to individual determinants in human society. Under the impact of the new Soviet emphasis on social factors in general, and Saussure's demonstration of the ineluctably social nature of language in particular, one projection of Bakhtin's phenomenology of self/other relations becomes increasingly sociological and linguistic, culminating in the appearance in 1929 of *Marxism and the Philosophy of Language*.

Far, then, from having an exclusively negative significance in dialogism, Saussure is one of the major constituents in its development. And if we look at some of the fundamental features of Saussure's thought through a dialogic lens, the reasons why this had to be so become quickly apparent. Saussure succeeded in transforming the ancient study of philology into the modern discipline of linguistics because he replaced the old basis for the study of language – history – with a new and different basis: society. Dialogism, too, is rooted in social experience, and before examining some of the reasons why, from a Bakhtinian point of view, Saussure's revolution, though epochal, was nevertheless incomplete, we should begin by marking this important affinity.

In order to shift from a historical to a sociological ground for linguistics, Saussure, like Bakhtin, argued that words should be studied not from the point of view of ancient (often hypothetical) languages, but from the point of view of those who actually use language: from the point of view, in other words, of the individual speaker. Both had the idea of looking at language from this new perspective, but having done so, the two thinkers drew diametrically different conclusions. These will be clearer if we first look at the similarities from which they diverged.

Similarities between Saussure and Bakhtin

Both thinkers begin with the revolutionary assumption that language should be looked at from the point of view of the individual speaker; having done so, each recognizes in that speaker many of the same characteristics. When Saussure turned to the individual member of society as the site of language activity, he discovered that the individual so conceived is subject to the law of placement: whatever he or she says is always uttered from a particular point, a unique perspective. To express his preference for a more localized point of view than had been assumed by previous scholars who studied the history of language as a whole, the Swiss linguist turns naturally to a mountaineering metaphor: "It would be absurd to attempt to sketch a panorama of the Alps by viewing them simultaneously from several peaks of the Jura; a panorama must be made from a single vantage point. The same applies to language."[1]

But as soon as he looks more closely at how the individual speaker does in fact relate to language, Saussure discovers in him an "inner duality." That duality is similar to Bakhtin's self/other distinction in so far as it is comprised of the simultaneous presence of features that are idiosyncratic to the speaker *and* features that he or she shares with others. Saussure articulates this duality of individual and social factors in terms of time and space, a parallel with Bakhtin's chronotopic emphasis that extends even to the particular terms both use to specify the individual speaker's inner time/space.

The individual speaker's experience of time is what led Saussure to isolate synchronic from diachronic linguistics, the first of several binaries that have since become a virtual catechism not just for linguists, but for most students of the social and human sciences. Saussure says "the first thing that strikes us when we study the facts of language is that their succession in time does not exist in so far as the speaker is concerned."[2] For the speaker, the history of the language that he speaks does not exist; the individual speaker is therefore the site of that synchronic "language state" upon which Saussure founds his whole system.

Both Bakhtin and Saussure emphasize the present moment of utterance: Bakhtin maintains that in cognition the time of the self is always a present state without beginning or end. Speaking as an epistemologist, he defines the "I" as an ultimate synchronism. Speaking as a linguist, Saussure also conceives the ruling time of the individual as a present that is always-already-there. And both men agree on the kind of space occupied by the individual speaker: it is always the specific point – what Saussure calls that single peak in the Jura – that the individual speaker (and that speaker alone) occupies in the physical and social worlds.

Differences between Saussure and Bakhtin

On closer examination, the apparent parallels between Saussure and Bakhtin conceal significant differences. For Saussure, the speaker's place is such that, in fact, it resists all attempts at generalization. This situation produces another Saussurian binary, the opposition of speech and language. Saussure characterizes speech (*parole*), as having a particularity so unsystematic and endless that it becomes virtually unstudiable. Speech, the realm of the individual "I", is one pole of the fatal "inner duality" at the heart of Saussure's system: speech for him is language as it is present *only* in a single speaker. Language is the other pole of the duality, the realm of the social: it is also, but not solely, in the individual. Saussure reserves the term language (*langue*) to refer to the general rules that exist for all present speakers of a particular language. These lend themselves to systematization and thus may "provide a fulcrum that satisfies the mind."[3] The individual aspects of the "inner duality" that Saussure began with are quickly consigned to an unanalyzable chaos of idiosyncrasy, and it is the social aspect of the duality alone on which Saussure founds his science of language. As a thinker whose paradigm is still dialectic (and thus binary) rather than dialogic, he cannot entertain both possibilities simultaneously. Having recognized the duality and its attendant complexities, he quickly retreats into the conceptual safety of an either/or opposition. In other words, Saussure abandons the self in the service of the other.

He must do so for, by his own admission, he lacks any conceptual means for relating the multiple – not just "dual" – phenomena that must be taken into account when speech is regarded from the point of view of the individual speaker: "Taken as a whole, speech is many-sided and heterogeneous; straddling several areas simultaneously – physical, physiological, and psychological – it belongs both to the individual and to society [the fatal 'inner duality']". Up to this point, Saussure sounds very much like Bakhtin. But Saussure then goes on to draw exactly the opposite conclusion from Bakhtin: "*we cannot put it* [speech] *into any category of human facts, for we cannot discover its unity*" (italics added).[4]

Saussure's failure to discover a dialogic relation between the self/other aspects of language as they are present in individual speakers produced a number of categories each with its own "symmetry" or "unity, such as his monologizing concepts of "synchrony," "the sign," and "society." The "natural order," as Saussure called it, of such concepts appears increasingly artificial on closer examination. This symmetry was achieved at the cost of suppressing the "inner duality" that had initiated Saussure's investigations of *both* idiosyncratic *and* social factors as they coexist in the individual speaker. Saussure concentrated almost exclusively on the shared, social aspect of language that enabled unity. The history of Saussure's reception has largely been the tale of chipping away at such perfect unities. Jakobson began his attack on the artificial unity of Saussurian synchrony as early as 1927, and by 1971 was justified in announcing that Saussure's "fallacious identification of two oppositions – synchrony versus diachrony, and statics versus dynamics – was refuted by post-Saussurian linguistics."[5]

Saussure's patent emphasis on difference and opposition, then, has somewhat obscured a subtler counter-tendency in his work toward symmetry, a tendency nowhere more present than in his insistence on the unified wholeness of the sign, the closure it achieves between sound and meaning, the union it forges between signifier and signified. But already in 1929 Karcevskij was successfully arguing that "A sign and its signification do not form a perfect fit."[6] And of course Lacan's rereading of Freud is enabled precisely by his destabilization of Saussure's formula for the sign – s/s – into S/s (thus indicating the asymmetrical priority of signifier over signified).

Bakhtin has his own way of mapping the relation between signified and signifier, one that constantly insists on difference and simultaneity, rather than symmetry. Moreover, the sign's variety inheres in the complexity of the social system. As a result, there is no neat, one-line definition of the motivated sign as it plays a role in dialogism. Rather, we shall have to pursue the work of signification as it manifests itself at different points in the hierarchy of levels where utterance is shaped.

The speaking subject as site of meaning

Dialogism begins by visualizing existence as an event, the event of being responsible for (and to) the particular situation existence assumes as it unfolds in the unique (and constantly changing) place I occupy in it. Existence is addressed to me as a riot of inchoate potential messages, which at this level of abstraction may be said to come to individual persons much as stimuli from the natural environment come to individual organisms. Some of the potential messages come to me in the form of primitive physiological stimuli, some in the form of natural language, and some in social codes, or ideologies. So long as I am in existence, I am in a particular place, and must respond to all these stimuli either by ignoring them or in a response that takes the form of making sense, of producing – for it is a form of work – *meaning* out of such utterances.

Bakhtin translates Dostoevsky's dictum that the heart of man is a battleground between good and evil into the proposition that the mind of man is a theater in which the war between the centripetal impulses of cognition and the centrifugal forces of the world is fought out. I can make sense of the world only by reducing the number of its meanings – which are potentially infinite – to a restricted set. A helpful analogy here is the way a given natural language selects out of all possible noises a limited number of sounds it will process as being significant. For instance, the "th" that we have in the English word "breath" does not exist as a meaningful sound in Russian; nor does English recognize as meaningful the Russian sound usually transliterated into Roman alphabets as "y" (ы). "Th" in Russian is as much mere noise as "y" is in English, because the two languages have selected out of all the potential noises available to human speech production a restricted number of particular noises they will recognize as meaningful and treat as sounds. The resulting sounds, or phonemes, are defined through an intricate set of phonic distinctions, not only as they are opposed to the noise of different possible sounds in other languages, but also to each other within the same language. In much the same way, the vastly more complex *meanings* I distinguish among the myriad utterances addressed to me are also made by discriminating among *values*. Phonemic differences are cut out of the physical fabric of the natural world's acoustic pressures; semantic differences are patterns cut from the ideological cloth of the social world.

"Ideology" and "social world" are terms best understood in the context of dialogism's emphasis on addressivity. To understand existence as "addressed to me" does not mean I am a passive receptacle into which events fall, as letters drop into mailboxes. Addressivity means rather that I *am* an event, the event of constantly responding to utterances from the different worlds I pass through. Addressivity implies not only that consciousness is always consciousness of something, but that existence itself is always (and no more than) the existence of something; dialogism resists the Heideggerian (and ultimately idealist) distinction between being as such (*das Sein*) and a particular being (*ein Seiende*). At a basic biological level, thirst does not just exist in the natural world, it *happens* to me (or, of course, to you); and lack of water means nothing without the response of thirst. And at the highest level of mental life it is still the case that nothing means anything until it achieves a response. In other words, addressivity is *expressivity*; what we usually call life is not a mysterious vitalistic force, but an activity, the dialogue between events addressed to me in the particular place I occupy in existence, and my expression of a *response* to such events

from that unique place. When I cease to respond, when there are
– as we say so accurately in English – *no signs of life*, I am dead.

Meaning as social value and as an event

It is here that we connect again with Bakhtin's ideas about the
nature of the sign as opposed to those of Saussure. In dialogism, life
is expression. Expression means to make meaning, and meaning
comes about only through the medium of signs. This is true at all
levels of existence: something *exists* only if it *means*. There are, of
course, things not known to anyone, but the mode of their
existence is to be in dialogue with what is known: knowing requires
unknowing. But unknowing is not absolute; for someone else, in
some other place, at some other time, it may be translated into
what is known. For a thing exists only in so far as it has meaning,
even if it is at any particular point only a potential meaning.
Anything that means is a sign, and since there is nothing that
may not function as a sign, everything has the potential to mean.

The sheer semioticity of the world calls into question certain of
our cherished beliefs, the most common being that the experiences
in our deepest psyche are unknowable, and that there must
therefore be a qualitative difference separating individual
(inner) experience from social (outer) experience. But Bakhtin
begins by assuming that the self does not coincide with itself: it
follows from the dialogic structure of consciousness (the I/other
relation) that "experience exists even for the person undergoing
it [the "I"] only in the material of signs [the other]" (*Marxism and
the Philosophy of Language*, p. 28).[7] Meaning comes about in both
the individual psyche and in shared social experience through
the medium of the sign, for in both spheres understanding comes
about *as a response to a sign with signs*. Since, therefore, there is no
sign in itself, every given sign is a link in the great chain
comprising all other signs: "And nowhere is there a break in the
chain, nowhere does the chain plunge into inner being, non-
material in nature and unembodied in signs." (ibid., p. 11).

The biology of meaning

The difference between inner and outer experience is not a single
difference, least of all one that is merely spatial; and it is certainly

not a difference that is absolute. The difference between the
(inner) individual and (outer) society is conceived in terms that
are *quantitative*: it is a graduated set of distinctions in the amount
of meaning signs convey at different levels of dialogue. Here, as in
many other ways, dialogism is very close to the thought of C. S.
Peirce, especially to the notion that meaning may be defined as
the translation of a sign into another system of signs.[8]

The lowest level of dialogue has meanings confined to the most
local circuits of the organism's physiology, such as binary
decisions at micro points in the neuronal chain that permit
stimuli either to pass or to be stopped. Reactions to external
stimuli such as light and dark, and reactions to internal activity
such as breathing or blood circulation, the intercommunication
by which the body's various systems are coordinated into a
unified organism – all operate by means of (and *communicate* with)
signs, as physiologists have known at least since Helmholtz'
investigation of the physiology of perception in the nineteenth
century. But the meaning of such signs is limited to the organism
in which they operate (this is the point Bakhtin makes in his
example of you feeling your own physical pain differently from
the way I feel your pain, no matter how much I may empathize
with you). Of course, at a higher level of semiosis, such as medical
research for instance, individual body signs take on enormous
significance for us *all*. But in order to do so they have had to
undergo many transformations (translations) from the original,
purely physiological system of primitive signs (that are really
closer to mere signals) into the different kind of sign system that
uses words as its medium of exchange.

That system serves as the subject of what Bakhtin calls the
science of ideologies, the study of differential relations between
"I" and others, where the meaning of "other" may range from
other individuals, through neighborhoods, classes, professions,
etc., all the way up to other culture systems. The main task of
such a science is to conceive the reality of both the individual and
society without doing conceptual violence to the status of either.
Bakhtin begins by recognizing the danger of going to one or the
other extreme:

> A sort of peculiar periodic alternation seems to take place
> between an elemental psychologism, which subjects all the
> ideological sciences to inundation, and a sharply reacting

antipsychologism, which deprives the psyche of all its content, relegating it to some empty, formal status . . . or to sheer physiologism.

(*Marxism and the Philosophy of Language*, p. 31)

Objective psychology

Dialogism's two basic categories for avoiding such reduction are "objective psychology" and "inner speech." As defined in *Marxism and the Philosophy of Language,* "objective psychology" can be understood as psychology with a new subject of analysis: the psyche not of the individual, but of the individual as striated by the social.

Objective psychology studies the relation of inner to outer speech in specific instances. It differs from conventional social psychology in that dialogism presumes all perception, including the higher forms of it which we call thinking, is accomplished through sign operations. And since signs can mean only if they are shared, it follows that the traditional individual/society opposition is best conceived not as a duel of mutually exclusive categories, but rather as a continuum in which differences between the two poles may be charted as varying ratios of intelligibility.

In other words, the individual/society opposition, like the self/other relation which contains it, must not be conceived as a dialectical either/or, but rather as *different degrees each possesses of the other's otherness*:

> The route leading from the content of the individual psyche to the content of culture is a long and hard one, but it is a single route, and throughout its entire extent at every stage it is determined by one and the same socioeconomic governance . . . [for] at all stages of this route human consciousness operates through words – the medium which is the most sensitive and at the same time the most complicated refraction of socioeconomic governance.

(*Freudianism: A Marxist Critique*, p. 87)[9]

The stages between individual and society are determined by their orientation toward either the pole of self or the pole of the other. At one extreme are incoherent associations so sunk in uniqueness that they do not achieve meaning even for the consciousness in which they occur: they are so particular to a given organism that they are unintelligible to the organism itself. At this level, perception is accomplished as a (relatively) unmediated stimulus/response mechanism with very little, if any, intervention from higher centers: there is no *selection* by the organism of the stimuli to which it will respond.

Above this inchoate level we begin to encounter the lower limits of inner speech. Inability to rise to higher levels of intelligibility after infancy (a stage without speech in which organisms have difficulty relating to otherness not directly tied to their biological needs) results in such disorders as autism or schizophrenia, conditions in which communication with others is impaired. It is not merely the inability to use language that is considered by the community of its users to be pathological; it is the inability to mediate between inner speech and the social dimension of language that is perceived as sickness.

Another pathology of language is "official discourse," at its purest a utopian language so compelling that no one would speak anything else. Official discourse in its most radical form resists communication: everyone is compelled to speak the same language (outer speech is all). It is a collective version of the mysterious disability called autism, victims of which cannot communicate with others because they (apparently) are not aware of them; or in other words, the individual exhausts the space of society (inner speech is all). Official discourse is autism for the masses. That is, extreme versions of official discourse are similar to autism in so far as they are totalitarian and do not recognize otherness: they abhor difference and aim for a single, collective self. This is why totalitarian societies seek a return to some primordial *Gemeinschaft*. Extreme versions of official discourse are totalitarian precisely to the degree that they assume no other selves beyond the one they posit as normative. In the totalitarian state, language seeks to drain the first person pronoun of all its particularity. Pathology provides examples of over-determined inner speech; history is full of examples of the over-investment in outer speech that results in the absolute language of totalitarian states.

Official languages, even those that are not totalitarian, are masks for ideologies of many different kinds, but they all privilege *oneness*; the more powerful the ideology, the more totalitarian (monologic) will be the claims of its language. Extreme versions of such language would be religious systems and certain visionary forms of government that have as their end that prelapsarian condition in which words are not necessary. Speech falls away because – in the state such ideologies wish to underwrite – no mediation is necessary since everyone's thought is in step with everyone else's. There is no difference between individual and society. Of course, such an extreme monologism is both theoretically and practically impossible: dialogism is a realism.

Self and other in Freud

Relations between inner and outer speech thus dramatize the interconnectedness of dialogism's various concerns, for though rooted in language, they cannot be examined without reference to psychology and social theory. To pursue this set of interrelated questions we need to clarify the way relations between inner and outer speech bear on relations between individual and society. We should begin by recognizing that Bakhtin is only one of several thinkers in the twentieth century who grappled with the question of how individual selves relate to social groups. Two among these others, Sigmund Freud and George Herbert Mead, will help us triangulate the specific contribution Bakhtin makes to understanding the problem.

Freud, like Bakhtin (and Saussure), sees the self as divided; it

is fallen apart into two pieces, one of which rages against the second . . . the piece which behaves so cruelly is not unknown to us . . . We have called it the "ego ideal," and by way of functions we have ascribed to it self-observation, the moral conscience, the censorship of dreams, and the chief influence in repression.[10]

The ego ideal is, then, immensely powerful, and would seem to work much as the otherness of society does in Bakhtin. But Freud stops short of directly relating the ego ideal to social force.

He must do so because his conception of the group is a very particular one that is difficult to extend to the more general level of what is usually meant by "society." Freud takes up the question of how individuals relate to groups as part of an attempt to extend his scenario of the family romance into the scenario of history, to make the Oedipal conflict between fathers, sons, and mothers the engine of change not only for individuals, but for whole cultures. And the Oedipal theory requires him to conceive society according to the model of the group we are given in his "scientific myth" of the primal horde. Thus he limits his discussion of social psychology to those groups (such as the church or the army) that have, like the horde in his just-so story, strong leaders: "A primary group . . . is a number of individuals who have put one and the same object in the place of their ego ideal and have consequently identified themselves with one another in their ego."[11]

This is a potentially powerful analytical assumption, but Freud betrays his essential commitment to isolated individuals by emphasizing group *leaders*, rather than focusing on groups as such. As a result, his account of the mechanism by which the group affects individual behavior (the movement from pleasure principle to reality principle) is most persuasive with regard to those particular groups that have such ruler figures. But it is obvious that many groups, indeed most groups, are not constituted as hordes. As such, the majority of groups bind individuals in more complex relations and have effects that are much subtler than those at work in religious or military organizations. By emphasizing leaders, Freud is psychologizing impersonal social force.

Freud makes a significant contribution to understanding the way in which individual persons are interpenetrated by group ideals. But what is lacking in his account of relations between individual and group is any concept of the *means* by which such relations are mediated: the scenario for interaction is over-personalized, made into a drama (a melodrama, really) involving real children and phantom parents. But, we may ask, by what means do the internalized phantoms communicate with the real actors? In what language does the internalized family romance play itself out in the theater of our minds?

Dialogism's answer to this question is that it is the same language as we use in the theater of society. The group as a collective and the individual members who comprise it all share the same language, which is whatever language (or more

accurately, whatever assemblage of possible discourses) they use
to communicate with each other in their day-to-day activity.
The essential clash between what Freud calls ego and ego ideal is
not an abstract tension between the former's libidinal spontaneity
and society's introjected demands in the latter. This description
is adequate so far as it goes, but it does not go far enough; what
needs to be added is that this opposition works itself out in highly
specific (and specifiable) circumstances as *a conflict between inner
and outer speech*. From this assumption flows Bakhtin's argument
for a necessary link between the study of psychology and the
study of language.

Self and other in George Herbert Mead

The doctrine that the nature of the psyche is best understood by
analogy with the nature of the sign is now closely associated with
Lacan's rereadings of Freud. We have forgotten that several
psychologies predating Lacan (and Bakhtin, too, of course) took
inner speech as a major a priori. At this point it will prove helpful
if we invoke another such psychology, the American school led
by James Mark Baldwin (1861–1934) (whose genetic stad-
ialism prefigures the work Piaget would later do on stages of
cognitive development), and James Rowland Angell (1869–
1949). In the decade preceding the First World War, Baldwin's
Mental Development in the Child and the Race and Angell's *Psychology:
an Introductory Study of the Structure and Function of Human
Consciousness* caused George Herbert Mead to ponder many of the
same questions that would preoccupy Bakhtin, particularly in
the area (neglected by Freud) of a language-based social
psychology.[12]

Baldwin distinguished between the ego, which resists social
pressures, and what he called the *socius*, a version of the self very
much like Freud's ego ideal, that accepts cultural norms and
adapts to its social surroundings. Mead recognized the essential
validity of such a division, but felt Baldwin had not sufficiently
taken into account its radical implications: "if the self-form is an
essential form of all our consciousness it necessarily carries with it
the other-form. Whatever may be the metaphysical impossibilities
or possibilities of solipsism, psychologically it is nonexistent.
There must be other selves if one's own is to exist."[13] Mead went

further than other American social scientists who were concerned with individual/group relations (and further than Freud as well), because he recognized that such relations were ultimately grounded in the medium shared by both individuals and groups, that is in language. Indeed, it was language that enabled the society which in turn permitted the existence of individuals: "consciousness of meaning is social in its origin . . . thought remains [even] in its abstract form *sublimated conversation*. Thus reflective consciousness implies a social situation which has been its precondition."[14]

Thus, not only does Mead, like Bakhtin, recognize that "In the process of communication the individual is an other before he is a self," but that "out of this process thought arises, i.e., conversation with one's self, in the role of the specific other and then in the role of the generalized other."[15] That is, the individual recognizes not only that thought is inner speech ("conversation with one's self") but that it is inner *dialogue*. Having recognized that language is the basis of thought, and thus the ground of all self/other relations, Mead failed to go further and say precisely what it was that gave language such enormous power.[16]

Thoughtful linguists have always been aware of the apparent contradiction between language's need of an invariant code (so that it may serve to convey meanings for everyone in the group) and its no less pressing need to be able to break the code (so that it may serve to communicate specific meaning for particular individuals in the group). Jakobson, for example, has argued that there is a hierarchy of different kinds of linguistic units in which the move from bottom to top represents "an ascending scale of freedom." At the bottom of the hierarchy are such units as phonemes, made up of even smaller "distinctive features." In deploying these, "the freedom of the individual speaker is zero: the code has already established all the possibilities which may be utilized in the given language." At the next level, there is some small freedom available in the way we combine phonemes into words. But this "liberty" is limited to the marginal situation of word coinage, as in Lewis Carroll's nonsense poems or the "trans-sense" vocabulary of such Futurist poets as Velemir Khlebnikov. At the higher level where words are combined into sentences, the speaker is less constrained. And finally, in the combination of sentences into utterances, the action of compulsory syntactical rules ceases, and "the freedom of any individual speaker to create novel contexts increases substantially."[7]

The great question left unanswered by Jakobson, Mead (and others) was this: what is it in language that binds individuals into groups and *at the same time* enables individuals to exist as selves? Put another way, the question becomes: what is the *particular* feature in language that serves as the threshold between selves and others? Bakhtin finds an answer in language's capacity to model addressivity and dialogue. He takes the implications of dialogue to their radical extreme and assumes that at no level where communication is possible is the subject ever isolated.

Non-Bakhtinian theories of dialogue

Bakhtin's relentless emphasis on dialogic relations sets him apart even from those other thinkers who, like him, have sought the essence of language in dialogue. What seems surprising is that there have been very few such thinkers. In the modern period, these have perhaps been only three: Gustave Tarde, Lev Yakubinsky, and Jan Mukarovsky. In 1901, Tarde, a French social philosopher, argued for the importance of dialogue, but he did so within the framework of *conversation*. By conversation he did not mean spoken speech in general, but the more restricted sort of exchange that takes place in forums set aside expressly for talk, such as the *salons* of Parisian society. Yakubinsky, a linguist and early member of the Russian Formalists, sought in 1923 to unpack the proposition (made almost in passing by his teacher, Lev Shcherba) that "*language reveals its genuine essence only in dialogue*."[8] Yakubinsky's essay influenced two later thinkers, Vygotsky and Mukarovsky, a leading theorist of the Prague Linguistic Circle. Arguing that "Dialogue . . . appears to be a more 'natural' phenomenon than monologue,"[19] Yakubinsky expanded dialogue's meaning beyond that of a conversational exchange between two speakers. But his emphasis is still narrowly linguistic, remaining on the formal syntactic and pronominal usages which have been developed to include other speakers. There is a hint in Yakubinsky of the potentially

revolutionary consequences dialogue as a *principle* might have
have for conceiving linguistics in a new light, but he does not go
on to articulate them.[20]

In his 1940 essay "Dialogue and monologue" Mukarovsky
seeks to go beyond Tarde and Yakubinsky by appealing to what
might be called the "Goldilocks" principle of not too hot, not too
cold, but just right. Tarde perceives monologue as primary and
plays down the role of dialogue; Yakubinsky claims too much
exclusivity for dialogue. Mukarovsky's formula is somewhere in
between. He says, "The relation between monologue and
dialogue can be characterized rather as a dynamic polarity in
which sometimes dialogue, sometimes monologue gains the
upper hand according to the milieu and the time."[21]

Working out the further implications of this position,
Mukarovsky comes extremely close to Bakhtin (and Vygotsky)
especially in formulating what the nature of the speaking subject
must be if dialogue is indeed so pervasive a force in language.
Unlike Yakubinsky, who limits the effects of dialogue to formally
observable linguistic elements such as pronouns, Mukarovsky
perceives the broader epistemological implications of dialogue.
In terms very close to those of Bakhtin himself, he says
the "essential feature of dialogue [the interpenetration and
alternation of several contextures] is already contained in the
mental event from which the utterance originates and . . .
therefore has priority over the utterance." He adds "it is now
clear where the source of the oscillation between the unity and
multiplicity of the subject in the individual's consciousness . . .
lies."[22]

Unlike Tarde and Yakubinsky, Mukarovsky's ideas are
obviously close to those of Bakhtin. There are differences as well,
of course, the most obvious being that for Bakhtin dialogue is the
central category informing all his work, whereas for Mukarovsky
it is merely the topic for two short essays. Why, if there are so
many similarities in their conception of it, did dialogue seem of
such importance to Bakhtin but play a relatively minor role in
Mukarovsky?

The major difference between the two – and it is fundamental
– is the way each conceived the relation of monologue to
dialogue. Mukarovsky perceived the two as of *equal* significance;
in other words, monologue has the same status in reality as

dialogue: "monologic and dialogic qualities are simultaneously and inseparably present in the psychic event from which the utterance originates."[23]

Bakhtin, on the other hand, conceives monologue as not only secondary in importance to dialogue, but as having a different ontological status. Dialogue is real, monologue is not; at worst, monologue is an illusion, as when it is uncritically taken for granted. Or at best, monologue is a logical construct necessary to understand the working of dialogue, as in the work of Yakubinsky and Mukarovsky:

> But the monologic utterance is, after all, already an abstraction. . . . Any monologic utterance . . . is an inseverable element of verbal communication. Any utterance – the finished, written utterance not excepted – makes response to something and is calculated to be responded to in turn. *It is but one link in a continuous chain of speech performances.*
>
> (*Marxism and the Philosophy of Language*, p. 72; italics added)

The study of language so conceived is properly not linguistics, but communication. The study of communication differs from the study of language as such (or at least as it is conceived in the practice of most professional linguists) in a number of ways, the most fundamental of which is that in communication there is no point at which the speaker may be thought of as an isolated entity. In the sphere of communication the individuality of the speaker is always and everywhere *relative*.

"Language" looks different when all of its components are conceived as in dialogue. For instance, it will become immediately apparent that at all levels from "distinctive feature" up through utterance, no unit exists in itself, but only in tension with all the others. The very capacity of such "invariant" features as phonemes to play a role in meaning presumes interplay with variance. The arena in which the identity and difference of even such apparently extrapersonal elements find themselves in conversation with each other is that of the specific utterance.

The fundamental role of utterance in dialogism: addressivity

Utterance (*vyskazyvanie*, высказывание) is the topic of analysis when language is conceived as dialogue, the fundamental unit of investigation for anyone studying communication as opposed to language alone. Since Bakhtin's idea of the utterance is active, *performed*, there is always a danger that it will be confused with the Saussurian concept of "speech" (*parole*) in which apparently willed performance is a key aspect. Utterance as it is used in dialogism is not the completely free act of choice Saussure posited. The Bakhtinian utterance is dialogic precisely in the degree to which *every aspect* of it is a give-and-take between the local need of a particular speaker to communicate a specific meaning, and the global requirements of language as a generalizing system. While there is some room for relative freedom in the utterance, it is always achieved in the face of pre-existing restraints of several kinds, some of which had always been recognized by linguists (such as those listed by Jakobson) and some of which Bakhtin was the first to recognize (such as speech genres, which we will take up in a moment).

A primary way in which the constraints on choice make themselves apparent is in the fact that an utterance is never *in itself* originary: an utterance is always an answer. It is always an answer to another utterance that precedes it, and is therefore always conditioned by, and in turn qualifies, the prior utterance to a greater or lesser degree. Before it means any specific thing, an utterance expresses the general condition of each speaker's addressivity, the situation of not only being preceded by a language system that is "always already there," but preceded as well by all of existence, making it necessary for me to answer for the particular place I occupy. The formal, objective way in which this need manifests itself is in the fact that discourse of any kind (spoken or written) is segmented not only by words and sentences, but also by protocols that establish whose turn it is to make the next utterance. The different ways in which speakers (and writers) indicate appropriate points for others to respond are enormously varied, of course, but relations between utterances, the context that makes them meaningful in specific situations, are always conditioned by the potential response of an other (a fundamental point sometimes played down in studying what is called turn-taking in current linguistics).

It is this fated in-between-ness of all utterance which insures that communication can take place only in society, for the rules that determine precedence in speaking develop out of group practice: they are not "wired into" the brain. The norms controlling the utterance are similar to other social norms, such as those found in judicial or ethical systems. They may vary in their details, but the nature of their existence remains the same: they exist only in the individual minds of particular people in particular groups. In dialogism, of course, the "I" of such individual minds is always assumed to be a function of the "we" that is their particular group.

An utterance, then, is a border phenomenon. It takes place between speakers, and is therefore drenched in social factors. This means that the utterance is also on the border between what is said and what is not said, since, as a social phenomenon *par excellence*, the utterance is shaped by speakers who assume that the values of their particular community are shared, and thus do not need to be spelled out in what they say. The simultaneity of the said and unsaid is most apparent in the area of intonation, which is where the repeatable, merely linguistic stuff of the utterance is stitched to the unrepeatable social situation in which it is spoken. Intonation is the immediate interface between said and unsaid: it "pumps energy from a life situation into verbal discourse – it endows everything linguistically stable with living historical momentum and uniqueness" ("Discourse in life and discourse in art," p. 106).[24]

Intonation clearly registers the other's presence, creating a kind of portrait in sound of the addressee to whom the speaker imagines he or she is speaking. A common illustration of this tendency is found when we hear someone talking on the telephone to another person whose identity we do not know, but whose relation to the speaker we can guess from his or her speech patterns. Intonation is a material expression of the shaping role the other plays in the speech production of any individual self. The community of shared values gives different semantic weight to the physically articulated acoustical shifts in pitch or volume. We never convey objective information in our speech; we always pass judgment on whatever information is contained in what we say: "The commonness of assumed basic value judgments constitutes the canvas upon which living human speech embroiders the designs of intonation" (ibid., p. 103).

Verbal discourse, then, is the means by which actual life situations structure themselves. They do so as scenarios dramatizing specific events. Any account of utterance must

> reproduce this event of the mutual [simultaneous] relationships between speakers, must, as it were, restructure it, with the person wishing to understand taking upon himself the role of listener. But in order to carry out that role, he must distinctly understand the position of the other as well.
>
> (ibid., p. 106)

To illustrate dialogism's principle that "in life, verbal discourse is clearly not self-sufficient," (ibid., p. 98), Bakhtin provides an analysis of a text. The text consists of a single word: " well." Or, more accurately, as the context makes clear, "Well!" Since this analysis is relatively short, and yet makes clear several points about the utterance, I will quote it in full:

> Two people are sitting in a room. They are both silent. Then one of them says, "Well!" The other does not respond.
>
> For us, as outsiders, this entire "conversation" is utterly incomprehensible. Taken in isolation, the utterance "Well!" is empty and unintelligible. Nevertheless, this peculiar colloquy of two persons , consisting of only one – although, to be sure, one expressively intoned – word [the word in Russian is *tak*, так], does make perfect sense, is fully meaningful and complete.
>
> In order to disclose the sense and meaning of this colloquy, we must analyze it. But what is it exactly that we can subject to analysis? Whatever pains we take with the purely verbal part of the utterance, however subtly we define the phonetic, morphological, and semantic factors of the word *well*, we shall still not come a single step closer to an understanding of the whole sense of the colloquy.
>
> Let us suppose that the intonation with which this word was pronounced is known to us: indignation and reproach moderated by a certain amount of humor. This intonation somewhat fills in the semantic void of the adverb *well*, but still does not reveal the meaning of the whole.
>
> What is it we lack, then? We lack the "extraverbal context" that made the word *well* a meaningful locution for the listener. This *extraverbal context* of the utterance is comprised of three

factors: (1) the *common spatial purview* of the interlocutors (the unity of the visible – in this case, the room, a window, and so on), (2) the *interlocutors" common knowledge and understanding of the situation*, and (3) their *common evaluation* of that situation.

At the time the colloquy took place, both interlocutors *looked up* at the window and *saw* that it had begun to snow; *both knew* that it was already May and that it was high time for spring to come; finally, *both* were *sick and tired* of the protracted winter – *they were both looking forward* to spring "and *both were bitterly disappointed* by the late snowfall. On this "jointly seen" (snowflakes outside the window), "jointly known" (the time of the year – May), and "unanimously evaluated" (winter wearied of, spring looked forward to) – on all this the utterance *directly depends*, all this is seized in its actual, living import – is its very sustenance. And yet all this remains without verbal specification or articulation. The snowflakes remain outside the window; the date, on the page of a calendar; the evaluation, in the psyche of the speaker; and nevertheless, all this is assumed in the word *well*.

(ibid., p. 99)

This little parable about the nature of the utterance is, of course, *itself* an utterance, and thus its lesson can be read in multiple ways. But one thing should be very clear: in so far as an utterance is not merely *what is said*, it does not passively reflect a situation that lies outside language. Rather, the utterance is a deed, it is active, productive: it resolves a situation, brings it to an evaluative conclusion (for the moment at least), or extends action into the future. In other words, consciousness is the medium and utterance the specific means by which two otherwise disparate elements – the quickness of experience and the materiality of language – are harnessed into a volatile unity. Discourse does not reflect a situation, it *is* a situation. Each time we talk, we literally enact values in our speech through the process of scripting our place and that of our listener in a culturally specific social scenario. Cultural specificity is able to penetrate the otherwise abstract system of language because utterances in dialogism are not (as in Saussure's *parole*) un-fettered speech: Saussure ignores the fact that "in addition to the forms of language there exist as well *forms of combinations of these forms*" (*Estetika*, p. 79).[25]

Speech Genres

A given culture makes itself felt in specific utterances at particular times through the work of three kinds of restrictions, which Bakhtin calls collectively "speech genres." They are: what is perceived as the immanent semantic exhaustiveness of the utterance's theme (how much elaboration and effort is felt to be adequate in speaking about the weather as opposed to speaking about the meaning of life); the speech plan of the speaker (what he or she intends to accomplish by saying this in just this way at this particular time); and the typical generic forms of finalization.

The first of these is relatively simple to grasp. Certain themes are typically dealt with in highly standardized ways in which the limits of exhaustiveness are rigidly determined, such as military orders: anything beyond the single-word utterance "Halt!" when one is seeking to bring marching soldiers to a stop would clearly be excessive.

Most other themes have much less constricting limits (i.e. are more independent of their context), which means that in most other forms of utterance the second restrictive aspect, the speech plan of the speaker, plays a larger role in shaping what gets said. In any utterance we posit what the speaker wishes to say, usually well before it has been completed:

> This is the subjective aspect of utterance; it is combined into an inseparable unity with its objective aspect, or what is inherently appropriate to the subject of the utterance, limiting this aspect by relating it to a concrete . . . situation of speech communication, with all its individual circumstances, its personal participants, and with the utterances that precede it.

> (ibid., p. 256)

Bakhtin sometimes calls speech plan (*rechevoii zamys'l*, речевой замысьл) speech will (*rechevaya volya* речевая воля), a term that seems at odds with the restrictiveness implicit in the governing concept of *genre*. In order to meet the danger of being so misunderstood, Bakhtin goes out of his way to underscore the restraining role played by the third category determining the structure of an utterance, the habitual forms of expression available for saying such and such a thing in such and such a situation.

In effect, the plan of the speaker can be realized only in his or her selection of *this* speech genre versus *that* one in any given instance. These typical forms of utterance come to us as we learn to speak (a process, of course, that does not conclude with the end of infancy but which continues all our conscious lives). In fact

> to learn to speak means to learn to construct utterances
> . . . We learn to cast our speech in generic forms and, when we
> hear others' speech, we deduce its genre from the first words;
> we anticipate in advance a certain volume (that is, the
> approximate length of the speech whole) as well as a certain
> compositional structure. We foresee the end; that is, from the
> very beginning we have a sense of the speech whole.
>
> (ibid., p. 258)

Speakers' evaluative attitudes toward what they are talking about (even attempting to be neutral is to enact certain values), plus their judgment of to whom they are talking, determine the choice of language units (lexical, grammatical) *and* communication units (the composition of the utterance, the speech genres employed). This evaluative component of speech is what determines the expressive aspect of the utterance. Words exist for the speaker in three possible relations that can be enacted toward them: "as a neutral word of the language [as a word in a dictionary, a word that signifies, but does not mean], as an *other*'s word, and as my word" (ibid., p. 268). These last two relations are those in which expressiveness – the individual style of the utterance – comes into play. It is here we see another difference between language and communication: phonemes and syntax have in common with speech genres a tendency to limit the freedom of individual speakers. Not only are words and sentences always already there, but so are the forms for their combination into utterances. The difference between the two is in the degree to which each is normative (speech genres are less restrictive than, for instance, phonemes).

The individual style of the utterance can be determined by its expressive side because the forms of communication are more open to play and intervention than the forms of language. Expressiveness is a different level of integration. Intonation, word choice, selection of a particular speech genre – all these are open to assimilation (*osvoenie*, освоение, making something one's own) by individual speakers as means for registering different values. Obviously, some genres are more malleable than others: the give-and-take at the information counter of a railroad station, or an air hostess's request for a passenger's choice of beverage and the response, will be maximally codified, whereas the possibilities for exchange between intimate friends having a heart-to-heart talk over a good wine at two a.m. will be considerably more diverse (but restricted, nevertheless, by such contextual factors as the generation of the speakers, the site of their conversation, and so on). Generic control may be more or less obvious, but it is always there.

We touch here on the aspect of utterance which comes closest to explaining why Bakhtin – who began his career with a long philosophical investigation of authorship – spent most of the rest of his life meditating on the social basis of language. For, as denizens of the logosphere, the sea of words in which we pass our lives, we are surrounded by forms that in themselves seek the condition of mere being-there, the sheer givenness of brute nature. In order to invest those forms with life and meaning, so that we may be understood and so that the work of the social world may continue, *we must all perforce become authors*.

4
Novelness as dialogue: The novel of education and the education of the novel

Bakhtin's literary studies, when taken together, constitute a manifesto proclaiming a cohesive body of ideas about the nature of literature.[1] Individually, each of his major books permits him a different perspective, and each is marked by different shadings and nuances; but their common trait is that each demonstrates a specific aspect of dialogism. Each of these works, in itself, has a certain manifesto-like quality, which is reflected first of all in the sweeping claims Bakhtin makes for the topics he addresses: for instance, he makes it clear that he has chosen to write about Dostoevsky, or Rabelais, because they have exercised influence on western culture as a whole, not just on literature. Such figures have, in Bakhtin's view, modified the nature of perception itself. Dostoevsky's innovations have a significance that "extends far beyond the limits of the novel alone" (*Problems of Dostoevsky's Poetics*, p. 3); and of Rabelais it is proclaimed that, "To be understood, he requires an essential reconstruction of our entire artistic and ideological perception" (*Rabelais and his World*, p. 3).

What is more, the larger significance of these figures has previously gone undetected, because misguided philologists have mistakenly studied them only because of the role they have played in a too narrowly conceived literary history: "The utter inadequacy of literary theory is exposed when it is forced to deal with the novel" ("Discourse in the novel," p. 8). The strongly implied assumption in such declarations is that Bakhtin's treatment of these subjects will remedy the mistakes of previous scholarship: after hundreds of years Rabelais will now finally be understood. Dostoevsky will now be rescued from all those other critics who failed to perceive the true nature of his achievement. And the novel will now cease to be perceived as merely one more genre among other literary genres. It will instead be recognized as the marker for a revolution in human perception.

These are extravagant claims, and in this chapter we will examine some of the reasons why Bakhtin felt justified in making them. Ultimately we will want to know why a thinker so concerned to understand the workings of discourse in general should assign such great importance to the particular form of discourse called literature.

For Bakhtin, the royal road to a better understanding of any particular literary topic is essentially the same, whether the topic be a figure such as Rabelais or Dostoevsky, or a genre such as the epic or the novel. Crudely stated, "literariness" (or, what Bakhtin calls "novelness") is the study of any cultural activity that has treated language as dialogic. The relation between literature and dialogue that Bakhtin posits is not the same as a relation between literature and *language*; in this we have one of the biggest differences between Bakhtin and the early Formalists, who were, in fact, looking for a one-to-one analogue between the system of literature and the system of language. The Formalist concept of literature was essentially *linguistic*: the literary text could be a self-contained object because words – the stuff out of which it was "made" – belonged to a unitary, impersonal language *code*. And in so far as it was a code, it belonged to no one.

For Bakhtin, on the contrary, literary texts are utterances, words that cannot be divorced from particular subjects in specific situations. In other words, literature is another form of communication, and, as such, another form of knowledge.

Literary texts, like other kinds of utterance, depend not only on the activity of the author, but also on the place they hold in the social and historical forces at work when the text is produced and when it is consumed. Words in literary texts are active elements in a dialogic exchange taking place on several different levels at the same time (it is this overriding feature of *simultaneity* that seems most difficult to grasp for those just coming to dialogism). At the highest level of abstraction, this dialogue is between the two tendencies that energize language's power to mean: the Manichaean opposition between centrifugal forces that seek to keep things apart, and centripetal forces that work to make things cohere. At another level, it is between language at the level of code, i.e. the level of prescribed meanings (where "tree" means any tree), and language at the level of discourse (where "tree" means *this* tree here and now, with all the cultural associations that cling to trees in this time and in this place). At still another level, simultaneity is a dialogue between the different meanings the same word has at different stages in the history of a given national language, and in various situations within the same historical period. And, of course, simultaneity is found in the dialogue between an author, his characters, and his audience, as well as in the dialogue of readers with the characters and their author.

Heteroglossia

The simultaneity of these dialogues is merely a particular instance of the larger polyphony of social and discursive forces which Bakhtin calls "heteroglossia." Heteroglossia is a situation, the situation of a subject surrounded by the myriad responses he or she might make at any particular point, but any one of which must be framed in a specific discourse selected from the teeming thousands available. Heteroglossia is a way of conceiving the world as made up of a roiling mass of languages, each of which has its own distinct formal markers. These features are never *purely* formal, for each has associated with it a set of distinctive values and presuppositions. Heteroglossia governs the operation of meaning in the kind of utterance we call a literary text, as it does in *any* utterance. Thus, before we ask what might be distinctive about "literary" discourse, it will be useful to know more about the general properties of heteroglossia.

Dialogism assumes that at any given time, in any given place, there is a set of powerful but highly unstable conditions at work that will give a word uttered then and there a meaning that is different from what it would be at other times and in other places. The conditions that make for such differences are to be found in the nature of language, but include other factors as well. Conventional forms of analysis would dismiss some of these other factors as inappropriate or trivial: details such as differences in the weather, in the physical condition of the speakers, for example. But dialogism assumes such contingent details are reflected in utterance and have an effect on the way formal linguistic features can convey meaning. All utterances are heteroglot in that they are shaped by forces whose particularity and variety are practically beyond systematization. The idea of heteroglossia comes as close as possible to conceptualizing a locus where the great centripetal and centrifugal forces that shape discourse can meaningfully come together.

Textual space and genres

Centripetal and centrifugal forces interact most powerfully with each other at the level where their mutual struggle creates the kind of space we call texts, space that gives structure to their simultaneity. Space of this kind is available only at the level where a given discourse coalesces into recognizable genres. This is so because genre is a collective phenomenon, whereas "style" may be conceived as individual style. The Formalist definition of "literariness" depended on an approach to language at the level of stylistics. "Novelness" treats language at the level of epistemology and of social dynamics. We may speak of a particular person's style; but an individual cannot, of course, constitute a genre. For the collective aspect of genre as such insures that the rise or fall of a specific genre will be a more accurate measure of the social and historical forces at work over long spans of time than the vogue for a style or (least of all) the reputation of specific authors, which would in any case be a subfunction of the fate of the genre in which they character-istically worked.

It follows from this that the major categories in Bakhtin's thinking about literature are genres, and he is uncharacteristically harsh in condemning other critics for ignoring the history of literature as the history of struggle among genres: "They do not see beneath the superficial hustle and bustle of literary process the major and crucial fates of literature and language, whose great heroes turn out to be first and foremost genres, and whose 'trends' and 'schools' are but second or third-rank protagonists" ("Epic and Novel," pp. 7–8.)

It is often assumed that a discourse finds its most lasting and comprehensive form at the level where it is conjoined with the particular institution that uses it. Thus the essence of legal language is to be sought in "the law," or the deepest meaning of other technical languages is to be found in the practice of "medicine" or the practice of "computer engineering," let us say. This assumption lies behind the Formalist prejudice that the essence of literary language (or, more accurately, what is perceived at a given historical moment as literary language) is to be found in the institutional practice called "literature." Such relations between particular discourses and institutions, are, of course, highly important and cannot be ignored.

The determining role of everyday speech in genre formation: Primary and secondary genres

However, the level where genres are deployed in professional discourses is not where their coalescence into recognizable patterns can best be seen. Dialogism assumes that the bases of genre formation are to be found, rather, in the rules that govern speech activity in our everyday conversations, since they take place beyond the restrictions that an isolated professional patois might seek to impose. Dialogism's assumption here is that in most conversations, one-to-one correspondences between discourses and institutions are not strictly observed. Because everyday speech is never narrowly technical, the genres that shape it are subtler and, paradoxically, more *normative* than those that are legislated by unitary institutional or professional usage. Thus, from the point of view of genre formation, the norms governing professional languages (or other forms of institutional argots) are *secondary* to another set of constraints that are even more fundamental: those genres that legislate language usage in all its spoken, everyday, transinstitutional variety.

The obligatory forms that govern everyday speech communication Bakhtin calls "primary speech genres," because they come into being *before* they are specified into institutional forms. The priority is obviously not as neat as this formulation would make it appear, and there is a constant give-and-take between primary and secondary genres that in any specific case makes it difficult to assign priority to either one or the other. It can be said in general, however, that speech genres constitute the primary material out of which all other particular kinds of utterances are constructed, including such secondary genres as are found in literature.

The distinctiveness of the novel among other genres

Bakhtin is particularly drawn to the novel, the genre least secure (or most self-conscious) about its own status as a genre. The kind of text we have come to call "the novel" has been most at pains to establish its generic identity not only relative to other literary genres, but as it relates to the norms of everyday speech, which are the bases of genre formation itself. And it does this by flaunting or *displaying* the variety of discourses, knowledge of which other genres seek to *suppress*. What marks the novel off as distinctive within the range of all possible genres (both literary and non-literary, as well as primary or secondary) is the novel's peculiar ability to open a window in discourse from which the extraordinary variety of social languages can be perceived. The novel is able to create a work space in which that variety is not only displayed, but in which it can become an active force in shaping cultural history.

In Bakhtin's treatment of it, the novel is sometimes a liberating *bogatyr*, hero, and sometimes a debunking trickster. In either case, Bakhtin makes some apparently inexplicable claims for his champion. These claims will sound wildly overblown if we do not recognize from the outset an important distinction Bakhtin makes between "novels" and "novelness," that is the distinction between actual examples of the literary genre we now recognize as the novel, and a characteristic feature they all share, but which is not confined to novels as such (although they manifest it in the highest degree): the feature of "novelness" (*romannost*'). Rabelais and Dostoevsky are significant for Bakhtin not merely because they write novels, but because they advance the work of novelness. And it is novelness – not the novel, not Rabelais, not even Dostoevsky – that is the name of his real hero.

The vision of novelness grows out of Bakhtin's conception of language, and his ideas about language are rooted in his epistemology. Novelness is a means for charting changes that have come about as a result of increasing sensitivity to the problem of non-identity. Greater or lesser degrees of novelness can serve as an index of greater or lesser awareness of otherness. The history of the novel has its place in literary history, but the history of novelness is situated in the history of human consciousness.

Novelness in the history of consciousness

Since at least the German Romantics, conflating the history of literature with the history of consciousness has been a move that characterizes most theories of the novel. Bakhtin provides several different versions of novel history, all of which are tied to the history of novelness, and thus they all appear to have some affinity with Hegelian ideas about history being the history of Mind. There are patent filiations in Bakhtin's concept of novelness to certain key ideas of Hegel, or at least to that Hegel who inspired the young Lukács of *Theory of the Novel*. Now, it is well known that Bakhtin was a thinker with little sympathy for Hegelian dialectics, which in his later notebooks he explicitly attacks. We are, then, confronted with a contradiction here that will require a bit of sorting out.

What all three thinkers (Hegel, Lukács, and Bakhtin) appear to have in common is a vision of history conceived as the history of consciousness. History is treated as a kind of *Bildungsroman*, in fact, that sees the ontogenetic growth of individual people from birth to maturity as a phylogenetic pattern for all human beings over the whole course of time, a kind of collective biography from prehistory to the present. Moreover, all three would appear to share the same sense of what it is that defines maturation: it is the development of consciousness in the specific form of self-consciousness. And just as various stages in the life of individual men and women are marked by particular kinds of achievements that are appropriate to, for example, youth or old age, so in the life of the species we may identify higher or lower stages of development on the basis of the works that are characteristic of each.

This pattern is most obvious in Hegel, where the story begins at a time when people, like infants, were aware of themselves only as undifferentiated subfunctions of an all-encompassing environment. The Egyptian pyramid is the great symbol of such an early stage, a pile of stony matter that offers (in Hegel's view) only minimal evidence of mind's separation from mere things. Ancient Greek statues represent a kind of middle stage, characterized by a harmony that renders visible the balance between marble and the activity of intelligence. The Gothic cathedral, with its upward surge of spires and flying buttresses, manifests a new stage in which the symmetry of matter and mind is shattered, as spirit seeks to liberate itself from the stone to achieve a purer state of consciousness. That stage will be reached when art, which cannot exist without manifesting itself in matter of some kind, ceases to be the characteristic expression of mind, and is supplanted by philosophy, the activity of pure thought unshackled by matter of any kind.

Hegel suggests that the novel is characteristic of a late stage in the history of consciousness. But it is Lukács who gives the most sustained account of the novel's role in the Hegelian scenario of the rise of self-consciousness. *Theory of the Novel* is a complex and beautiful book in many ways, but its implicit narrative scheme is fairly simple. The story begins at one state of human consciousness and ends at another. More specifically, it begins with the Homeric Greek heroes who have very little, if any, sense of having unique selves. They do not sense a distinction between themselves, their society, and nature. And the story ends with modern men, so saturated with self-consciousness that they seem to wander the world alone, alienated from themselves and their culture – and alienated ultimately from the cosmos itself.

Lukács tells this story as a journey from one genre, the epic (in which men have little sense of themselves as unique identities but are at home in the universe), to another genre, the novel (the form which is "like no other, an expression of transcendental homelessness").[2] In Hegel and Lukács, development in consciousness means greater and greater awareness of one's self as a unique self: the inner form of the novel is perceived as "the process of the problematic individual's journeying towards himself . . . towards a clear self-recognition."[3] Such individuality is so radical that it condemns the novelistic hero to loneliness and alienation: he finds out "through experience that a mere glimpse of meaning is the highest life has to offer."[4]

Bakhtin's differences with Hegel and Lukács

Bakhtin differs fundamentally from Hegel and Lukács, although his dialogic history of the novel is also tied to a history of consciousness. In Bakhtin's history, the criteria by which higher degrees of consciousness can be judged are not singularity and unity as in Hegel and Lukács, but rather multiplicity and variety. Another fundamental difference consists in the conception of progress that obtains in dialogism: instead of the unitary and constantly upward-moving surge of progressive consciousness that we find in Hegel and Lukács, dialogism conceives history as a constant contest between monologue and dialogue, with the possibility of reversions always present. The novel is the characteristic text of a particular stage in the history of consciousness not because it marks the self's discovery of itself, but because it manifests the self's discovery of the other.

At first glance, this may appear merely to be a difference in emphasis, but Bakhtin's story about the novel differs substantially from that of Lukács: first of all in its conception of how literary forms calibrate with levels of self-awareness. More fundamentally, dialogism's sense of maturation, as well as how it comes about, is radically at odds with Hegelian models of development.

Hegel and Lukács are working with what is essentially a base/superstructure model; it is precisely the opposite of Marx's version of base/superstructure, which is one of the things Marx had in mind when he said he had turned Hegel on his head. Hegel and the early Lukács (he rued it in his later, Marxist phase) see the movement of developing Mind as the great engine of change in the universe: Mind is the whole of which all particular events are always only a part. Mind is the basis on which all specific acts of creation (whether they result in material objects or aesthetic objects) form a mere excrescence. But the separation of spirit and matter will – in the end – be overcome in a final sublation-of-sublations that will have as its result Mind in its purest state. Thus the course of history is from the oneness of brute matter, through the struggle of mind to free itself from all that is not itself, to pure mind or, in other words, to *another oneness*.

In dialogism, the course of history is also conceived as a history of greater or lesser awareness, but it is a sequence that *has no necessary telos built into it*. It is a narrative that has the appearance of being developmental only from a present point of view. From that point of view it is a tale that can be recapitulated in the history of the novel as a genre. The novel can be used in this way not because it is a register for some mysterious property called Mind or Consciousness, but because of its unique relation to the primary genres of everyday speech. All secondary genres – including literary genres – bear a mediated relation to spoken speech. But the novel's relation to everyday talk is particularly significant, because it is the very variety of language, the constant reminders of otherness in speech, that constitute the novel's characteristic subject, as well as its formal features.

The history of primary genres controlling everyday language has no necessary direction built into it – ideas about "progress" in the development of languages have long been discredited. Therefore, the history of the novel, the secondary genre having the most intimate connection to spoken speech, will not be wired for any specific line of development. Instead of a teleology whose course is a movement from one unitary state to another, Bakhtin's historical masterplot opens with a deluded perception of unity and goes on to a growing knowledge of ever-increasing difference and variety that cannot be overcome in any uniting synthesis (Kant's heteronomy of ends, as opposed to Hegel's triumph of *Geist*).

In the aboriginal state, mind and world were *already* cut off from each other, as they always will be, but people failed to perceive the gap. At that early stage they deluded themselves with myths of unity (the unity of a single word and its meaning, the unity and uniqueness of a whole specific language, the unity of culture and nature). With the rise of the novel, "Two myths perish simultaneously: the myth of a language that presumes to be the only language, and the myth of a language that presumes to be completely unified."[5]

As ethnography has demonstrated again and again when discovering new aboriginal communities all over the globe, tribes that have had little or no contact with other cultures more often than not designate themselves by a term that means simply "the people," or "human beings." Assuming they were the only people in the world, it followed logically that their language was the only one in existence. Whether such societies had what we might now call epics or not, it is this sense of oneness that

Bakhtin has in mind when he invokes unity as the basic determinant of epic consciousness. In Lukács' Hegelian scheme the move from epic to novel is irreversible (the epic has been *aufgehoben*). In stark contrast, Bakhtin's history conceives a *constant* struggle between two impulses that may be labeled epic and novel for purposes of convenience, but the real struggle is not confined to these two super genres. Thus novelness can in local instances still be overcome by epic-ness (the so-called Socialist Realist novel under high Stalinism being a case in point).

The epic is, then, not a genre confined to a moment in the distant past. It is historical precisely in the sense that it represents an always-still-available possibility. It is the genre typical of societies in which diversity and change either go unrecognized or are actively suppressed: "The epic world is constructed in the zone of an absolute, distanced image, beyond the sphere of possible contact with the developing, incomplete and therefore re-thinking and re-evaluating present" ("Epic and Novel," p. 17.)

Summing up this part of our argument, we can say that the biggest difference between Bakhtin and the Hegelian/early Lukácsian model of the history of consciousness is that for Bakhtin this history has no clearly defined end or telos. This open-endedness generates not only a contrasting sense of the novel's role in history, but an opposed sense of what the novel is. While Bakhtin and Lukács both assume that the development of humans as a species is similar to the development of a single human being, they interpret this development in quite different ways: each reads the novel as if it were a clock, but they fundamentally disagree about the time that clock tells. If we are prepared to grant that history records changes in how humans have perceived themselves and the world, then it soon becomes obvious that Bakhtin and Hegel/Lukács cannot agree on the question of how such changes reflect themselves at earlier and later stages. In other words, while both sides conceive history as a *Bildungsroman*, they operate with *fundamentally opposed theories of education*.

Differing historiographies as different versions of the educative process: Hegel, Lukács, and Piaget

In Hegel's dialectical version of history there is an iron law of entelechy at work. We get something similar to the theory of

cognitive development as it unfolds in human children found in
Piaget. For the Hegel/Lukács view of historical development
might also be called, in Piaget's terminology, a "genetic
epistemology" in so far as that theory assumes for humans
as a species what Piaget assumes for the child as individual, that
is a distinct teleology that progresses through preordained
levels.[6]

Both approaches offer a version of determinism. Piaget shows
that a child of 4 or 5, no matter how gifted, who has been shown
two equal amounts of liquid in similarly shaped containers, and
is then shown the liquid from one container poured into a taller
one, will always conclude that there is a difference in the amount
of liquid in the last container. Piaget concluded that at this level
of development the child simply does not think as adults do: for
children, such categories as "amount" and "sameness" are not
logical, but merely functions of appearance. A year later,
however, the same child, seeing the same experiment performed
in the same laboratory, will not only perceive that the amount of
liquid in the taller container has not changed, but will "ridicule
the idea that anyone, least of all himself, could ever entertain
another interpretation of these phenomena."[7] Every child must
go through the same structure of cognitive development, the
levels of which are logically ordered in a fixed sequence (Piaget
was greatly influenced by Poincaré's work on mathematical
group theory), whose six stages are precisely graduated.

The dialectical (Lukácsian) concept of cognitive development
for the human race is similar to Piaget's for the individual child:
the growth of consciousness is *stadial* and *irreversible* (what
happens at a later stage is enabled by what happened at earlier
stages in a progression that never repeats itself). The novel
"arises" suddenly in the modern period because the cognitive
conditions that make it possible were lacking in earlier ages.
It had not, as it were, been prepared for. The novel as a
specific kind of text merely reflects developments occurring at
the base level of collective Mind. Thus, the novel has little active
role to play in the development of *Geist*: it is merely an index, a
number on the face of a clock, not part of the motor that turns the
hands.

Bakhtin and Vygotsky

Bakhtin's historiography is also deeply implicated in psychological theories of child development, though not those of Piaget. Given Bakhtin's emphasis on inner speech, it should come as no surprise that the version of child development closest to his history of the novel belongs to another philosopher of inner speech: Lev Vygotsky, who was one of Piaget's greatest critics.

Piaget and Vygotsky differ in the way each configures the part/whole relationship: for the former, the part has no initiative in itself, existing as a mere subfunction of the whole; for the latter, the part may – within strictly limited parameters – be creative and have recursive effects on the whole. Its history is not an irreversible sequence. What this means, in effect, is that the dialectic constitutes a form of logic, the subject with which Hegel always began his lectures after 1817. As such, its movement is global and structural, always pre-existing the local activity of any part within its whole, much as Piaget's idea of progress in the development of the child is predicated on a static structure of graduated epistemological levels. In Piaget change is motivated extra-individually; development is pre-coded and "genetic." Therefore, the goals that might be served by education, the attempt *intentionally* to accelerate individual development, are highly restricted: there is very little room for the kind of initiative that is envisioned in the concept of tutoring.

In Vygotsky, by contrast, there is a very definite role to be played by actively directed learning, both in the maturation of individual human beings and in the history of human culture. Vygotsky called the mechanism that enables such learning the "zone of proximal development" (*zona blizhaishevo razvitiya*, зона ближайшего развития), hereafter referred to as the "zoped."[8]

Before going on to suggest how this concept might be appropriated for historiography, and its crucial relevance in any attempt to grasp Bakhtin's concept of the novel, it will be helpful to know something about how the zoped works.

The zoped

Prior to Vygotsky's research on the learning potential of young children, investigators (including Piaget) had almost universally assumed that learning and development were the same thing.

Or, if they were different, it was felt that advances in the former could follow only upon progress in the latter. Individual children were conceived as local instances of a general algorithm. It was not surprising that the social aspect of a child's coming to consciousness was not given prominence.

Vygotsky made the revolutionary decision that tutoring was a necessary aspect of the child's journey to a ground of higher consciousness. Tutoring and learning could be treated separately from factors inherent in the "natural," "spontaneous," or "biological" development of mind in young children. Tutoring represents a way of overcoming some of the effects of the iron determinism built into the child's biological growth. Vygotsky, much like Bakhtin, saw the child unfolding in a massively social environment in which the determining aspects of growth were shaped not only by genetic directives, but by other people in the community to which the child belonged. Vygotsky went so far as to articulate this idea as a law: "higher mental functions [i.e. thinking] appear on the inter-psychological plane before they appear on the intra-psychological plane."[9] Thus the child was conceived not as an isolated entity making its lonely way through the maze of a preprogrammed cognitive design, but as an organism intrinsically tied to a community of others: "the true direction of the development of thinking is not from the individual to the socialized, but *from the social to the individual*."[10]

Both Bakhtin and Vygotsky emphasize social factors – and thus the radical significance of education – in the child's coming to consciousness, because both assume that thought is inner speech.[11] Bakhtin says "consciousness itself can arise and become a living fact only in the material embodiment of signs" (*Marxism and the Philosophy of Language*, p. 11). Language is the means by which parents organize their thoughts about the world, and when they teach their children to talk, they pass on such organizational patterns: the process normally described as "learning to talk" is really learning to *think*. It is a process that begins very early in childhood, in fact from the moment when the child is born, as has been demonstrated in studies of how mothers talk to their babies and carry on extended dialogues with them immediately after birth.[12]

From his earliest work as a mature thinker, at least a decade before he published *Marxism and the Philosophy of Language* and other texts that overtly discuss the importance of social conditioning, Bakhtin insisted on the shaping importance of parental language for the child:

> The child receives all initial determinations of himself and of his body from his mother's lips . . . [her words] are the first and most authoritative words the child hears about himself; they for the first time determine his personality *from outside*; they *come to meet* his indistinct inner sensation of himself, giving it a form and a name in which, for the first time, he finds himself and becomes aware of himself as *something* . . . [such words] come to meet the dark chaos of my inner sensation of myself: they name, direct, satisfy, and connect it with the outside world – as a response that is interested in me and in my need. And as a result, they give plastic form . . . to this boundless, "darkly stirring chaos" of needs and dissatisfactions, wherein the future dyad of the child's personality and the outside world confronting it is still submerged and dissolved.
>
> ("Author and hero in aesthetic activity," p. 211)

The work of recent investigators such as Roger Brown[13] and, pre-eminently, Jerome Bruner has shown in greater detail how the "loan of consciousness" from parent to infant is accomplished in little playlets or "formats" which the mother usually teaches the child to perform with her. Bruner identified and studied a number of these, such as the ritual of "book reading" in which the mother "phases her questions in a regular sequence: (1) Vocative, (2) Query, (3) Confirmation. Or, (1) Oh look, Richard! (2) What's that? (3) It's a fishy. (4) That's right."[14]

Language acquisition as intertextuality

Family culture is, then, every child's first culture. But the transmission of the signs and values constituting that culture should not be thought of as a direct relay from an actively sending adult to a passively receiving child. It is rather a complex act of *translation* between the enormous language capability of the adult and the relatively weak capabilities of the child. The process, as Lotman has pointed out, is an exercise best understood in terms of intertextuality:

On the basis of some contextual-situational equivalence (situations: "good," "pleasant," "bad," "dangerous," etc.) the child establishes a correspondence between some texts familiar and comprehensible to him in "his" language and the texts of "adults" (for example, on the principle "incomprehensible but pleasant," or "incomprehensible but frightening"). In such a translation – of one whole text by *another* whole text – the child discovers an extraordinary abundance of "superfluous" words[15] in "adult" texts. The act of translation [from the point of view of the child] is accompanied by a semantic reduction of the [adult] text.[16]

Children see the world through the signs of their parents, reducing the complexity and number of their repertoire to the greater simplicity imposed by a smaller stock of meanings (so that the word "poison" may come to signify for the child a particular patch of peeling lead paint in the bedroom). Not only do children thus limit the scripts of the playlets their parents enact with them; they also limit the size of the cast. That is, for children all possible players in the world's drama are reduced to the characters experienced in the family culture: at first usually only mummy, daddy, and "I"; slightly later, the cast may be expanded to include siblings. Thus children live in a world of words and actions that are – by comparison with the words and actions available to adults – not only highly restricted in number, but extremely limited by comparison with the immense diversity of possible roles which society at large forces even a child to confront.

Education is the process of overcoming both of these restrictions in the child through active intervention by adults who make a "loan of consciousness" from their "monopoly of foresight."[17] The child needs to cross the distance from one state to another in cognitive space, which is precisely the point where Vygotsky's concept of the "zone of proximal development" becomes crucial. He defined the zoped as

the distance between the actual developmental level as determined by independent problem solving and the level of potential development as determined through problem solving under adult guidance or in collaboration with more capable peers. . . . Human learning presupposes a specific social nature and a process by which children grow into the intellectual life of those around them. . . . Thus the zone of proximal development enables us to propound a new formula, namely that the only "good learning" is that which is in advance of development.[18]

It is the existence of this zone that makes tutoring – the activity by which those with more consciousness aid those with less consciousness – possible.

We now have the components that will let us formulate more clearly the opposition between dialogism's account of the role literature plays in the history of consciousness and that role as it had been formulated in the Hegelian account of the early Lukács. Instead of conceiving the space between two different levels of consciousness as a gap that is overcome only through an activity determined by a preordained telos – an activity in which the initiative of parts in affecting the whole is highly limited – dialogism sees the gap between higher and lower levels of consciousness as a zone of proximal development, a distance that may be traversed (at least partially) *through the pedagogical activity of the parts in a dialogic simultaneity relating to each other in time.*

On this account, literary texts do not merely reflect changes in development, but also serve to bring them about. Literary texts are tools; they serve as a prosthesis of the mind. As such, they have a tutoring capacity that materially effects change by getting from one stage of development to another. The tutoring is not intentionally directed in any trivial sense toward specific goals, beyond that of teaching the world's difference and diversity. Novelness, and not just the novel, is the name of Bakhtin's hero because it is the force that enables such particular texts as *Don Quixote* or *The Brothers Karamazov* to be "great expectations," i.e. good education in the Bakhtinian sense of putting the future into dialogue by being always in advance of current states of consciousness. Literature, when it enacts novelness (which it does, of course, not only in the form of the novel), is a loophole through which we may see a future otherwise obscured by other forms of discourse. The acquisition of language is for Vygotsky the best example of how the child learns not only to speak, but also to think; by extension, literature is a particularly potent means by which consciousness transmits itself in the form of coherent and durable patterns of culture. Literature enables the future of culture to be exploited as a zone of proximal development. These are big claims to make for literature. What then, we may ask, is the capacity of literary discourse that underwrites its epistemological privilege?

Let us recapitulate for a moment: dialogism assumes that every individual constitutes a particular place in the master dialogue of existence; he or she is compelled by the structure of addressivity (the overwhelmingly social nature of communication) to be responsible for the activity of meaning in his or her local environment. Dialogism conceives that environment as a site of constant struggle between the chaos of events and the ordering ability of language. The effect of order which language achieves is produced by reducing the possible catalogue of happenings, which at any moment is potentially endless, to a restricted number that perception can then process as occurring in understandable relations. What happens in an utterance, no matter how commonplace, is always more ordered than what happens outside an utterance. We discharge our responsibility by putting meaningless chaos into meaningful patterns through the authorial enterprise of translating "life" outside language into the patterns afforded by words, by sentences – and above all, by narratives of various kinds.

The relation of language to life in literary activity is another projection of the structure of self/other relations: much as we can perceive ourselves only in the categories of otherness, so it is that the "self" of a text can be seen only through the eyes of the other. It will be remembered that the time of the self is always open, unfinished, as opposed to the time we assume for others, which is (relative to our own) closed, finalizable. And yet, in order to be known, to be perceived as a figure that can be "seen," a person or thing *must* be put into the categories of the other, categories that reduce, finish, consummate. We see not only our selves, but the world, in the finalizing categories of the other. In other words, we see the world by authoring it, by making sense of it through the activity of turning it into a text, by translating it into finalizing schemes that can order its potential chaos – but only by paying the price of reducing the world's variety and endlessness: novelness is the body of utterances that is least reductive of variety.

Literature has a particularly important role to play in the economy of dialogism, then, because it affords opportunities of a unique power to explore, to *teach* possibilities of authorship, where authorship is understood as consummating or "finalizing" the unsigned world into an utterance in a manner that least restricts the world's possible meanings.

Literature is essentially a perceptual activity, a way to see the world that enriches the world's communicability. In a literary text, the normal activity of perception, of giving order to chaos, is performed at a heightened degree. The difference between perceiving the world by textualizing it into an utterance in everyday speech on the one hand, and, on the other, perceiving it by authoring a literary text, is not absolute, but rather one of degree. Every time we talk we give order to the world; every time we write or read a literary text we give the greatest degree of (possible) order to a world.

Literature and life

In saying so much, we must be careful not to fall back into the traditional opposition of "literature" vs. "life." Some of Bakhtin's most energetic and intelligent Russian admirers, the so-called Tartu semioticians, have at times oversimplified dialogism's gradualist and historical distinctions between everyday spoken utterances and literary utterances; they have hypostatized a difference of quantity (the *relatively* greater amount of order available to a literary text as opposed to other text types, such as everyday speech utterances) into a difference of quality (literature does something that no other activity performs). Their assumption is that "literature" differs from "life" in so far as "literature, unlike everyday life possesses a high degree of internal organization."[19] As we have seen, dialogism assumes that *all* speech activity possesses a high degree of internal organization: the distinctiveness of the kind of utterance we call a literary text is that it manifests this quality in the *highest* degree. The opposition is not between something called literature and something called life that is not literature, but between different kinds of utterance. Literary utterances, like all other forms of utterance, constitute themselves as utterances precisely by doing what traditionally has been thought to be the work exclusively of "literature": by reducing and (relatively, always relatively) finalizing the roiling chaos of the world outside language into the ordering categories inside language.

The distinction between utterances nominated as literary, as opposed to other kinds of utterance, is relative at any given point in time, and therefore it is a distinction that constantly changes over time. If so much is assumed, we can go on to say with the Tartu group that

> if the structural ties that exist among the elements of a literary work are imposed onto the chaos of everyday life, they reveal in that chaos a certain *model* with a distinct structure and meaning. When the highly organized and conscious world of a literary work touches the endless continuum of human life, certain of the latter's discrete and interlinked elements are singled out.[20]

Other theories of the difference between society and the individual

In dialogism, literature is seen as an activity that plays an important role in defining relations between individuals and society. Although dialogism thinks of the levels in terms of self and other, there are several different ways to nominate these levels. Three examples drawn from the tradition that most occupied Bakhtin in his early programmatic work would be: Windelband's distinction between nomothetic knowledge (knowledge of general laws) and idiographic knowledge (knowledge of specific events); Dilthey's more complex distinction between systematic studies that seek to arrive at general principles and historical studies that seek to understand the temporal succession of unique events; or Durkheim's distinction between psychological states which are registered by individuals, and social facts which comprise the behavior of whole communities.[21]

Each of these thinkers – and, of course, many others could be cited – perceives a difference between the particularity of individual human experience and the generality of social or natural events. Ultimately, the difference is between two different kinds of knowledge, perceived by most as antithetical to each other. The difference is perhaps most starkly formulated in Durkheim's 1897 study of suicide, where he draws an opposition between realms appropriate to the psychologist, who may be able to explain why *this* person killed himself, but could never grasp the principles that enable sociologists to perceive conditions that affect the behavior of whole communities. The study of individuals cannot say why more persons of one group constituted by a certain age, class, or profession commit suicide more frequently than do persons in other groups.

The knowledge of sociologists and psychologists differs because the discourse of each is defined by only one of several levels of possible perception; the language practices that define sociology and psychology as distinct professions are mutually exclusive. On this point Durkheim is quite explicit: "society is not a mere sum of individuals; rather, the system formed by their association represents a specific reality which has its own characteristics."[22] The reality serving as the specific subject of sociology is to be sought in this collective reality, not in any of the individuals subject to it, who are assumed to be the proper subjects of psychology. Dialogism abhors such categorical claims to exclusivity, but it understands that any discourse able to set one professional practice off from another will be condemned to make claims of this kind.

Why literature (novelness) is important

Dialogism assigns so much importance to literature because the kind of authoring that is characteristic of discourses that have been labeled "literary" is not – and can never be (despite what some poets and novelists may have thought) – narrowly professional in the same sense that the institutionalized languages of the human sciences generate such professions as psychology or sociology. Novelness is the name Bakhtin gives to a *form of knowledge* that can most powerfully put different orders of experience – each of whose languages claims authority on the basis of its ability to exclude others – into dialogue with each other.

And in this sense, Bakhtin conceives the history of the novel – novelistically. He is doing two things at once, so it helps to read him at two different levels simultaneously. At a first level (an *object* level) he seeks to clarify a particular type of literary text, the novel, and he discusses characteristic examples of the genre. At a second (*meta-*) level, he seeks to clarify the workings of novelness, and sets out the conditions that make his own inquiry possible. The two levels not only depend on each other, but in so far as they may be said to have separate existences, each depends on *otherness itself*. What this means in more conventionally literary terms is that the simultaneity of both levels is insured by the role in each of intertextuality, this being understood as a specific instance of a more comprehensive dialogue between selves and others which shapes whole culture systems.

Novelness and intertextuality

In attempting to understand the relation between novels and novelness in terms of intertextuality, we may usefully invoke a distinction introduced by one of Bakhtin's more sensitive British readers, as he extends the work of one of Bakhtin's more acute French readers. Tony Bennett writes that Julia Kristeva's concept of intertextuality comprehends references "to other texts which can be discerned within the internal composition of a specific individual text [whereas] we intend the concept of *inter-textuality* to refer to the social organization of the relations between texts within specific conditions of reading."[23]

In this sense, a novel is always a combination of these phenomena. Novels are overwhelmingly intertextual, constantly referring, within themselves, to other works outside them. Novels, in other words, obsessively *quote* other specific works in one form or another. In so doing, they manifest the most complex possibilities of the quasi-direct speech that so preoccupies Bakhtin in *Marxism and the Philosophy of Language*. But in addition, they simultaneously manifest inter-textuality in their display of the enormous variety of discourses used in different historical periods and by disparate social classes, and in the peculiarly charged effect such a display has on reading in specific social and historical situations. Among the more powerful *inter*-textual effects novels have is the *extra*-literary influence they exercise on claims to singularity and authority made by other texts and discourses.

The objection will be raised that such effects are not unique to the novel. And in the light of dialogism, of course, it is true all texts must be assumed to be interrelated. It is also true that genres other than the novel characteristically contain explicit references to works outside themselves. However, none of these is so completely dependent as the novel on intertextuality for its very

existence. The manifold strategies by which the novel demonstrates and deploys the complexities of relation – social, historical,
personal, discursive, textual – are its essence. Heteroglossia is a
plurality of relations, not just a cacophony of different voices.

Carnival and novelness

Dialogism assumes that intertextuality and inter-textuality are
the novel's hallmarks, and therefore that otherness is at work in
the genre's very heart. It is no wonder, then, that carnival is one
of Bakhtin's great obsessions, because in his understanding of it,
carnival, like the novel, is a *means for displaying otherness*: carnival
makes familiar relations strange. And like the novel, carnival is
both the name of a specific kind of historically instanced thing –
the popular social institution of early modern Mardi Gras, for
example – and an immaterial force which such particular
instances characteristically embody. *Embody* is, of course, precisely
what carnival does to relations, as it, like the novel, draws
attention to their variety, as well as highlighting the fact that
social roles determined by class relations are *made* not given,
culturally produced rather than naturally mandated.

In such emphases – and particularly in Bakhtin's insistence on
their interconnectedness – we can discern vital parallels between
his concept of the novel and his vision of the body as set forth in
the Rabelais book. That vision, which he calls the "grotesque
body," is

> a body in the act of becoming. It is never finished, never
> completed: it is continually built, created, and builds and
> creates another body. Moreover, the body swallows the world
> and is itself swallowed by the world. . . . Eating, drinking,
> defecation and other elimination (sweating, blowing of the
> nose, sneezing), as well as copulation, pregnancy, dismem-
> berment, swallowing up by another body – all these acts are
> performed on the confines of the body and the outer world, or
> on the confines of the old and new body. In all these events, the
> beginning and end of life are closely linked and interwoven.
>
> (*Rabelais and his World*, p. 317)

The body is, if you will, *intercorporeal* in much the same way as the
novel is intertextual. Like the novel, the body cannot be

conceived outside a web of interrelations of which it is a living part.

In dialogism, the novel is the great book of life, because it celebrates the grotesque body of the world. Dialogism figures a close relation between bodies and novels because they both militate against monadism, the illusion of closed-off bodies or isolated psyches in bourgeois individualism, and the concept of a pristine, closed-off, static identity and truth wherever it may be found. But historically that illusion seems to have had its richest career in post-Renaissance western Europe, in the bourgeois "egotism of the West" that Bakhtin deplored (and that Dostoevsky so loved to denounce).

There is a certain inevitability about the novel's originating in western Europe, and in its becoming the predominant prose genre in the nineteenth century. For, surely, one of the more radical versions of monadic self is that of the Romantic artist as lonely genius that became virtually a cult in Germany, France, and England at that time. The solipsism of much early nineteenth-century German philosophy, the figure of the artist peering down from Alpine heights into misty valleys below, provides perhaps the most fully realized figure for the illusions that must be overcome in both the vision of the grotesque body and the theory of the novel as quintessentially an intertextual genre. Why dialogism insists on this particular confrontation may be made clearer through a brief examination of a particular case. We will conclude this chapter, then, with a short reading of a novel that, more than most, offers itself as a parable about relations between otherness, bodies, and intertextuality: perhaps all too predictably, given these emphases, it is a novel written by a woman: Mary Shelley's *Frankenstein* (an example, I hasten to add, not used by Bakhtin himself).

Frankenstein: The novel monster

The novel has two titles, whose relation to each other is a first indication of its intertextual preoccupations. The two titles accurately nominate the poles of the opposition that shapes the novel as a text: *Frankenstein* is a proper name, unique not only to a particular figure, Victor Frankenstein, but to a figure who embodies (with all the irony that attends the use of this word in the novel) the *principle* of uniqueness: he is the quintessential Romantic artist. The novel's subtitle, *The Modern Prometheus*, on the other hand, opposes the presumption of such radical singularity by highlighting *Frankenstein*'s indebted relation to another text. No matter how new Frankenstein the *scientist* may conceive his creation, he must do so in *Frankenstein* the *novel*, which on its very title-page announces that he is anciently preceded.

A first lesson of Mary Shelley's book is, then, that while much has been made of the urge toward newness and singularity inherent in the genre's very name (in English, at any rate), it, like Victor Frankenstein's creature, is still stitched together out of older materials. *Frankenstein* embodies the paradox of a Prometheus that is "modern." As such an embodiment, it constitutes a prior justification for (and an expansion of) the indictment Henry James made of Russian novels: the lesson of *Frankenstein* is that all novels are baggy monsters.

The contradictory relation between the two titles of Mary Shelley's novel (the uniqueness of "Frankenstein" subverted by the subtitular "modern Prometheus") is replicated in the relation between Victor Frankenstein and his creature. Both the scientist and his monster make claims to an unexampled aloneness, while it is perfectly obvious that they are in a relation of the most immediate intimacy: in an urgent sense, it is precisely *each other that they share*. An over-determined sense of uniqueness is what makes them the same.

More programatically, from the point of view of inter-textuality, each is made out of other books: the monster claims again and again that "I am alone," – never more hauntingly than when he employs the rhetoric of Milton's *Paradise Lost*: "[I am] the fallen angel [who] becomes a malignant devil. Yet even that enemy of God and man had friends and associates in his desolation; I am alone."[24]

It is equally obvious that he is less a monster than he is a classical instance of the "homme de la nature de la vérité": the creature is at home in nature as only an uncorrupted man *à la* Rousseau is *supposed* to be. The description he gives of his life comes almost directly out of Rousseau's novel of education, *Émile*. We can see this in his account of his existence before he acquired language and was merely an animal wandering the hills. But Rousseau is there as well as he describes the future to Frankenstein in his plea for a mate:

> I do not destroy the lamb and the kid to glut my appetite; acorns and berries afford me sufficient nourishment. My companion will be of the same nature as myself and will be content with the same fare. We shall make our bed of dried leaves; the sun will shine on us . . . and will ripen our food.[25]

If the monster is the only creature to have been born without a mother, then Frankenstein is a very singular kind of father, one no less unique than his progeny. Frankenstein's assumption is that he is the sole begetter of the monster: the secret of imparting life to dead flesh is "one secret which I alone possessed."[26] Frankenstein's judgment that he is an original *author* is the source of the monster's conviction that he is an unprecedented *character*.

The intimacy, indeed the complicity, of maker and made who conspire in this theory of originality is grounded in the concomitant and shared assumption of both that not only was the monster unique in his inception: he was *complete* in his origin as well. They share a confusion about the precise point at which the creature becomes the creature. The steps leading up to both the discovery of the secret of life and its application in animating the monster are progressive: "the *stages* [italics added] of the discovery were distinct and probable. After days and nights of incredible labor and fatigue, I succeeded in discovering the cause of generation and life; nay, more, I became myself capable of bestowing animation upon lifeless matter."[27]

But in the case of the discovery, Frankenstein ignores process to concentrate on its end:

> After so much time spent in painful labour, to arrive at once at the summit of my desires was the most gratifying consummation of my toils . . . this discovery was so great and overwhelming that all the steps by which I had been progressively led up to it were obliterated, and I beheld only the result.[28]

This emphasis on arriving all at once, at *only* the result, is present not only in Frankenstein's discovery of the "secret of life." The same emphasis also legislates his relations with the monster, who is thrown into the world having only the *appearance* of a result, in so far as his mind is that of a child but his body is that of a mature adult. He is "obviously" grown up, and it is as an adult, something finished, that Frankenstein regards him. In other words, the monster's mode of being is comprehended in the two phrases "all at once" and "a result only."

All the non-encounters creator and created will endure are figured in the moment when the monster opens his eyes for the first time, for while the scientist looks at the monster as if he were finished, the monster does not even perceive that Frankenstein is there: he is still so very *unfinished* that he has not yet learnt to discriminate between figure and ground, light and dark.

The monster is thrown into the world with the body of an eight-foot adult man. As he says, "From my earliest remembrance I had been as I then was in height and proportion."[29] He is born as a physically mature man whose mental condition is that of an infant in the literal sense of that word – a child in the earliest period of its life, still without language (from the Latin *infans*: *in-*, "not," plus *fans*, the present participle of *fari*, "to speak"). Because the monster, at his inception, is a giant who cannot speak, Frankenstein will assume that he is an idiot, not only in the general sense of being unintelligent (he speaks of the monster's "dull yellow eye"), or even in the more technical sense used by psychologists (or alienists) already at the end of the eighteenth century, meaning that he is incapable of connected speech ("His jaws opened, and he muttered some inarticulate sounds").[30] Rather, Frankenstein's emphasis on the absolute singularity of what he calls his creation makes it clear that the scientist in his philology, as in his biology, is going back to first principles, to the root of idiot in Greek *idiotes*, private person, one cut off from affiliation (even after the monster acquires speech, he himself feels the need to "become linked to the chain of existence and events from which I am now excluded").[31]

But of course the monster is not as alone as he fears, nor is Frankenstein as original as he thinks. It is only the first of several ironies that haunt relations between the monster and Frankenstein that the claims to uniqueness made by each are most seriously brought into question by the other. And the claims to uniqueness both make are in turn undercut by the universal pattern of metamorphosis they – and not only they, but all the other characters in the text – enact. It is not only the case, as has been pointed out so many times, that they share certain character traits (such as a love of nature, or that the speech of each is unusually eloquent), or that they can exchange roles (as the monster says, "You are my creator, but I am your master")[32], or that either or both of them can credibly be said to be the eponymous hero of the novel that has as its subtitle *The Modern Prometheus*. It is not the specular image each provides of the other that is the most powerful witness against the singularity of either, but the *secondariness* of all their actions when perceived within the structure of change and renewal that they share with everyone else, a structure whose presence in the text is made unavoidable through its constant literary allusions. The secondariness and the multiplicity that stand over against Frankenstein's and the monster's patent claims to firstness and singularity – that oppose such claims by the novel itself – are enacted as an intertextuality that can nowhere be avoided.

Frankenstein is not only the modern Prometheus, he is only a *modern* Prometheus: his story is known before he acts it, his fate has been thought before in the myth whose hero's name, Prometheus, means forethought. (Although it could be argued that Frankenstein is also the modern version of that other Titan who was the brother of Prometheus, Epimetheus, who married Pandora, and whose name means afterthought, for is not Frankenstein's whole activity after opening the coffins that he rifles to create the monster one long afterthought? Is not the monster precisely an afterthought?)

Of the several allusions to previous narratives that make the tale of Frankenstein recognizable, Prometheus is the first, but of course far from the last: the threads of the story stretch out before Prometheus to what was thought even before the Titanic forethinker, and those threads stretch as well into a posterity that includes not only a version which Mary Shelley could call modern, but which we in our day may credibly recognize as postmodern.

The Prometheus myth

In the tangled skein of *Frankenstein*'s pretexts, it will be best to start with the classical myth, not only because it is chronologically prior, but because it makes clear the paradox of all claims to priority: for the story of Prometheus is already impossible to separate into a discrete text that can stand apart from the other tales that run through it. Prometheus was a friend of the gods before he became a friend of human beings (in some versions, the creator of the first human): he belonged to what might be called the second generation of Greek deities, the first generation having comprised Uranus and Gaia, the sky and earth spirits who gave birth to the Titans, including Prometheus, who participated in the revolt first against his father, and then, after Uranus was castrated and deposed by Kronos, in the revolt of the Olympian gods against the new leader. Prometheus was a traitor to the race of Titans before he became a traitor to Zeus. The race of humans, which he either creates (or at least enables) through the stolen gift of fire, represents, then, at least a fourth generation of beings brought forward by revolts against the parents.

Revolt against predecessors is, of course, an obsessively repeated pattern in relations between virtually all the major fathers and the sons in *Frankenstein* (excluding Ferdinand De Lacey, who is, in any case, a quite minor figure): Walton's father's dying injunction was that his son should not go to sea. So not only does Walton go to sea; he goes as far as he can in his search for a polar passage. Frankenstein blames his father, in effect, for permitting him to embark on the course that culminates in the creation of the monster. As a boy he finds a copy of an alchemical treatise by Cornelius Agrippa, about which his father remarks, "My dear Victor, do not waste your time on this sad trash."[33] And the grown-up Victor laments that his father failed "to explain to me that the principles of Agrippa had been entirely exploded, and that a modern system of science has discredited its predecessors."

All these elements play a fairly obvious role in the novel, so I will not dwell on them, mentioning only in passing that it is not only their thematic content of generational revolt and religious heresy, of how responsibility is shared between parents and children, but the formal feature of the myth's structure that is important for reading *Frankenstein*, which is a tale no less impacted with other tales than is that of Prometheus.

An obvious way to see the inevitability of the intertextuality that calls the singularity not only of this text but of all texts into question is to look at the four books that shape the monster's

education. The first of these is *Ruins of Empires*, first published
in 1791 by Volney, a true child of the French Enlightenment who
was inspired by Gibbon's demonstration of Christianity's harm-
ful effects on the Roman state to show the role of religion in
the decline of other empires. The doubling effect of
intertextuality is dramatized in the way this text is produced
for the monster: Felix thinks he is instructing Safie, but hidden
behind the wall, anticipating the underground of Dostoevsky's
underground man, is the monster, much as Gibbon is behind
Volney, and as both are behind Mary Shelley's novel. It is then
not only the case that the monster learns history from this text,
but it also gets lessons in the kind of metamorphosis we call
revolt; it is the kind of education calculated to produce
the expected result dramatized when the monster orders his
maker to do his bidding: "Slave, before I reasoned with you, but
you have proven unworthy of my condescension . . . obey!"[34]
And as he leads Frankenstein into the icy deserts of the north,
the monster, parodying the miraculous gift of manna to the
Israelites as they wandered in the wilderness in the book of
Exodus (16: 14–36), leaves food for his former master, boasting
in an accompanying note of his power: "My reign is not yet
over."[35]

The other books that constitute the monster's library are in the
Pandoran portmanteau he finds in the woods. They include
Paradise Lost, Plutarch's *Lives*, and Goethe's *Sorrows of Young
Werther*. It adds to the central role of intertextuality in this novel
to note that the particular versions of these English, Latin, and
German texts that the monster reads are all translated into
French. And of course each of these books will be recapitulated in
one form or another in the further course of the narrative. For
Frankenstein is in many ways a novel of education, but
education of a particular kind: the monster discovers the need to
become "linked to the chain of existence and events."[36] But this
need for linkage is itself linked to another set of questions about
connections: "My person was hideous and my stature gigantic.
What did this mean? Who was I? What was I? Whence did I
come? What was my destination?"[37] His goal is to find one of
"these histories," as he calls them, which will have a place for
him in it. The process is made clear in his rumination on *Paradise
Lost*: the book

moved every feeling of wonder and awe that the picture of an omnipotent God warring with his creatures was capable of exciting. I often referred the several situations, as their similarity struck me, to my own. Like Adam, I was apparently united by no link to any other being in existence; but his state was far different from mine in every other respect.[38]

In the logic of the monster's *Bildung*, to become linked to the chain of existence means becoming interwoven with a pre-existing narrative. The question of who he is – and in this he is an emblem for the text of the novel that seeks to contain him, is a narrative problem involving beginnings, middles, and ends, which is why in the closing pages of the novel he worries about what he calls the need to "consummate the *series* of my existence" (italics added).

We are arguing that a major gap in the novel is between the repeated, almost hysterical claims to original authorship made by virtually all the narrators in the text, and the existence of other texts prior to them in the "series of their existence" to which such authors are linked, and thus whose claim to priority and uniqueness is made suspect. Frankenstein's monster springs from the library as much as he does from the charnel house and laboratory: he is made up not only of other bodies from the past, but, like Mary Shelley's novel, from other books from the past. And in so far as he is an emblem of that novel, the instinct of generations of moviegoers who refer to the monster as Frankenstein is sound – the monster's name is Frankenstein not because he is the mad scientist, but because his hybrid form is Mary Shelley's novel. That novel, like the monster, is made up of *disjecta membra*, story inside framed story, as Walton's letters surround Frankenstein's spoken tale that surrounds the monster's tale, that includes the story of Safie and the De Laceys, all encompassed at the end in Walton's diary. Not only is there a mix of narrators, there is a compound of genres – letters, diaries, and a variety of oral tales. Thus the monster who complains he is without a link to existence is in fact tightly enmeshed in a chain of narratives.

The most important of these in his own formation are the copy of *Paradise Lost* he finds in the woods and the copy of Frankenstein's journal that he finds in the pocket of the clothes he takes with him when he flees Ingolstadt on the night of his birth. For the purposes of pursuing our argument against the oneness that both the monster and his creator claim for themselves, the aspect of both these narratives that has the greatest resonance in *Frankenstein* is their over-determined emphasis on instantaneous creation and their principled opposition to change. Milton's God in his relation to Adam, and Frankenstein in his relation to his monster, seek to deny the capacity of the creatures they spawn to change. Both God and Frankenstein suspect the possibility of change that sleeps in temporality: the God who says "I am that I am" is superior to creatures who can only say "I was that then, but I am this now," because his authority is defined by the fact he always is. And Frankenstein, in one of the many changes rung on the biblical assumption that men are created in the image of God, shares this sense of the priority of stasis. He curses his own changeling status again and again, as when he says: "Nothing is so painful to the human mind as a great and sudden change."[39]

Valorizing stasis over change, both Milton's God and Mary Shelley's scientist conceive the transition from non-being to being as a moment of creation, an instantaneous transformation that occupies no time.

> And God said, Let us make man in our image, after our likeness. . . . So God created man in his own image . . . there went up a mist from the earth and watered the whole face of the ground. And the Lord God formed man of the dust of the ground and breathed into his nostrils the breath of life; and man became a living soul.

And Frankenstein says, "I collected the instruments of life around me, that I may infuse a spark of being into the lifeless thing that lay at my feet . . . I saw the dull yellow eye of the creature open; it breathed hard, and a convulsive motion agitated its limbs."[40] In Genesis it is a breath that instantaneously breaks the barrier between being and non-being; in Mary Shelley it is a spark, but in both cases what we get is a transformation from one state to another that is presumed to be both timeless and complete.

But of course Adam does change – he experiences a second creation at the moment he eats of the tree of knowledge, as he moves from the timelessness of edenic space to the time of the world into which he is exiled. And of course the monster, too,

experiences a second creation as he moves from the undifferentiated state of his first awareness (the "original era of my
being" as he calls it). The tree of knowledge was dangerous
because its fruit made Adam aware not only of the knowledge of
the difference between good and evil, but of difference *as such*.
Similarly, it is the gradual discovery that the world is not all one
that constitutes the first in a series of transformations that
result in Frankenstein's creature falling from innocence into
monstrousness. He begins to be aware of difference, thus change,
and thus time, even before he acquires language. In the
beginning, all is one: "all the events of that period appear
confused and indistinct . . . I saw, felt, heard, and smelt at the
same time." But soon, "changes of day and night passed, and the
orb of night had greatly lessened, when I began to distinguish my
sensations from each other."[41]

This is only the first of many transformations through which
the monster passes, the next important one being the acquisition
of language, a process he completes so successfully that he is
briefly able to put himself in the place of his own creator. Having
determined that his physical appearance is what gets in the way
of commerce with others, he resolves to use old De Lacey's
blindness in a moment when the old man is alone to mold an
image of himself in words that will win human sympathy. He
decides, in other words, to author another version of himself.
And because he is so very eloquent (another aspect he shares with
his creator), his words do indeed compel the old man's empathy,
but only momentarily as De Lacey's children return to beat him
away from the cottage.

At this point, what up till now has been only a creature
becomes the monster: "from that moment I declared everlasting
war against the species, and more than all, against him who had
formed me and sent me forth to this insupportable misery."
These are "the feelings which, from what I had been, have made
me what I am." He has gone from being a Rousseau-
style "homme de la nature et de la vérité" to being a
vicious murderer. In the apologia he frames for Walton, the
monster draws out all the rhetorical stops to characterize his
fall:

> Once my fancy was soothed with dreams of virtue, of fame
> and of enjoyment. Once I falsely hoped to meet with beings

who, pardoning my outward form, would love me for the excellent qualities which I was capable of unfolding. I was nourished with thoughts of high honor and devotion. But now crime has degraded me beneath the meanest animal . . . I cannot believe that I am the same creature whose thoughts were once filled with sublime and transcendent visions of the beauty and the majesty of goodness.[42]

Notice the repetitive pattern formed by sentences that begin with the word "once." This is an ancient rhetorical trope known as anaphora, from the Greek verb "to repeat." A famous example, that is very much to the point in our discussion of generation and repetition, is the so-called "begats" section of the Bible. In Genesis 5, the generations following Adam are listed: "And Seth lived an hundred and five years and begat Enos. . . . And Enos lived ninety years and begat Cainan. . . . And Cainan lived seventy years, and begat Mahalaleel," etc.

A less famous but pithier example is Gertrude Stein's summation of her philosophy after she left Oakland: "There ain't any answer. There ain't going to be an answer. There never has been an answer. That's the answer."[43] Stein's example makes clear another turn on repetition that is conspicuously avoided in the creature's rhetoric – repeated endings. In her quote, Stein repeats not only the word "there" at the beginning of several sentences, but the word "answer" at the *end* of those sentences (which is technically a figure called epistrophe). Although the monster is a master of rhetoric, and rhetoric knows many patterns of repetition, the one that he uses most is particularly apt for figuring his condition: anaphora is the monster's characteristic trope because it is the figure of *repeated beginnings*.

Another way to conceive such radical changes as the monster undergoes is to be found in a concept that everywhere informs *Frankenstein* but is nowhere spoken in it (much as in the old adage that you do not mention death in the house of the undertaker). It is the word that serves as the translated title of another narrative: metamorphosis. Metamorphosis literally means changing shape suddenly. It thus has an obvious relevance for a creature who is made of the changed shapes of other men, as well as one whose gigantic proportions change the shape of man. But it is the more figural use of the word that will help us to understand the changing shape of the text's narrative: in that sense, a metamorphosis is any sudden transformation, as if by magic or sorcery, or more generally a marked change not only in appearance, but in character, condition, or function.

A concern for metamorphosis is as old as myth, but it finds its first extended, self-consciously literary elaboration in Ovid's long poem devoted to transformations of mortal men and women into animals or natural objects through the power of the Olympian gods. Ovid's text is another of the books out of which *Frankenstein* is made, another of the secret sharers in this novel about doubles. Of the many metamorphoses Ovid recounts, none is perhaps more apt for understanding the nature of sudden change in *Frankenstein* than the tale of Arachne, the girl who is transformed into a spider. It is particularly fitting not only because Arachne is, like Mary Shelley when she wrote the novel, a young woman, or because one of Victor Frankenstein's favorite epithets for the monster is "You insect," but because it comes up in Book VI of Ovid's poem, at the point where "human beings are beginning to prove themselves by defying the Gods." The species Arachnidae, which includes spiders and scorpions, is known as such because a mortal girl named Arachne, famous for her weaving, was transformed into a spider by the goddess Athena (or Minerva, as Ovid calls her). What is perhaps less well known is why Athena transforms the girl.

Athena is the goddess not only of wisdom but of several of the domestic arts as well, including weaving. When Arachne boasts that her skill is superior to that of the goddess, Athena challenges her to a duel. Ovid makes clear that the girl's crime is less mere pride in her achievement than ignorance of the limits of humanity: or, as we might say in the context of *Frankenstein*, she is guilty of Promethean pride.

> You could know that Pallas had taught her. Yet she denied it, and offended at the suggestion of a teacher even so great, she said, "Let her but strive with me; and if I lose there is nothing which I would not forfeit."[44]

In the contest itself, Athena weaves a tapestry showing scenes that dramatize the majesty of the gods, enclosed by four scenes depicting acts of presumption against them, with the offending mortals then violently transformed. Arachne, for her part, weaves scenes that show the gods engaged in scandalous acts which are permitted by their transformation into other things, such as Leda's rape by Zeus in his disguise as a swan, or the rape of Deo's daughter also by Zeus, this time in the form of a snake, or his ravishing of Danae in the form of a golden shower. Since Arachne's work equals her own, Athena tears the girl's tapestry to shreds and beats her with the shuttle. Arachne hangs herself and is transformed by Athena into a spider.

There are several details from Ovid that might illuminate our reading of Frankenstein, above and beyond the obvious (Promethean and Miltonic) theme of transgression against the gods, or the hierarchization that metamorphosis always enacts (the power relation from gods to humans dramatized in the Jovian rapes of mortal women). Most of all, it is the different ratios of mutually defining differences between gods and humans that needs to be emphasized.

Notice that Zeus – or Athena – can be many things, but that the mortals are apportioned only *one* transformation: Arachne is still a spider. When the monster complains that he is alone, is it not the case that he is lamenting his lack of continuing mutability? When he seeks to transform himself into a new identity in the tapestry of words he weaves for the blind old De Lacey, is it not rage at his inability to become something other than his present body that triggers his metamorphosis from mere creature, the Rousseauesque noble savage, into a monster? He is indeed, as Frankenstein calls him, "a vile insect," one who belongs to the class Arachnidae, because like Athena's victims, he has been denied the right to metamorphosis. The people who attack him when he saves a child from drowning, the children of old De Lacey who attack him as he seeks to save that other child who is himself, all insist the monster must be read literally. He must be, to return to our opening concern for the obviousness of the text, always scrutable. He is frightening, but not mysterious, because *he is always perceived as known*. The rule of the text for perceiving the monster is that he must be seen as he is, his appearance must be identical with his character. He cannot, in other words, attain the power to metamorphose because he cannot attain the status of a sign, that order of recognition where things never coincide with themselves.

Frankenstein's final decision not to create a mate for the monster is a result not only of his all-too-apparent suspicion of women ("she might become ten thousand times more malignant than her mate . . . she also might turn with disgust from him to the superior beauty of man"), but above all because she might enable the monster to reproduce:

> Even if they were to leave Europe and inhabit the deserts of the new world, yet one of the first results of those sympathies for which the demon thirsted would be children, a race of devils would be propagated upon the earth who might make the very existence of the species of man a condition precarious and full of terror.[45]

It is the possibility that the monster might exceed itself that disturbs Frankenstein, whose decision accords with the prejudice of that Borgesian heresiarch of Uqbar who said: "mirrors and copulation are abominable, since they both multiply the numbers of men."

It is of course not a Malthusian fear of overpopulation that actuates either the heresiarch or Frankenstein: the latter's terror is not merely that the monster will reproduce itself (for both mirrors and copulation are means of mediation, neither produces identities); what he fears is the figurative power to become other, the possibility that the monster may not, even without a mate, be alone. In other words, Frankenstein refuses the monster's right to metamorphosis because he is opposed to that particular form of transformation we call metaphor. He repeatedly claims uniqueness for himself, and yet he has in common with most of the other figures in the text that he is a bad reader; he is constantly, like the De Lacey children, judging a book if not by its cover, then at least by its most apparent and literal meaning. He complains that his father is a superficial reader: when the elder Frankenstein attempts to deter his son from reading the alchemist and magician Cornelius Agrippa, Victor says: "My father looked carelessly at the title page of my book and said, 'Ah! Cornelius Agrippa! My dear Victor, do not waste your time upon this; it is sad trash.'" Frankenstein is, however, unpersuaded: "But the cursory glance my father had taken of my volume by no means assured me that he was acquainted with its contents, and I continued to read with the greatest avidity."[47]

But it turns out that the son is no more acute a reader than his father: previously, he says,

I had gazed upon the fortifications and impediments that seemed to keep human beings from entering the citadel of nature, and rashly and ignorantly I had repined. But here were books [he is still speaking of Cornelius Agrippa and Albertus Magnus], and here were men [notice the automatic homology he draws] who had penetrated deeper and knew more. I took their word for all that they averred, and I became their disciple.

This episode is described in Frankenstein's account of his life to Walton, an autobiography that assumes the formal shape of a confession, and so is tied to the structure of that particular kind of metamorphosis we call conversion . Thus, in the passage just quoted, the adult Victor Frankenstein (the present or narrating self) is describing young Frankenstein (the past, or narrated self), who stands on the other side of the conversion (Frankenstein's turn at university to "natural philosophy") that marks transformation into a new identity. So it could be said that when Frankenstein describes the bad reading habits of (what Mel Brooks might call) "the young Frankenstein" he is talking about somebody else; and that the narrating Frankenstein has now metamorphosed into a better reader than the narrated Frankenstein. Such, of course, is not the case.

Proof that Frankenstein will be a literalist to his death (will, in a sense, die of literalism) is confined not only to those incidents after his conversion when he stupidly misreads a fairly obvious situation, such as his assumption that the monster's warning – "I will be with you on your wedding night" – means that the monster intends to kill *him* instead of Elizabeth, who is the metaphorical equivalent of the monster's bride Frankenstein has torn into pieces. After abandoning the "exploded systems" of the alchemists, Frankenstein gives himself over to his age's version of modern science. After he hears the chemist Waldmann claim that the new science has "indeed performed miracles," we get an almost technical description of a conversion experience:

As he went on I felt as if my soul were grappling with a palpable enemy; one by one the various keys were touched which formed the mechanism of my being; chord after chord was sounded, and soon my thought was filled with one thought, one conception, one purpose.

I quickly pass over the ironies implicit in his use of the trope of anaphora.

It is now that the ineluctability of figuration begins to undermine his literalism and his dream of oneness. Singlemindedly pursuing "natural philosophy" and especially chemistry, that branch of it most concentrated on compounds and transformations brought about by mixing elements, Frankenstein comes upon the secret of what appears to be the greatest metamorphosis of them all, "the change" as he says, "from life to death, and death to life," a secret announced in terms of sudden illumination: "from the midst of this darkness a sudden light broke in upon me – a light so brilliant and wondrous, yet so simple, that for a while I became dizzy."[48]

Whence this light? From Frankenstein's earlier conversion, that point at the age of fifteen, when he experiences the power of lightning:

> When I was about fifteen years old . . . we witnessed a most violent and terrible thunderstorm. It advanced from behind the mountains of Jura, and the thunder burst at once with frightful loudness from various quarters of the heavens. . . . As I stood at the door, on a sudden I beheld a stream of fire issue from an old and beautiful oak . . . and so soon as the dazzling light vanished the oak had disappeared, and nothing remained but a blasted stump . . . I never saw anything so utterly destroyed.[49]

A "man of great research in natural philosophy" is in the neighborhood, and from him Frankenstein learns about electricity "which was new and astonishing to me." He turns to mathematics as sounder science, but soon gives it up and thus is ripe for his turn to the chemistry of Professor Waldmann. And it is from this point (the blasted tree and the unsuccessful turn to mathematics) that Frankenstein dates his work on the monster, work that he from now on figures as a storm:

> When I look back, it seems to me as if this almost miraculous change of inclination [toward mathematics] . . . was the last effort made by the spirit of preservation to avert the storm that was even then hanging in the stars and ready to envelop me. . . . Destiny was too potent, and immutable laws had decreed my utter and terrible destruction.[50]

The monster, too, in whose metaphors of light burn flames from the blasted oak, has been a literalist and unitarian, so it is not surprising that he should realize his maker's master metaphor in his own end. Addressing the corpse of Frankenstein, he says,

> Blasted as thou wert, my agony was still superior to thine. . . . But soon these burning miseries will be extinct. I shall ascend my funeral pile triumphantly and exult in the agony of the torturing flames. The light of that conflagration will fade away.[51]

Amidst the ice that Walton has figured as "a country of eternal light" there is blackness: Walton says of the monster in the novel's final lines, "He was soon borne away by the waves and lost in the darkness and distance."[52] It is in that distant darkness that the monster will immolate himself.

Frankenstein as a novel of changes, as a text that self-dramatizingly makes itself out of the remnants of other books and other discourses, is not only about the making of a monster. It is an enactment of the monstrosity of novelness itself. The flames that will spring from the funeral pyre of the monster, as it courses its way through the polar gloom, cast an eerie light. It is finally the light of allegory, the tale of the genre that the monster so beautifully exemplifies. It is, of course, the genre that gives the force of novelness its name in dialogism, the novel that speaks the dilemma of knowing that its constitution is always incomplete and ineluctably other.

5

The dialogue of history and poetics

Books such as *Problems of Dostoevsky's Poetics*, *Rabelais and his World*, and the essays published in English as *The Dialogic Imagination* have established Bakhtin as a leading theorist of the novel. Dialogism, however, resists being confined to any exclusively "literary" application. Indeed, the fixity of boundaries between "literary" and "extra-literary" discourse is precisely what it questions, even in those of his works that seem most conventionally "literary." There is a certain Russian broadness that clings to dialogism, making it difficult to use in restricted doses. In the light of dialogism, literature can never be completely disentangled from its capacity to serve as a metaphor for other aspects of existence.

Nevertheless, it is obvious that topics bearing on conventional literary concerns such as narrative structure, point of view, the status of the author, diction, style, and so on, play an enormous role in dialogism. A legitimate question for anyone first coming to dialogism, then, would be, "What kind of a literary theory is it?" "How does it differ from any of the other theories now contending in the great market-place of ideas?" These questions usually mean, "What kind of methodology is it?" Or, in other words, "How will this way of doing things help me read more effectively?" At this level, the honest answer has to be that there are no easy prescriptions for interpretation or quick fixes to be found in dialogism. It is no theoretical steroid. It is important to stress this, for at first blush many seem to feel (as a student once said to me), that "Bakhtin looks easy!"

Readers often experience this initial impression because dialogism has relatively few technical terms. Its vocabulary is characterized by a seeming simplicity, and thus it appears to be easily assimilated, especially by comparison with some of the formidable difficulties so immediately apparent in other current theories. But those who have been deceived by dialogism's appearance of ease have always paid a price in analytical rigor. Such categories as "Bakhtinian carnival" or "polyphony," come to mean nothing more than a liberating licentiousness in the first case and no more than multiple point of view in the other. In such hasty appropriations it is all too clear that previous reading habits have not been changed. An immersion in Bakhtin's thought will indeed transform the way one reads, but only after some time has elapsed, and in ways that are not predictable.

Once so much has been admitted, however, certain generalizations about dialogism in its character as a literary theory can be made. As a "method," it is perhaps best grasped as a historical poetics, and before going any further, the potential scandal of a poetics that claims historicity should be faced openly. The formulation contains a paradox: how do we overcome the apparent contradiction between a "history" and a "poetics"? Are change, difference, and uniqueness not the stuff of history, while stasis, sameness, and similarity are the matter of poetics? However else it might be understood, history surely means nothing if it does not attend the particular and the unrepeatable. By contrast, a poetics is defined by its focus on patterns that are unchanging and by norms whose authority resides precisely in their ability to legislate uniformity. Poetics, as usually understood, is the study of figures that recur, and as such poetics is opposed to the manifold differences that are the essence of history. In so far as poetics addresses static shapes, is it not then a spatial science? How can it coexist with history, the most radically temporal form of knowledge? Some insight into this paradox can be gained if we look more closely at Bakhtin's key monograph "Forms of time and of the chronotope in the novel," which has as its subtitle, "Notes toward a historical poetics."

The chronotope: a device, a function, a motif?

Chronotope is one of the very few non-Russian words Bakhtin uses as part of his technical vocabulary, *khronotop*, хронотоп, being recognizably Greek in Russian, as it is in English. It was far more common for Bakhtin to use an existing Russian word in an unusual way (as in his use of *vnenakhodimost'*, вненаходимость, "outsideness"). The markedness of the very noun he chooses is only one way the special importance of chronotope for Bakhtin is made apparent. Sometimes expansive in his use of terms, he was anxious to define this one with relative precision: he specifies when he first heard it ("summer of 1925"), and from whom (the distinguished Leningrad physiologist Ukhtomsky).

Nevertheless, at the conclusion of the 200-page monograph on the chronotope – a small book really – many readers will find themselves hard pressed to answer the question, "What exactly is a chronotope?" On the one hand, it is "the intrinsic connectedness of temporal and spatial relationships that are artistically expressed in literature" ("The chronotope," p. 84).[1] As such, one would expect the concept of chronotope to be a contribution to our understanding of narrative. And in a fundamental sense it is: "The chronotope is the place where the knots of narrative are tied and untied" (ibid., p. 250). In this first, restricted use of the term, it refers to particular combinations of time and space as they have resulted in historically manifested narrative forms. A number of examples are given, demonstrating how the term may be "applied" when appropriated as a technical constituent of plot.

Bakhtin (who trained as a scholar of Greek and Latin literature) is perhaps at his clearest in discussing the type of plot typical of the ancient romance. Such tales as the *Aethiopica* or *Daphnis and Chloë* are grouped together as the "adventure novel of ordeal": the plot usually opens with a catastrophe (a new bride is abducted by pirates, for instance); the main body of the story consists of a potentially endless number of adventures as the hero repeatedly attempts to save the bride from monsters, brigands, and so on; and in the conclusion the two lovers are united. It is, in other words, the archetypal idea of "boy meets girl, loses girl, gets girl." The time is "empty" in the sense that events are not connected to each other in any causal relation; none of the events is linked in a sustained consequence. No matter how frequently the hero has rescued his intended bride from earthquakes, floods, dragons, or pirates, he gets no older or wiser: "These hours and days leave no trace, and therefore, one may have as many of them as one likes" ("The chronotope," p. 94). And the space of this chronotope is "abstract" in the sense that the adventures in it could occur anywhere (when there are eruptions, it could be any volcano; when pirates appear, it could be on any sea).

Chronotope at this elementary level of application seems to have something like the status of "motifs" or "functions" in Structuralist analyses, a kind of recurring formal feature that distinguishes a particular text type in such a way that – no matter when it is heard or read – it will always be recognizable as being *that* kind of text; for instance, "quest object" and "benefactor" serve as distinctive features of the fairy-tale in morphological studies of that genre.

Using chronotope in this restricted sense, Bakhtin treats three other plot types that are characteristic of ancient prose forms. The first of these is "the adventure novel of everyday life." Its exemplar is Apuleius' *Golden Ass*, chiefly important for exploring new, more "realistic," or less abstract areas of space through which Lucius wanders after he has been transformed into an ass, such as the everyday sites inhabited by muleteers, bakers, and low-ranking soldiers. The time of this chronotope is characterized by its effects on the life of an individual person; unlike characters in earlier Greek romances, such a hero bears some responsibility for the changes in his life. These changes may be abrupt metamorphoses, similar to mere adventures, but they do more than articulate an abstract pattern of rearrangeable events: they create a pattern of development in the biography of the hero as he moves from guilt through punishment to redemption.

In these analyses of ancient texts, Bakhtin uses chronotope as a unit of *narrative* analysis, a time/space figure that is typical of certain types of historically instanced plots. At this level, the chronotope would seem to be a recurring "structure," differing very little from the kind of technical feature of literary texts which the Russian Formalists called a "device." Bakhtin specifically invokes it as "a formally constitutive category of literature" ("The chronotope," p. 84)

If chronotopes are transcultural, how can they be historical?

But chronotopes are not merely devices (any more than most Formalist devices turned out to be "merely" devices). Chronotopes in literary texts are not cut off from the cultural environments in which they arise: "Out of the actual chronotopes of our world (which serve as the source of representation) emerge the reflected and *created* chronotopes of the world represented in the work." (ibid., p. 253). Bakhtin is careful to avoid the proposition that there is a direct, "realistic" reflection of the experienced world in literature – after all, his first published essay is based on the proposition that "When a man is in art, he is not in life, and vice versa" (*Estetika*, p. 5).[2] But this does not mean that there is an utter cut-off between art and life (in which case the chronotope could, indeed, be merely a device): just as when I am in the kitchen I am not in the bedroom but nevertheless I am still in the same house, so art and life are recognized by Bakhtin to be different places contained by a larger unit of which they are constituents. Both art and lived experience are aspects of the same phenomenon, the heteroglossia of words, values, and actions whose interaction makes dialogue the fundamental category of dialogism. For while art and life, when conceived as abstract topics *in general*, have no connections between them, in the experience of particular living subjects who consume works of art, who, as it were, "utter" them, there is a possibility for effecting exchange. Art and life are two different registers of dialogue that can be conceived only in dialogue. They are both forms of representation; therefore they are different aspects of the same imperative to mediate that defines all human experience. There is a presumption, then, that some kind of correlation exists between the characteristic plots inside Greek romances and the world of experience outside those texts, if only because the literary text would lack any meaning were this not the case.

When conceived as more than a narrowly technical narrative device, then, the chronotope provides a means to explore the complex, indirect, and always mediated relation between art and life. For instance, in nineteenth-century French novels a "fundamentally new space" opens up in literature, the "space of parlors and salons." But this newly opened possibility is explained not only by Balzac's "ability to 'see' time" ("The chronotope," p. 247), but by the peculiar importance such space assumed in Paris at that particular time. And yet those salons were not "the same" as in Balzac's novels. Nor are they "the same" as the meanings those salons have had in subsequent readings of Balzac's novels. Nevertheless, all the meanings that can be assumed by the Balzacian salon will bear on the institution of the salon as it historically manifested itself in the early nineteenth century (and not as it did, let us say, in eighteenth-century Paris, any more than medieval fortresses are the same as castles in Gothic novels, which constitute a different chronotope).

The example of Balzac would seem to indicate that literary chronotopes are highly sensitive to historical change: different societies and periods result in different chronotopes both inside and outside literary texts. If, as seems the case at one level, specific chronotopes do indeed shape themselves in some kind of relation to the exterior conditions in which they arise, one might reasonably assume that this correlation between a particular, historical intra-textual world and an equally particularized extra-textual world must in each case be unique. And it is – up to a point. What that point is, we must now explore.

Certain chronotopes are treated by Bakhtin as if they were transhistorical structures that are not unique to particular points in time. There is a tension, if not a downright contradiction, between these examples and the claims Bakhtin makes elsewhere for the chronotope's ability to be in dialogue with specific, extra-literary historical contexts. It is in such a juxtaposition we can best perceive the tensions inherent in a "historical poetics." For instance, the adventure chronotope (in which sheer contingency of events determines the plot) is the formal feature that best defines the peculiarity of the ancient Greek romance. But such a chronotope – and here is the rub – can also be generalized to include the seventeenth-century baroque novels of D'Urfé and La Calprénède. It can also serve to distinguish even later works, such as the novels of Sir Walter Scott (ibid., p. 95). In a 1973 addendum to his original essay, Bakhtin provides a long catalogue of such recurring patterns (the chronotope of the road, of the trial, of the provincial town, and so on).

We seem to be faced with apparently contradictory claims: on the one hand, the adventure chronotope defines the place of the Greek romance in a historical sequence. But the same chronotope is also treated as a transhistorical feature to be found in works separated from each other by many centuries. In seeking to understand such antinomies, we should keep in mind the varying functions that are served by chronotopes at different levels of specificity and generalization. Chronotope, like most terms characteristic of dialogism, must be treated "bifocally," as it were: invoking it in any particular case, one must be careful to discriminate between its use as a lens for close-up work and its ability to serve as an optic for seeing at a distance. But once the outside limits of specificity and generality defining chronotope have been established, it should be possible to conceive some of the more common and useful applications the term might have in the many different "middle distance" registers between the extremes.

At one extreme, chronotope has a relatively restricted set of applications that apply to literary texts conceived as single units. But chronotope may also be used as a means for studying the relation *between* any text and its times, and thus as a fundamental tool for a broader social and historical analysis, within which the literary series would be only one of several interconnected types of discourse. It is at this level that the chronotope's contribution to a historical poetics may best be seen.

The chronotope as a category of narrative

However, if we for the moment restrict ourselves to viewing chronotope as a formal constructive category, it might most economically be defined as *the total matrix that is comprised by both the story and the plot of any particular narrative*. I am, of course, invoking a well-known distinction, first proposed by the Russian Formalists as the difference between *fabula* (фабула) and *syuzhet* (сюжет): the distinction between the way in which an event unfolds as a brute chronology (fabula), and as the "same" event, ordered in a mediated telling of it, a construction in which the chronology might be varied or even reversed, so as to achieve a particular effect. It is only by putting the order of the plot against a background of a (hypothetical) story that the figural, textually imposed aspect of the former becomes apparent. *Chronotope is the indissoluble combination of these two elements*. As such, it is another illustration of how Bakhtin's emphasis on simultaneity in his early philosophical writings, continues to make itself felt in later, more 'pragmatic' works. In "Author and hero in aesthetic activity," the figure/ground (self/other) distinction was charted precisely in spatial and temporal terms as "the *spatial* form of the hero" and "the *temporal* form of the hero." In Bakhtin's later work on the novel, the simultaneity and difference of time/space works itself out in the story/plot ratio (chronotope) he deploys as a category of narrative.

The chronotope as the ineluctability of simultaneity: The dialogue of figures and ground(s)

Stated in its most basic terms, a particular chronotope will be defined by the specific way in which the sequentiality of events is "deformed" (always involving a segmentation, a spatialization) in any given account of those events. It is this necessary simultaneity of figure (in this case, plot) and ground (or story) that constitutes the dialogic element in the chronotope. But even when reduced to this elementary narratological definition, there are certain difficulties that cannot be completely elided. We can better grasp these if we see some of the complexities that Shklovsky's concept of story (fabula) takes on when inter-illuminated by Bakhtin's concept of chronotope.

Shklovsky, at least in his early (and most characteristic) work, assumed that there could be such a thing as "pure" chronology (in the sense that it would be a sheer sequentiality independent of interpretation, and thus something that could be universally recognized even in different eras and cultures). For instance, the story (or fabula) of even such complex narratives as Tolstoy's *War and Peace* or Proust's *Remembrance of Things Past* could be easily recovered by simply answering the question, "What happened first, and what happened next?" In other words, although events in such complex narratives do not occur in a sequence arranged by chronology, such an unproblematical order of events could be "recovered," as it were, by rearranging the "distorted" pattern of events back into their "proper" or, as it is sometimes said, their "real-life" chronology.

Not only could an unproblematic beginning, middle, and end thus be extracted from the narrative, but it *must* be, for the whole effect of the text's "literariness" depends on readers perceiving precisely *how* the chronology is deformed (and Shklovsky provides a virtual gazetteer of such deformations). Thus, in a famous example adduced by Shklovsky, Pushkin's *Evgeny Onegin* is composed not of the events comprising "Onegin's love affair with Tatyana, but rather the artistic treatment of this fabula, achieved by means of interpolating digressions."[3] The assumption here seems to be that we all carry around in our heads a narrative scheme for love affairs as they happen outside literature; Pushkin insures the literariness of his project by "braking" this progression with numerous interpolations that distort the "logic" of love affairs in "real life."

The conventionality of time: Parallels with relativity theory

Underlying this conception of separation between story and plot, then, is the assumption of a prior and more fundamental discrepancy, that between literature and life: the assumption that in literature events can be arranged in any sequence, whereas in real life they are always chronological. In the restricted area of narratology, this principle reflects what is in fact a general tendency of the early Formalists to make absolute distinctions between literature and lived experience. A founding prejudice of the Formalists as a school (one they in varying degrees overcame) was the assumption that something natural called everyday language stood over against the language of literature, which was distinguished by its distortion of everyday usage. The language of literature and everyday language were completely cut off from each other because of fundamental differences in the functions and conventions of each. This difference extended to *time* as it worked in "literary" as opposed to "everyday" practice: "Literary time is pure convention. Its laws do not coincide with the laws of time in 'real life.' "[4]

Bakhtin differs from the Formalists in not accepting (at least at this level of relative simplicity) a distinction between "conventional" and "real" time. In his Neo-Kantian view, *time in real life is no less organized by convention than it is in a literary text.* As a category in dialogism, the chronotope is grounded in simultaneity at *all* levels, including those of both "literature" and "real life." Dialogism does not envision an absolute separation between existence free of conventions outside texts, and a world comprising only conventions within texts. There is no purely chronological sequence inside or outside the text. It is in any discussion of this sort that Bakhtin's immersion in Einsteinian ideas about the inseparability of time and event must be remembered.

For Einstein there is no chronology independent of events. The movement of the clock's hands, if that movement is to be an event – if it is to mean anything to a human being perceiving it – must always be correlated with something happening outside the clock. An event, in other words, is always a dialogic unit in so far as it is a *co*-relation: something happens only when something else with which it can be compared reveals a change in time and space (which is why, in his early works, Bakhtin flirts with tediousness by constantly reiterating the phrase *sobytie bytiya*, событие бытия, meaning "the event [or co-being] of existence" at those points where others less obsessed with the eventfulness of being would say simply "existence").

As soon as co-being is recognized as an event's necessary mode of existence, we give up the right to anything that is immaculate, *in-itself*, for everything will depend on how the relation between what happens and its situation in time/space is mediated. That is to say, not only are particular happenings subject to different interpretations – for instance, is a battle won or lost? The very question of whether an event has occurred at all is already an act of interpretation. Bakhtin's early emphasis on the distinction between "given" and "made" is useful here, reminding us that an event is always a dialogue between both possibilities.

In other words, and this point cannot be stressed enough, the means by which any presumed plot deforms any particular story will depend not only on formal ("made") features in a given text, but also on generally held conceptions of how time and space relate to each other in a particular culture at a particular time ("given" features). It follows that the apparently unproblematic definition of plot (fabula) provided by the early Formalists, that is the chronological order of events, is always interpreted in different ways at different times. Bakhtin is practicing a historical poetics precisely in this: he assumes that forms are always historical.

Take the simple example of adventure time, which, in his studies of detective stories (and of Laurence Sterne's *Tristram Shandy*) so fascinated Shklovsky, and which is at the heart of Bakhtin's definition of the Greek romance. Events are deployed in the Greek romance, as we have seen, as a series that can best be rendered: "and then *x* happened, and then *y* happened, and then . . ." It is a sequence in which, as Bakhtin says, nothing in fact happens: nothing happens in the sense that there could always be more or fewer events without their relative priority or posteriority to each other being significant.

For instance, it is not significant in the romance known as the *Ephesiaca* that any of the several abductions of the heroine, Anthia, occurs before or after any of her other abductions, for none of the rapes or captures has any progressive effect: all the actions and adventures that fill the Greek novel "constitute time sequences that are neither historical, quotidian, biographical, nor even biological and maturational" ("The chronotope," p. 91). In other words, there is only the *appearance* of what purports to be a chronological sequence, because there is only the *appearance* of change. That is, the timing of the narrative does not correspond to events that are significant enough to order what (in English) are so revealingly called "priorities." The only real changes occur at the formulaic beginning of such a sequence (the first time Anthia is separated from her lover Hebracomes, let us say, in the *Ephesiaca*) and at its equally ritualized end (when the two get married). All other changes fail to register on the figures who (quite literally in this way of regarding them) "carry the story": the adventures do not affect their bodies, which do not age nor do their minds develop. It is as if the hands on the clock in Einstein's exemplary railroad station moved, but the trains all remained stationary on their tracks.

As we saw, this pattern, is not confined to Greek romances. It can, for instance, be found in almost all the characteristic plots of post-industrial popular culture, whether the short films that were shown in the United States on Saturday mornings in weekly "chapters" from the 1920s to the 1950s about the adventures of singing cowboys and mad scientists that were so properly called "serials," or whether the eternal triangle of Ignatz Mouse, Offisa Pup, and Krazy Kat in George Herriman's great comic strip of that name (whose surrealistic desert backgrounds offer perfect illustrations of what Bakhtin means by "abstract adventure space'). Most so-called "formula fiction" (Harlequin romances, *Heimatsromane*, much spy and detective fiction) is formulaic precisely in the degree to which it deploys what Bakhtin calls "abstract adventure time."

Thus, at one level, a chronotope that found its earliest textual embodiment in the first centuries after Christ (roughly from the early second to the fifth century AD) continues to organize later texts up to and including those of the present day. As such, it would appear to be the kind of transhistorical, universal pattern of which early Russian Formalists (and later French Structuralists) dreamt.

In the sphere of literary studies, such a pattern has important parallels with the kind of ahistorical forms that were identified in linguistics by those Bakhtin attacked as "abstract objectivists," particularly the assumption in both cases that the chronotope (or linguistic unit) can be studied *in itself*. But even the most elementary form of the chronotope, abstract adventure, is subject to intertextual and historical conditions that make any appropriation of its repeatable features an *utterance*, that is, a text with a particular meaning in a specific situation.

Superman

Consider the case of Superman; what narrative could be more formulaic and repeatable than the tale of this comic strip hero who for fifty years has been disappearing into phone booths, changing his clothes, and in a flurry of speed-lines emerging once again to save the world? The story (fabula) both of Superman's macronarrative (the demise of the planet Krypton, Superman's flight to Earth) and of his various micronarratives (Lois Lane is in trouble, Clark Kent changes into Superman, Lois is saved, Superman becomes Clark Kent again) would seem to have a simple enough chronology, one that is recognizably the accordion structure of abstract adventure time: between Lois Lane's abduction (let us say) and the transformation of Clark Kent into the Man of Steel at one pole, and at the other the heroine's rescue combined with the ritualistic reappearance of the mild-mannered reporter, any number of events could unfold. But the abstract adventures that are common (at the merely formal level) both to

Greek romances and to comic strip heroes have a different meaning in each. Their time/space is similar, but they constitute quite different events.

Superman's strivings occur against the background of genres *within* literature that were unknown or relatively undeveloped in the first centuries AD (such as, most importantly, the modern novel and autobiography). *Outside* literature, his adventures unfold within the context of quite different ideas about the relationship of space to time. The adventures of Superman occur in a time and place in which it is widely assumed by most people (and not just physicists such as Reichenbach or philosophers such as Heidegger) that time is a structure of possibility. As such, time's action is perceived as a form of consumption: every time we act, a little more is revealed about who we are, and thus each event in our lives consumes not only a certain chronological duration, but also other possibilities of who we might become. Such a way of conceiving time has an effect on the way adventures unfold. In the case of Superman, as Umberto Eco has pointed out, it means that there is an ineluctable paradox built into the narrative: in spite of all his powers, Superman is

> a creature immersed in everyday life, in the present, apparently tied to our own conditions of life and death, even if endowed with superior faculties. An immortal superman would no longer be a man but a God, and the public's identification with his double identity would fall by the wayside. Superman, then, must remain "inconsumable" and at the same time be "consumed" according to the ways of everyday life.

Eco concludes from this paradox that "In Superman stories the time that breaks down is the *time of the story*, that is, the notion of time which ties one episode to another."[5]

However, as the time which ties one episode to another, or, in other words, as brute seriality, Eco's "time of the story" turns out to be a temporality that is really *extra*-temporal. It is a kind of sequencing that, in so far as it is merely sequential, is always the same. A different possibility comes into play if we see "the time that breaks down" not as the kind of time that is "the time of the story" (which assumes once again that a purely temporal sequence is somehow possible), but rather as an effect comprising *both* time and space. If, in other words, we conceive it as a chronotope, we may draw an inference from the Superman paradox which will be different from Eco's. It would then not merely be the case that "the time of the story" (or, in the terms we have been using, the chronological arrangement of the story) somehow "breaks down," as in Eco's account, or "gets deformed," as the Formalists would say. Rather, the breakdown or deformation would then be seen not as chronological, that is as taking place in a time so pure as to be self-evident and therefore beyond interpretation (the dream of a sheer fabula), but rather as unfolding in a *space* (as all time must). It is a space, moreover, that is not merely that of "everyday life" or of "our conditions," but the space of a constantly changing relationship: the relationship *between* such a theoretically presumed order, and the order in which events are actually deployed in a particular text (its unique *syuzhet*). Much as in the sphere of general semantics the normative, repeatable meaning of a word opposes its unique significance on specific occasions, the opposition between normative stories and particular plots in the sphere of narrative manifests itself in the larger contest between centrifugal and centripetal forces that is the dialogue of dialogues in our heteroglot world.

Thus the problem that Eco perceives in Superman, lack of correspondence between the two poles of narrative, story and plot, is a problem that haunts all texts – and not just literary texts, where it has most frequently been studied. The definition of the simplest chronotope of all – that of abstract adventure time – may be said to contain in it the pattern that is basic to all chronotopes. At different times and places authors and readers will be working with different sets of time/space co-ordinates, and thus the *relationship* between time and space – and therefore the relationship between a presumed chronology and its "distortion" in any given narrative progression – will vary.

In the chronotopic study of a particular text, attention will always be focused on simultaneity: a corollary of dialogism's emphasis on the dynamism of texts is that no single time/space can be definitive for any one of them. Instead of the text's being a "prisonhouse of language," it is seen as a three-ring (at least) circus of discourse. The tension between story and plot will have a meaning at the time of a text's first production that will be different from the one accruing to it in later readings. In addition

(and thus unlike reader reception theories), dialogism stresses
the role played by temporal and spatial frames of reference
inherent *in formal properties of the text*, not in the psychology of the
reader. A historical poetics will attend to all these different
relationships, and then seek to establish a hierarchy among
them.

The need for a temporal and spatial standard

Such a hierarchy will require a basal chronotope, a kind of
standard space as well as a standard time for orienting other
time/space relations that are appropriate to the discussion of a
given text. This Greenwich Mean Chronotope, as it were, is
usually provided by the co-ordinates deployed in the text itself.
But the "text itself" is never, of course, itself; it is always a
composite of what the author produced at one given time and in
one given place, and the meanings that accrue to the formal
features of that text in its later appropriations at subsequent
times. A reading undertaken in the light of historical poetics
will not concentrate (at least initially) on lexical or stylistic
features of traditional literary analysis. It will give attention
to details often dismissed as trivial: spatial and temporal
markers in the text such as "before" and "after," or "here" and
"there."

All texts use such indicators to make their meanings, but these
will be different in every text, and for the same reasons that they
are different for every speaking subject. Such universal markers
have meaning in any particular situation because they are
conventionally taken to have as their standard for distinguishing
between before and after, or here and there, the present moment
of the speaker who uses them. By analogy, the standard for
making such distinctions in a written text has been – also
conventionally – taken to be the time and place of a work's
first appearance. The text is in this sense an utterance.
Differences in time and place are never merely temporal or
spatial, of course, but have meanings – and literary texts are
especially powerful in deploying these. But no matter how
complex such meanings may be, it will be necessary first of all to
"place" their differences by establishing the sites of here/there
and now/then.

Example of Gogol's "Notes of a madman"

Before continuing, it will be useful to have an example. Bakhtin himself is not overly generous in providing these, so we shall choose a story by Nikolai Gogol called "Notes of a madman" ("Записки сумасшедшего," 1833). I select this particular work not only because Gogol is a recurring interest of Bakhtin's, but because it seems to me to illustrate both the possibilities and the problems inherent in chronotopic analysis. It also has the advantage of being more complex than the Greek romances or comic book narratives dealt with so far.

"Notes of a madman" is, ostensibly, the diary of a petty clerk in Petersburg of the 1830s (the decade in which the story was written). One basic chronotope we shall have to deal with, then, will be the space of Russia in the time of the early years of the nineteenth century. While we must recognize the initial abstraction and conventionality of such categories, they will none the less serve to orient the tale's manifold other time and space combinations.

Important among these is the fact that the tale unfolds as diary entries. These are chronological in the sense that they follow a calendric sequence of day and month: "October 3rd," "November 6th," and so on. But as this chronology unfolds, the clerk who is authoring the diary becomes more and more deranged: he first hears dogs talking to each other, and then he reads a number of letters he has stolen from a pair of dogs named Madgie and Fidèle. In other words, a tension grows between the coherence of the steadily marching dates as they unfold with all the logic of chronological sequence, and the growing chaos in the entries beneath their predictable order.

The clerk's increasing distance from those around him is emphasized in a number of incidents involving his tardiness (at the office, in meetings with fellow clerks). Despite the orderly parade of dates that organize his daily entries, the clerk falls further and further away from a time and space that can be shared. The tension between the calendar's order and the clerk's growing disorientation finally becomes unbearable, until the time/space of the headings becomes as disordered as the clerk's entries beneath them: the principle of chronological ordering finally breaks down completely as the clerk decides one day that he is not a clerk at all, but the king of Spain, an announcement made under the heading, "The year 2000, April 43." From this point on, the lack of system in the clerk's fantasies is matched by the disordered dates he uses to put them into chapters ("martober 86" or "January of the same year which happened after februarius").

Gogol takes the tension between story and plot to an extreme that results in what Eco calls the breakdown of "the *time of the story*, that is, the notion of time which ties one episode to another." In so doing, he brings into relief the degree to which such normally unquestioned categories as "sheer" chronology (the "notion of time which ties one episode to another") are not, in fact, *given*. The task of Gogol's clerk – to calibrate his personal rhythms with those ordained by his particular society at a particular time in its history – is one we all share outside literary texts. And *within* such works, the task of co-ordinating the time/space of a constructed self with all the givenness of its historically assigned social demands is what provides the general, shared ground against which any particular pattern of discrepancies between story and plot becomes a recognizable figure. *The dialogue between story and plot is in this sense the enabling condition for narrative as such.*

Gogol's laying bare of chronology, or story, as a conventional device (even if a necessary device) in this particular tale typifies much of his other work as well: so much so, that Nabokov, in his little volume on Gogol (*Gogol*, New Directions, 1958), merely imitates his hero in beginning with his death and ending with his birth. Gogol's experiments with story/plot opposition are pertinent to any attempt to understand the history of chronotopes, in their capacity as recurring, transcultural narrative patterns.

Biographical chronotopes

In so far as its form is that of a diary, "Notes of a madman" may be said to belong to a subgenre of autobiography, a genre whose norms provide Bakhtin with a number of exemplary transhistorical models in his monograph on the chronotope. Particularly important among these is "biographical time" as it is articulated in ancient Greek encomia, speeches read over the graves of eminent citizens of the polis and usually including an account of their major achievements.[6] In these, battlefields or the agora provide the usual setting for outstanding acts of military or political prowess. But they also serve to measure time, in so far as they catalogue the progress of heroes defined by their completely exteriorized careers. Public events that unfold in such places serve to mark differences in the rise or fall of figures who have no lives independent of their careers as generals, rhetors, tyrants, and so on.

A good deal has been written (following Hegel) about the differences between heroes in ancient (especially Greek) texts and heroes as they appear in later works. A common assumption has been that the most fundamental of these differences is an increase in self-consciousness; earlier heroes are frequently said to lack the interiority of later characters. And there is a certain amount of historical and literary evidence for such an assumption. Bakhtin himself is seduced into something like this view, although as I shall argue, the logic of his positing the chronotope as the basic unit of study in any historical poetics would seem to militate against such a prejudice. In order to read "Notes of a madman" in the light of a historical poetics, we shall certainly have to recognize differences between classical and modern texts. But differences in degree of *interiorization* will not figure among them: though living in a post-Romantic world, Gogol's clerk is as externalized as any of the ancient heroes whose lives unfold in public places.

The imperial ministries, the thronging main street of a modern capital, and the insane asylum which comprise the characteristic public spaces of Gogol's story are, of course, not the same as those found in ancient Greece. Moreover, we may briefly glimpse the clerk in his apartment, whereas we do not see a Greek general in the intimacy of his villa. In Gogol, the institutional space will be more diverse, superficially personal, and the hero will be of humbler station. Nevertheless, the pattern of public space that structures biographical narrative in nineteenth-century Petersburg will have certain features in common with the chronotope of public spaces in fifth-century BC Athens.

Bakhtin's argument, it will be recalled, is that the encomium's public spaces are the appropriate site for the biographies of characters who, in effect, have no lives outside their careers: in this "all-encompassing chronotope [of the agora], the laying

bare and examination of a citizen's whole life was accomplished." In such a chronotope nothing was

> intimate, or private, secret or personal, anything relating
> solely to the individual himself, anything that was, in
> principle, solitary . . . [therefore] the individual is open on all
> sides, he is all surface, there is in him nothing that exists "for
> his sake alone," nothing that could not be subject to public or
> state control and evaluation. Everything here, down to the
> last detail, is public.

("The chronotope," p. 131)

The most important effect of this public chronotope is to blur a
fundamental distinction between narrative types: "under such
conditions there could not in principle be any difference between
the approach one took to another's life and to one's own, between
the biographical and autobiographical points of view" (ibid., p.
132).

At a later period, a special relation is assumed between the
person relating events and the person who is the subject of those
events in autobiography, and therefore it is usually distinguished
from other forms of life writing. The special intimacy the author
enjoys *vis-à-vis* his narrative is the distinctive feature of autobiography. Others lack this intimacy, being mere biographers.

But in "Notes of a madman," Gogol's clerk lacks precisely the
kind of privileged knowledge about himself that is autobiography's most basic convention. His earliest diary entries are
peppered with the kind of questions that autobiography as a
genre presumes its author has already answered: "Why am I a
clerk? Why should I be a clerk? Perhaps I'm really a general or a
count and only seem to be a clerk? Maybe I don't really know
who I am? (December 3.)"[7] In other words, the clerk is in the
condition of being an I without a self. It is that condition, indeed,
in which there can be no difference "between the approach one
[takes] to another's life and to one's own" ("The chronotope,"
p. 132).

An important feature of ancient encomia was their tendency
to rub smooth the rough edges of particularity in the life of the
statesmen or warriors being praised: there was a small stock of
generic prescriptions defining the narrative patterns of public
life. Every effort was made to mold the specific details of a man's

existence into the contours of such a normative paradigm. These patterns pre-existed the particular individuals whose lives would be shaped to fit them. A distinction developed between a life that was unique and lacked generic forms for its telling, and the concept of *career*, which had available to it the formal time/space categories of the encomium. The names of particular battles or the themes of particular political debate might change, but the morphology of the exemplary public figure's career – unlike the events of his life – remained pretty much the same.

Life stories and career patterns

The encomium's tension between life stories and career patterns is a feature of its genre that will help us understand the dialogue between history and poetics, for it points both forward and backward to other narrative types. Like other major aspects of dialogism, it is an undertaking in which nothing can be treated as complete in itself. For instance, certain aspects of the tension between life and career as they are present in the ancient encomium are derived relatively unchanged from mythic forms that preceded it as a genre, while other aspects expose new shadings and nuances of the tension that will feed the development of later versions of biographical writing. In the chronotopic analysis of any genre, it is necessary to discriminate between features that – in retrospect have (so far) – proved unproductive in later transmutations, and those features that (once again, so far) continue to generate new forms:

> a literary genre, by its very nature, reflects the most stable . . . tendencies in literature's development. Always preserved in a genre are undying elements of the *archaic*. True these archaic elements are preserved in it only thanks to their constant *renewal*, which is to say, their contemporization. A genre is always the same and yet not the same, always old and new simultaneously.
>
> (*Problems of Dostoevsky's Poetics*, p. 106)[8]

A historical poetics will seek to specify in any given text its relation to the morphological and semantic changes of the class to which it belongs (it being taken for granted that every text belongs to *some* genre).

The encomium's emphasis on generalized careers, for example, is a structural inheritance from the past of ancient myth: it translates into stories about humans a pattern already present in older tales about demi-gods. In those, too, names signified certain well-known career narratives rather than individuals with unique lives. "Hercules," for instance, is not a proper name as such, but is rather the *title* for a story about twelve labors.

But the encomium has features that look forward as well: by appropriating a chronotope for historical persons that had previously been reserved for mythic heroes, the encomium performed a service that would give it immense importance in subsequent biographical narrative. It continued to shape such later genres as the saint's life, where its influence is obvious. However, variations on the pattern can be perceived as well in such militantly secular autobiographies as those of Jean-Jacques Rousseau (whose *Confessions* seek to resist the pattern by obsessively emphasizing their author's uniqueness on every page) or Henry Adams (whose life is treated as the exemplary career of a certain type of modern man). Nevertheless, the particular aspect of the encomium which we have been calling its depersonalizing tendency lost much of its strength in subsequent literary history.

Before returning to "Notes of a madman," we shall briefly look at the decline of this tendency, because its movement will illuminate yet another aspect of historical poetics, one that is implicit in Bakhtin's concept of the chronotope, but which he never explicitly developed at any length. I refer here to the obvious parallels between evolutionary principles in natural history and in a historical poetics. We do not know why Bakhtin failed to articulate the inherent link, a lacuna that is all the more puzzling when we remember how attracted in general he was to the natural sciences: it was, after all, Bakhtin's biologist friend Kanaev who took him to the lecture on physiology where, in 1925, he first heard the term chronotope. This is not the place to establish Bakhtin's motive for ignoring irresistible parallels between his concept of a historical poetics and natural history, but we might speculate in passing that in this, as in so much else, he was marking off his own work from that of the Formalists, who were obsessed by evolutionary models which Bakhtin considered over-simplified.[9]

Despite Bakhtin's own reticence, it is perfectly obvious that his historical poetics is intertextual, relative, and comparative in all its findings. Historical poetics is, in other words, a form of comparative morphology. As such, it ineluctably shares certain (but, of course, not all) features with evolutionary theory. None of these parallels is closer than the emphasis given in both undertakings to determining which present features of the object being studied will prove conducive to its future development, and which will not. In other words, history may be understood in both as the search for features in the past that evolutionists now call preadaptive.

Yet another metaphor for history drawn from biology: Preadaptation

Preadaptation, as understood by evolutionists, is a way to answer the thorny question of how intermediate steps toward an organ's ultimate evolution could be possible, if – as classical evolutionary theory asserts – there is no teleology governing natural selection. Similar questions have been raised about Bakhtin's insistence on the connection between modern texts and prototypes that are separated from them by hundreds or thousands of years and many intermediate steps (such as the relation between Dostoevsky and Menippean satire, or Rabelais and primordial carnival).[10] We can answer some of these criticisms in much the same way that Darwin did, when much the same question was raised as an objection to his theories. Darwin's great breakthrough was to propose natural selection as the mechanism that drove evolutionary development. But the principle of natural selection flew in the face of certain commonsense objections, as explained by Stephen Jay Gould:

> Natural selection has a constructive role in Darwin's system: it builds adaptation gradually, through a sequence of intermediate stages, by bringing together in sequential fashion elements that seem to have meaning only as parts of a final product. But how can a series of reasonable intermediate forms be constructed? Of what value could the first tiny step toward an eye be to its possessor?

Or, as Gould puts it in a pithier formulation, "The dung-mimicking insect is well protected, but can there be any edge in looking only 5 percent like a turd?"[11]

Preadaptation takes into account the argument against incipient stages "by admitting that intermediate forms did not work in the same way as their perfected descendants. We avoid the excellent question, What good is 5 percent of an eye? by arguing that the possessor of such an incipient structure did not use it for sight."[12] For instance:

> Most fishes build their fins from slender parallel rays that could not support an animal's weight on land. But one peculiar group of freshwater, bottom-dwelling fishes – our ancestors – evolved a fin with a strong central axis and only a few radiating projections. It was admirably preadapted to become a terrestrial leg, but it had evolved purely for its own purposes in water – presumably for scuttling along the bottom by sharp rotation of the central axis against the substrate.[13]

Stated most broadly, "the principle of preadaptation simply asserts that a structure can change its function radically without altering its form as much. We can bridge the limbo of intermediate stages by arguing for a retention of old functions while new ones are developing."[14]

But there are, of course, great differences between bottom-dwelling fishes and books; and as Bakhtin suggests by stressing the central role of genre memory in literary dynamics, the most fundamental of these differences is no doubt the ability of authors consciously or unconsciously to reach back to earlier stages in a way that human organisms can no longer effect a return to their fishy state. Although conscious retrospectivism is enormously important in literary history in such schools as neoclassicism, or in such writers as Walter Scott, it is perhaps the *unconscious* turn to the past that has proved most frequent and most consequential. In the particular case of carnival forms, for instance, it would be difficult to say they exercised

> a direct and vital influence on Dostoevsky . . . [rather] carnivalization acted on him, as on the majority of other eighteenth and nineteenth-century writers, primarily as a literary and generic tradition whose extraliterary source, that is, carnival proper, was perhaps not even perceived by him in any clearly precise way.
> (*Problems of Dostoevsky's Poetics*, p. 156)

That is, while present vestiges of earlier genres are never precisely what they were, connections to their ancient identity can still more or less be achieved. In the world of culture, selection, because it is not natural, is, up to a certain point, a matter of memory and choice.

Preadaptation has the following relevance to our inquiry about the relation between ancient biographical forms and Gogol's "Notes of a madman": depersonalization shapes the morphology of both ancient forms of biography and relatively recent life-writing experiments. It would seem that the tendency to emphasize careers over lives in ancient forms was preadapted to meet the quite different social context of Russia in the 1830s. Otherwise, the survival of this particular formal feature is inexplicable, for a long trend of events that militated against depersonalization intervened between Greek encomia and Gogolian narrative.

The decline of depersonalizing tendencies would seem to be especially steep after the seventeenth century, when new forms for displaying the intimate details of particular lives begin to appear with ever growing frequency. For instance, in the eighteenth-century British novel, the life/career ratio of ancient biographical narrative would seem to be completely reversed: *Tom Jones* is a common name that could nominate many men; in itself, it signifies nothing except "a common English proper name." It lacks meaning until fleshed out by the novel details of the unique life of this Tom Jones. The narrative of *Tom Jones* and the name Tom Jones form a unique bond; they cannot be known independently of each other.

By contrast, the public chronotope that structured earlier forms had the effect of draining all individuality out of proper names. Names had meaning only in so far as they could be coupled with well-known career formulas that pre-existed any particular bearer of any specific name. The radical exteriority characterizing the generic careers of ancient biographies had the effect, then, of distancing their heroes from the uniqueness nominated by their own names. As a result, a man's name ceased to be his own, ceased, in the technical grammatical sense, to be "proper": no longer the appellation of a unique life, it became another title for the oft-repeated tale of an exemplary career.

Such a depersonalized name was, in effect, transformed into a version of eponym, which the dictionary defines as "a real or imagined person from whose name the name of a nation is derived or supposed to derive" – William Penn founds Pennsylvania, Romulus originates Rome. In other words, eponyms are the names of individual people – the kind who have *biographies* – that are translated into the names of collective, extrapersonal entities, the kind that have *histories*. Romulus' name is similar to the names of ancient biographical subjects in so far as the sign "Romulus" does not name a man so much as a story. But the eponym is a special case among all other possible name/biography, story/plot, life/career relations: as in encomia, we have names nominating careers rather than individual persons, but the careers of eponymous heroes are of a special kind. They are foundational, always associated with origins, and thus the transformation of a name into an eponym is always fraught with political implications.

Eponyms are spectacular reminders that the name of every person is first of all a sign, something standing for something else that it, in itself, is not. While this is true of all words, the kind of words we use as names for our selves present particular problems when regarded as signs. It is here that the relation between ancient biography and modern narrative of a certain kind can be perceived.

In "Notes of a madman," we shall examine vestiges of the encomium, particularly as they relate to the transformation of proper names into eponyms. A poetics that is *historical* will make note of these, and then pursue some (but obviously, never all) of the specific meanings such general patterns might have in a text far removed from ancient biography. In order to pursue this line, it will be helpful to have in mind one or two additional details from Gogol's text and certain facts of Russian history.

'Notes of a madman" as an experiment in autobiography

"Notes of a madman" is a meditation on biography as a particular project within the horizon of possible narrative types: more specifically it is an experiment in *auto*biography, a self in search of a writing that could be its life. For the moment I defer the question of whose autobiography, since this, precisely, is the fundamental question for its author, the keeper of the diary. While there may be several answers to the question of who he is, we might well begin with the most conventional answer to the question of identity: a proper name. In this particular case the name of the clerk – or general or count – is Poprischin. Probably because it is difficult for most non-speakers of Russian to pronounce, this name is often left out of English translations. The omission is unfortunate for a number of reasons, not least because it obscures an overall feature of Gogol's work, his obsession with the powerlessness of names to fix meanings.

Gogol had a Dickensian gift for inventing euphonious names. But there is an important difference in the function such names serve for the two writers: Dickens' names are memorable not only because of their alliterative sound combinations (Mister Pickwick, Nicholas Nickleby, Newman Noggs) but because they are so well suited to their subjects. Such names as Gride or Gashford are tiny essays on the negative features of the characters they name; their capacity to signify makes them *proper* names in the fullest sense of the word. By contrast, the names of Gogol's characters are usually improper. Gogol uses the arbitrariness of names to interrogate the idea of self-identification. For instance, the hero of "The Overcoat," another story from the collection in which "Diary of a madman" was first published, is called Akakii Akakievich, a name so peculiar Gogol feels the need to explain it. When the new baby arrived, his mother

> was given her pick of the following three names for her son: Mochius, Sossius, and that of the martyr, Hotzazat. "That won't do," Akakii's mother thought. "Those names are . . . how shall I put it. . . ." To please her, the godparents opened the calendar at another page and again three names came out: Strifilius, Dulius, and Varachasius. "We're in a mess," the old woman said. "Who ever heard of such names? If it was something like Varadat or Varuch I wouldn't object . . . but Strifilius and Varachasius. . . ." So they turned to yet another page and out came Pavsicachius and Vachtisius. "Well, that's that," the mother said, "that settles it. He'll just have to be Akakii like his father." [The narrator then helpfully adds,] So that is how Akakii Akakievich originated.[15]

The scandalous logic of Akakii Akakievich's nomination at his birth is then realized in the fits and starts and gaps that mark his progress toward a death that is as arbitrary as his name. Gogol, in other words, experiments with the ratios of meaning assumed in most symbolic names: a name is right because it points to something wrong – something wrong, moreover, that has to do with names themselves.

The diarist of "Notes of a madman" also has a name at his beginning, one no less strange, and whose power to, as Gogol says, *originate* him, is no more assured. Poprischin, as one of the dogs he monitors says, is "a funny name." It contains a pun blurring suggestions of *pryshch* (прыщ), the Russian for pimple, and *poprishche* (поприще), field, as in "the field of medicine."

Both the suggestions of "pimple" and "field" are to the point. *Poprischin* nominates a site of discourse, a place from which the time/space of a particular existence must be organized in the time/space of shared words. "Pimple" and "field," especially in their punning relation to each other, constitute a chronotope in themselves: if the *pryshch* of Poprischin points to a time that is temporary (the fleeting existence of pimples that come and go), *poprishche* points to a space that is not only bounded ("field"), but linear: its most common translation is "career," one's progress through life or through a particular vocation.

For instance, what in the dictionary definition of an eponym is a mere conjunction ("real *or* imagined person"), is in "Notes of a madman" the fundamental question: Poprischin cannot decide whether he is himself real or imagined. Poprischin nominates the person who bears that name only because the chance event of his birth threw him into the biological series locally referred to as Poprischin. Is his name a word that has a meaning, or is it only nonsense?

The concept of the eponym organizes our reading of the "Notes of a madman" first of all, then, because it so militantly draws attention to questions about the relation between a name and the identity of the person who, as we so accurately say in English, *bears* that name, when the name is perceived as being a sign like any other sign, such as "tree" or "stone." The *pryshch* aspect of the pun, then, describes Poprischin's mode of being as a pimple on the surface of his name.

Name as story

But the power of the eponym resides more in its evocation of *poprishche*. The biographical institution of the 'walk of life' or career relates to the name, Poprischin, as the political institution of Rome relates to the name, Romulus. In both cases, a proper name is used to signify not a person but a place, a place that is a story; in each case, the putative subject *is* a story. Although Poprischin belongs to the genre "career," while Romulus belongs to the genre "history, they are similar kinds of stories: in the case of each, some authority outside the flux of time must be found to legitimate what otherwise is merely a brute chronology of disconnected events. "Poprischin" and "Romulus" are shorthand notations for narratives about origins, about founding projects. In other words, they are about the kind of power that can authorize the authority of their authors. The biographical institution called Poprischin, the project of a single citizen of the Russian empire, proves to be no less governed by politics than the imperial project called the Roman state. A homology between the politics governing the life of a puny individual and the politics at work in the life of a populous state is, of course, absurd; indeed, it is precisely the absurdity that grounds the decline and fall of the Spanish empire ruled by the author who calls himself both Poprischin and Ferdinand VIII.

Madness in this tale is defined not as an absolute condition binarily opposed to another absolute condition called normalcy, but as a difference that is relative in the horizon of possible relations between self and other, interdiction and dialogue. Madness is the result of a self's not being able to work out a treaty governing ratios of authority between itself and the other. Madness is then modeled in Gogol as a problem in the politics of communication, the statecraft in small that legislates who may speak, when and how. The general problem of authority is worked out in the specific categories of authorship. When society decides that one of its citizens is no longer in harmony with its expectations, he is judged not to be competent; he loses his status as the author of his own identity because others judge him to be no longer able to answer for his own utterances, utterance being understood as both word and deed. The self's identity needs to be legitimized by some agency outside itself: sanity in the diary is framed as the ability to negotiate a point of view, a conceptual space, from which self and other can interact in a simultaneity.

Simultaneity always involves the question of proportion: when two things or consciousnesses are together in a simultaneous relation, how much of each is present? In other words, the simultaneity of self and other is a contested space, and as such is mediated by politics. In the specific case of life writing, politics will be present as a negotiation between an individual self's attempt to convey as much of its uniqueness as possible in a narrative whose otherness is constituted by formulaic career patterns. Such formulas always pre-exist any individual existence and thus rob unique lives of their authenticity. The other side of the coin, however, is that only through some such formula can the particularity of any life be made coherent to others. The question (and it is a political question involving the mediation of authority) always must be: how much uniqueness can be smuggled into a formula without its becoming unrecognizable to others?

In Gogol's tale, this problem is paradigmatically present in Poprischin's relation to the two dogs whose correspondence plays so large a role in his diary. The dogs are remarkable not only for their ability to write (although, as Poprischin remarks, "there *is* something canine about the handwriting"), but for their ability to *correspond*: not just to each other, but with the surrounding society, in a manner precisely opposite to Poprischin's iconic attribute of dis-correspondence. He is moved to observe that "A dog is an extraordinary politician," and on the next page that, "Dogs are a clever race, they understand politics."

The dogs are political in the sense they successfully negotiate their places not only in society, but in perception: the observation point from which they view the world lets them be both inside and outside the social space Poprischin seeks to know; thus they are the perfect optic for Poprischin who cannot find a place to situate his self either inside or outside.

In any biography, there is a formal distinction between a writing self and a self who is written about. The distinction between the two is most grossly framed in the temporal discrepancy between them (biographer is always later than subject). In Gogol's tale, this distinction is modeled as a contrast between genres (diary vs. letter). But more importantly, the distinction between the writing self and the self written about is completely elided in the purloined letters. Poprischin, who merely reads texts about himself that are written by others, as well as addressed to others, disappears as biographer – and as subject. As neither the sender nor the intended addressee of the letters, Poprischin's role as both their writer and their reader is completely masked (he is, as he will later say, 'incognito'). The author is masked by the structure of address. The dual relation he normally bears to his words in the diary (where he is both writer and reader) is parodied in the abnormal relation he bears to his words in the letters, where he is both sender and receiver. The censoring power of the interdict has become so great that in the dog letters it literally *speaks* between his self as self-addressee and his self as addressee of the other. The diary as characteristic genre of his utterance begins to break down because there is no identity to which a form so ineluctably predicated on its author's selfhood can be addressed.

Before coming back to what Poprischin does with space/time in the rest of the diary (or what it does to him), it will be useful to ask certain questions, such as why does he choose to become a king? Why does he choose to exercise politics precisely in Spain? And why, having become a king, do the diary entries he now records become so non-sequential?

Poprischin is the eponym for a problem: how to find a meaning that is not merely sequential in the chronological series that is one's life. In ancient Greek encomia, the problem was solved by dividing the text into two parts: one would recount the life sequentially from birth through youth to old age; a second part would then concentrate on the essence of the dead man's character, the degree to which he was a model statesman or warrior, let us say. In later times this division which the Greeks formally marked between the time and the meaning of a life was eroded, and attempts were made with increasing urgency to conflate the two. However, the source of authority to which the Greeks had always appealed – the death of the subject, the stasis at the end point of his life's chronological sequence – remained unchanged. Such an arrangement would seem to preclude autobiographies for obvious reasons, but St Augustine in his *Confessions* found a structural solution in conversion experience: he told his life before conversion as a temporally sequential narrative that ceases on the day when he hears the voice of God in a Roman garden; after that point in his twenty-first year he gives no more chronology, but an unplotted meditation on the mystery of time. The authority to interpret his life still derives from death, in this case the death of the subject he was before his conversion *and* his birth as the subject who writes the auto-biography.

The genre memory of "Notes of a madman" includes both encomia and Augustine's twist on ancient biographical narrative. In a bravura exercise in perspective by incongruity, Poprischin's entry announcing that he is the king of Spain reads very much like a parody of Augustine:

> I am the king. I discovered it today. It all came to me in a flash. It's incredible to me now that I could have imagined that I was a Titular Councillor. How could such a crazy idea ever have entered my head. Thank God no one ever thought of slapping me into a lunatic asylum. *Now* I see everything clearly . . . *then* things loomed at me out of a fog [italics added].[16]

Poprischin's madness is another version of conversion, or more accurately it is an inversion of Augustine's confessional strategy: instead of the break between time and timelessness marking translation to a higher authority, the rupture between his diary entries that are sequential and those that are not mark Poprischin's descent into increasing domination by others.

But death of the old subject is still the means by which he attempts to usurp authority; concealed below the non-sequence of the insane dates (such as "Martober 86, Between day and night") sleeps a quite rigorous logic of sequence: it is of a kind available only to royalty. Poprischin has read that Ferdinand VII of Spain has died: in other words, the king, Ferdinand VII, is dead; long live the king, Ferdinand VIII. The doctrine known as the king's two bodies – according to which the ruler has both a body physical and a body politic, so that while his physical body may die, the other body is immortal and is immediately invested in the dead king's successor – provides a powerful legitimacy.[17] There is a certain inevitability, then, in the events that impel Poprischin, who has always perceived bodies through the optic of politics, to be a king.

But why king of *Spain*? A first and obvious answer would have to be that current events in Spain provide the most convenient succession into which Poprischin can insert himself. While Gogol was writing "Notes of a madman," (in 1833, a year in which he was, by the way, still officially a history professor) the Bourbon king of Spain, Ferdinand VII, died, leaving the throne to his infant daughter, Isabella II. This precipitated the first Carlist war, as supporters of Ferdinand's brother, Don Carlos, sought to establish him on the throne. The scenario for contested legitimacy of identity (who is the real ruler, the true heir?) could not have been more tailor-made.

But another, and less obvious, reason why Poprischin chooses precisely Spain to rule suggests itself if we remember that Gogol, like many Russians of his generation, was an uncritical admirer of the German Romantics: his first published work was called *Hans Kühelgarten*, and most of his early stories are Kunstmärchen. So, as Gogol would have known, the phrase (in Russian as well as English) "It's all Greek to me" (meaning "I do not understand") is rendered in German as "It is Spanish to me" (*"Es kommt mir spanisch vor"*). By a logic more Gogolian than macaronic, we may then say that the Spain over which Poprischin rules is the German Spain. First of all because Poprischin's Spain is known to be interchangeable with other countries: as he says

> I have discovered that China and Spain are the same thing
> and it is only ignorance that makes people take them for two
> separate countries. I advise anybody who doubts it to take a
> piece of paper and write the word "Spain" and they will see
> for themselves that it comes out "China."

Any doubts we may have had about his disputed authorship of the correspondence between the dogs are here laid to rest, for the ease with which the written form of Spain becomes the written form of China is made possible by the same formula that enables the written form of Poprischin to become the written form of the dog Madgie – or, for that matter, the dog Fidèle. A more precise reason for supposing that Poprischin's Spain is German is that the space he comes to occupy after he enters the non-linear time sequence of diary entries initiated by "Year 2000, April 43" is one where the grammatical, syntagmatic, and semantic rules that order the meaning of differences in language have lost their power, with the consequence that everything is Greek – that is, Spanish; that is, *unintelligible* – to Poprischin.

The concluding entries of the diary teem with references to lost authority and usurped legitimacy, not merely in the Carlist war of succession that obsesses Poprischin, but in the repeated references to other examples of dispossessed power. Wellington is perhaps less the "English chemist" that Poprischin thinks he is than the chief means by which the emperor Napoleon, himself a notorious dethroner, was dethroned. Polignac, who comes up several times in the tale, is the ultra-conservative statesman under Charles X (himself a token for the broken sequence of Bourbon kings – not only of Spain but also of France – who rule after the supreme discrowning of the revolution) whose excesses led to the later revolution of 1830. But earlier in the year that Polignac lost power, he organized the invasion that brought the French into Algeria, bringing about the fall of yet another monarch, Hussein Pasha, the last Dey of Algiers.

The last Dey of Algiers comes up in the last line of the diary: "And by the way, did you know the Dey of Algiers has a wart under his nose?" The appearance of the wart in the rhetorically privileged place of the text's last line (and in Russian, "wart" is even more final, since it is the last word) brings us back to the eponym with which we began: a wart is semantically related to pimple, in so far as both are unnatural growths that protrude from the skin. Once again Poprischin's eponymous attribute of protruding, of standing out from the body of his culture, is highlighted.

The inability to find a proper relation, figured in the failure of Poprischin to relate in any sequence of any kind, is what accounts for the tale's final discrepancy: Poprischin is once again exploring fantastic points of view from which to observe his self as an object that his self as a subject cannot sustain: "I have no strength left. I can't stand anymore . . . I have no strength, I cannot bear this suffering," an utterance all too commensurate with the place from which it is spoken. There is a pathetic if momentary fit between text and context for the first time in the diary, but Poprischin characteristically takes off from the time and space of the present to a more cosmic point of view: "Soar upward my horses, carry me away from this world . . . Further, further where I will see nothing." But then he sees his mother;

"Mother, save your wretched son! Let your tears fall on his sick head! . . . There is no room for him in this world . . . Mother, take pity on your sick child . . . And by the way, have you heard that the Dey of Algiers has a wart under his nose?"[18]

The inability to find a common term between the levels of discourse appropriate to his situation and those involving the Dey of Algiers marks an ultimate rupture between the temporal, spatial, and linguistic parameters of his self and the time, space, and language coordinates of others. Can any sequence so incoherent tell us anything about sequences coherent enough to be called narratives?

To the degree that the tale's very incoherence is significant as a deviation from expected narrative conventions, it can. Gogol, a great eccentric who always had trouble giving coherence to his own name, provides in "Notes of a madman" a textbook on the politics at play in the forging of a narrative able to negotiate between the desire of the self and the demands of others. Poprischin is deposed as ruler of the space that is the time of his own biography, because he is an inept legislator in the language kingdom of which we are all citizens, and in whose politics we are therefore players. Poprischin's diary engages the basic problem that slept in the ancient encomium, but which takes on new significance in the particular time and place of Gogol's tale.

The multiplicity of chronotopes to be found in a single text

Gogol's tale illustrates first of all that no text will ever have a single chronotope. Vulgar Marxist critics such as Pereverzev, the early Soviet historian of literature who explained all of Gogol's texts by reference to his parents being small landholders in the Ukraine, take as normative a time/space within a work that can most readily be associated with the period and place in which it was written. Only slightly less vulgar proponents of what has come to be called Reader Reception theory take as normative a time/space that derives from the point at which a work is read. The early Formalists presumed reified time/space patterns that somehow existed ahistorically and independently of both authors of works and their readers. What both of these (admittedly hypostatized) views have in common is that they privilege (monologize) *one* point in the history of a text's existence as a normative time/space pattern.

We might then add to Bakhtin's list of chronotopes three others: that of vulgar Marxism, in which the time/space of the text's author is determining; a Reader Response chronotope in which the time/space of a text's reader is determining; and an early Formalist chronotope, in which a time/space configuration perceived in a given text at a given time – the time of its analysis by a Formalist critic – is taken to be a universal pattern not dependent on the contingent factors of its reception.

Dialogism – and this is why the concept of chronotope is so important in any attempt to grasp its difference from other available concepts of the text – assumes by contrast that the text is always in production, that there is no single point of normalizing stasis, or at least none that is determining in quite the way assumed by the three possibilities outlined above. Each of those theories assumes a static element in their analyses: a point, variously nominated, that would transhistorically be able to serve as the unchanging figure against which all or any particular arrangement of events could be perceived as a "distortion" (it is of course ironic that such a static element is more often than not conceived as a "chronology," a figure of pure time). Chronotope, on the other hand, begins by assuming that *both* the pattern and its distortion are constructs.

On the other hand, unlike some Reader Reception theories, dialogism does not assume that either the author or the reader is absolutely free to construct his or her own relation between a pattern and its distortion. It argues that the time/space relation of any particular text will always be perceived in the context of a larger set of time/space relations that obtain in the social and historical environment in which it is read. This emphasis on the text's groundedness in a social and historical context *at every point of its existence* is one of dialogism's distinctive features. One of the more important of these contextual considerations will always be the manner in which – at a particular place and in a particular time – the nature of "Time itself" is assumed to work. We all live in a world of assumptions so basic that they are rarely (if ever) expressed, for they are unconsciously taken for granted.

This is a truism in our age, when we are so sensitized to the workings of ideology. But what is often overlooked is that there is

not only a "political unconscious," but what might be called a
"chronotopic unconscious," a set of unspoken assumptions about
the coordinates of our experience so fundamental that they lie
even deeper (and therefore may ultimately be more determining)
than the prejudices imposed by ideology. In fact, the two may be
coterminous. The deepest layers of our assumptive world are
probably those where we unreflectingly conceive the nature of
time and space: at a banal level, it is obvious that today the
overwhelming majority of men and women organize their
behavior as they always have – on the assumption that the sun is
going to rise again tomorrow and that they will awake in the
same space as that in which they went to sleep. But beyond such
gross and unacknowledged expectations, people at different
times and places have held different unconscious beliefs about
the nature of time and space that are unique to their *own* time
and space. These beliefs manifest themselves in a number of
different ways, from the differing shapes of cosmologies to
varying attitudes toward farming.

Beliefs about the nature of time/space itself arguably condition
the very language people speak. In closing this chapter, we will
pursue this last suggestion because if it has any validity at all, the
implications for understanding how chronotopes outside texts
relate to intratextual chronotopes will be considerable.

The best-known formulation of how language is affected by
time/space as it is conceived in the assumptive world of
particular cultures is, of course, the so-called "Sapir–Whorf
hypothesis." Through his great authority as a linguist, Edward
Sapir attempted to give disciplinary respectability to the
Romantic idea that each language had a spirit, which, in turn,
formed the national character of those who spoke it. Avoiding
the crude directness of this analogy, Sapir nevertheless argued
that: "Human beings are very much at the mercy of the
particular language which has become the medium of expression
for their society ... the 'real world' is to a large extent
unconsciously built up on the language habits of the group."[19]
His student, Benjamin Lee Whorf, sought to specify what such
a language-influenced world might look like by attempting
to extract from the formal features of the Hopi language
(tense markers, spatial indicators, and so on) a Hopi world
view.

There are many holes in the theory, which will not occupy us here. Suffice it that the hypothesis was in many ways conceptually naive; most damagingly, it lacked a full-blown theory of knowledge that could provide a base to support the effects it describes. Dialogism, on the other hand, is fundamentally an epistemology; one, moreover, that not only supports such effects, but requires them. Dialogism, like the Vygotskian model of cognitive development with which it has so much in common, assumes that thought is fundamentally a language activity. As we saw in chapter 3, the dialogue in dialogism attains its importance because of Bakhtin's assumption that the acquisition of language is in fact the acquisition of the ability to think. What might be called Vygotsky's law, i.e. "higher mental functions [complex thought processes] appear on the interpsychological plane before they appear on the intrapsychological plane" also animates Bakhtin's assertion that, "Speech had first to come into being and develop in the process of the social intercourse of organisms so that afterward it could enter within the organism and become inner speech."

Bakhtin's whole "objective psychology" is based on the assumption that

> The psyche enjoys extraterritorial status in the organism. It is a social entity that penetrates inside the organism of the individual person ... [but it is also the case that] the sign, whose locus is outside the organism, must enter the inner world in order to implement its meaning as a sign. Between the psyche and ideology there exists, then, a continuous dialectical interplay.
>
> (*Marxism and the Philosophy of Language*, p. 39)[20]

While this may sound hopelessly abstract, the exchange between semiotic activity at the level of society and at the level of the individual member of the group is in fact rendered with the greatest particularity every time someone actually speaks or writes. An important difference, though, between the two levels is that while "the process of speech, broadly understood as the process of inner and outer verbal life, goes on continuously [knowing] neither beginning nor end" (ibid., p. 96), the same process perceived at the level of any specific speech act made by a particular person in a unique situation *does* know a beginning and an end. And it is in pursuing the way in which beginnings and ends frame discrete utterances in everyday speech situations that we shall begin to perceive the relevance of questions (fundamental to any historical poetics) about how time is shaped outside literary texts to questions about time/space operations within the literary text.

Any actual utterance

> is an island rising from the boundless sea of inner speech; the dimensions and forms of this island are determined by the particular *situation* of the utterance and its *audience*. Situation and audience make inner speech undergo actualization into some kind of specific outer expression that is directly included into an unverbalized behavioral context and in that context is amplified by actions, behavior, or verbal responses of other participants in the utterance. (ibid.)

In other words, the utterance is a narrative unit in so far as it always has a beginning and an end. But it is a social unit as well in so far as what constitutes the proper beginnings and endings are agreed upon by the participants. And as a unit defined by socially determined norms, it is also generic. For in order to concur as to whether a particular utterance is appropriate – neither too long nor too short, neither too formal nor too informal – we must have agreement about the *general* form utterances should have when made in that specific situation.

As sociolinguists and ethnographers have begun to suspect only very recently, everyday speech appears to be no less governed by normative ideas about form than is literature. We need a poetics of everyday speech no less than we do a poetics of literature. And both poetics will be *historical* in the same sense. Ideas about norms which in a particular time and place have the appearance of being timeless and universal are in fact period-specific and peculiar to specific culture systems.

A poetics always involves normative ideas about form. Dialogism adds that ideas about form are themselves predefined by ideas about time/space relations. Moreover, these relations are culture specific: the concern for precise placement of words and careful timing of delivery in classical rhetoric, or the debates about whether a play's action should last longer than twenty-four hours in Renaissance appropriations of Aristotle, are only

some of the better-known examples of the basically chronotopic –
that is local *and* transhistorical nature of all poetics.

Genre is a master category in dialogism, then, because the way
time and space characteristically relate to each other will always
be in units larger than any particular text in itself. Genres are
different ways to codify the rules assumed to govern time/space
relations in the class to which any given text belongs. For by the
same dialogic law (nothing exists in itself) that says both a figure
and its elaboration are required to understand how a text works
"internally," so must it be put into relation with other texts
externally. In poetics, no less than in physics, time/space
categories are relative in so far as they can be known only by
contrast with at least one other set of coordinates that can serve
as a system of reference. Much as the narrative is always between
its "own" time and space and another conceived as the
background which makes its particular "distortion" coherent, so
is the text as a whole always between other texts whose patterns
render *its* particularity intelligible. These other texts will fall into
roughly two categories, those that are similar to "this" text, and
those that are not. Those that are similar constitute, of course,
the genre to which any particular text will be presumed to
belong. "The chronotope in literature has an intrinsic *generic*
significance" ("The chronotope", pp. 84–5) not only because it
determines genres, but because the reverse is also true: genres
determine it, both for authors and readers, all of whom entertain
it as a background against which their own dialogue with a
particular work can be made meaningful.

The importance of genres

It is at the level of genre that *relatively* transhistorical figures are
possible, enabling a pattern against which perception of any
particular text at any particular time allows us to see it as
distinct. The way time and space are organized in the text
requires attention not only to its own temporal and spatial
categories, but also to those of a presumed norm. Genre as norm
is related to individual texts in much the same way that story as
norm is related to plot in the narrative of any particular text.

And if a genre is defined as a gross possibility for arranging
time and space in a pattern that individual members of the class

deploy in more or less different versions, we may begin to see how interconnected are not only the categories Bakhtin is describing directly, but also those "meta-categories" he uses to frame such a description in his own discourse. What holds such fundamental figures as genre and chronotope together in the historical poetics that dialogism proposes is the same emphasis in each on a particular relation in them all: a constant dialogue between uniqueness and generality, that which is unrepeatable, and that which can be repeated. It is a relation that obsesses Bakhtin both early and late: the non-psychologistic interdependence that obtains between self and other.

By taking up self and other in a discussion of chronotope, story, plot, and genre, we may perhaps see more clearly the degree to which all of these categories specify different versions of a relation common to them all. The dialogue of dialogues is the relation of fixity to flux, of same to different that Bakhtin in the 1920s in his work on *Marxism and the Philosophy of Language* and on Dostoevsky, and in the 1930s in his various essays on the novel, came to recognize as a fundamental problem of all cognition that is mediated through language (as he assumes is all human cognition, including that of the self). The pole of invariant norm assumes different guises throughout Bakhtin's career: among others, it sometimes appears as self, as story, or, more to the point for our purposes, as generic chronotope. Against the normative background these categories provide, another set may be perceived as individual variables which "distort" them: the other permits the self, plot permits story, or the generic chronotope enables the chronotope specific to a particular work.

Language provides the common substrate to all these categories. It is thus in the conditions that govern the borders between same and different, stable versus mutable operations *in language* that the basal dialogue between unity and diversity may most clearly be charted:

> The strength and at the same time the limitations of such basic [categories as we have discussed above] become apparent when [they are seen] as conditioned by specific historical destinies. . . . These categories arose from and were shaped by the historically *aktuell* forces at work in the verbal-ideological evolution of specific social groups. . . . These forces are the

forces that serve to unify and centralize the verbal-ideological world.

(*The Dialogic Imagination*, p. 270)

The fixative power of such centripetal forces is what enables sense to be made out of the flux of experience. But the authority that enables such fixity is not real, or at least not real in the same way that variety, change, all those heteronomous effects which Bakhtin labels centrifugal forces, are real. They are given (*dan*, дан), whereas systematic claims to stability never exist as a given: their existence must always be made up, conceived (*zadan*, задан).

For instance, in English we assume the sound aspect of the sign "horse" always refers to a large quadruped. We posit a connection between a certain sound we can produce in our mouths and a certain kind of animal we encounter in experience. But in between the word in the mouth and the animal on (let us say) the race track is a set of imposed rules insuring that every time we see such a quadruped it will not be a completely new or random occurrence: rather, it will be an event that can be stabilized through our capacity to name the animal "horse." We may know at some level that there is no necessary connection between the sound and the thing – that what we call horse can also be called *Pferd* or *cheval*, but, when speaking English, we will still assume the power of the (conceived, *zadan*) sound "horse" to fix into a meaning any (given) appearance of a certain kind of quadruped.

As is well known, at this merely lexical level, change can occur fairly rapidly, particularly in those nouns that belong to the mysterious realm of slang, where different words meaning "good," for instance, can replace each other almost every ten years: in the United States the "cool" of the 1960s gave way to the "awesome" of the 1970s and the "serious" of the 1980s. But other aspects of language, such as grammar or syntax, change much more slowly, and even most other lexical elements, such as our initial example of "horse," are more stable. For most people, the oldest thing they will ever encounter in their lives is the language they speak every day, a constant and intimate reminder of immutability amidst the rapidly shifting contingencies of lived experience.

But of course even the relatively stable system of grammar changes over time, and, on a scale of centuries, whole languages give way to others. At any given point in its history, speakers of a natural language can have the illusion that the meaning of the words they use is stable. But even this stability, which lasts much longer than almost any other human institution, is *un*stable in the sense that it, too, changes and thus has a history. It is "conceived," not given, like the centrifugal forces in experience, and the reality of flux and indeterminacy that are at work in nature and in ourselves. Thus, although language can provide the basis for giving the appearance of stability to the world, the forms by which it does so are themselves mutable: the very forms by which we seek to slow the quickness of experience are themselves in flux.

In making this assumption, dialogism defines itself as a Neo-Kantian heresy: with Kant, it assumes that time and space shape all perception. But most emphatically unlike Kant, dialogism makes a radical commitment to the historical particularity of any act of perception as it is actually experienced by living persons from their unique place in existence. Thus, in addition to, and more important than, the general, repeatable aspects of perception to which Kant gives exclusive attention, dialogism argues that there is an unrepeatable – read, historical – dimension that Kant's abstraction omits. In other words, time and space, or more accurately, time/space, for their simultaneity is the whole point here, are not transcendental. Or at least they are not so at the level of knowledge defined by our lived experience of them.

What we need, then, is a category that can comprehend the necessity of time/space as recurring elements in all perception, but which will also take into account the non-recurring particularity of any specific act of perception. That category is the chronotope. And because it is sensitive to both repeatable and unrepeatable aspects of the means by which human behavior is mediated, the chronotope is the basic unit of study in Bakhtin's conception of historical poetics.

6

Authoring as dialogue: The architectonics of answerability

A major concern in Bakhtin's early work is architectonics. It is a topic to which he returned in his last essays. In Bakhtin's work architectonics constantly takes on new meaning in the different contexts in which it is invoked. In general, architectonics concerns questions about building, questions about how something is put together. Architectonics provides the ground for Bakhtin's discussion of two related problems. The first problem is how relations between living subjects organize themselves into the master categories of "I" and "another." The second problem is how authors forge a tentative wholeness out of the relation they articulate with their heroes – the kind of wholeness we call a text. More particularly, architectonics helps provide a conceptual armature for Bakhtin's more partial readings of specific works and authors, in all of which, in one way or another, the relation of parts to wholes figures prominently. In his disputations with other schools (such as Formalism and, in his last years, Structuralism), Bakhtin's argument usually includes the charge that his opponents have not completely theorized their position. He criticizes their lack of philosophical thoroughness largely because they fail to provide a conceptual framework for their pronouncements of the kind he himself provided in his early works.

The importance of architectonics

Aesthetics, a major topic of Bakhtin's early essays, is treated as a subset of architectonics: architectonics is the general study of how entities relate to each other, whereas aesthetics concerns itself with the particular problem of *consummation*, or how specific parts are shaped into particular wholes. In dialogism wholeness, or consummation, is always to be understood as a relative term: in Bakhtin, consummation is almost literally in the eye of the beholder in so far as it is always a function of a particular point of view. When invoking the term "consummation," one should always keep in mind questions about *position*: "consummated by whom for whom?" "consummated where?" and "consummated when?" Consummated wholes may be various kinds. But it should be kept in mind that for Bakhtin – the thinker who sought to make loopholes into (almost) metaphysical categories – their wholeness can never be absolute.

Dialogism's distinctiveness, however, is not to be found in any one of its individual components, but in the particular combination Bakhtin makes of them all. Architectonics of one kind or another, for instance, is a necessary item on the agenda of most thinkers who define themselves in a Kantian context. Bakhtin's distinctiveness lies in the particular areas in which he combined architectonics with other of his characteristic subjects: as the relation of parts to the whole containing them in individual texts (as in his early reading of Pushkin's lyric "Parting" ("Разлука")); as the relation of disparate individual texts to a whole that constitutes their genre (as in his various attempts to define the novel); as the relation of different genres to a whole called "literature" (as in his exercises in historical poetics, such as the Rabelais study); and as the relation of different discourses to a whole called language (in such metalinguistic works as *Marxism and the Philosophy of Language* and the monograph on speech genres).

The main components of dialogism, such as self/other, author/hero, transgredience, the utterance, and several others including dialogue itself, can all be seen, then, as tools for what is essentially an architectonic enterprise. The need is always to specify relations between individual persons and particular entities as they constitute a simultaneity. Because relations can be established only in terms of temporal and spatial parameters, the

chronotope will be of the greatest importance in Bakhtin's
architectonics. Space and time are, for Bakhtin as for Kant, "the
indispensable forms of cognition." In dialogism, however, they
are not (as in *The Critique of Pure Reason*) transcendental
categories, but "forms of the most immediate reality" ("Forms of
time and of the chronotope in the novel," fn., p. 85).[1]

This formulation contains the major paradox of any poetics
that claims to be historical: how can the givenness of "the most
immediate reality" be coupled with the madeness of "forms"?
The linkage at first appears to be a contradiction: how can reality
appear to be immediate if it comes to us in *forms*? Is not form
always a representation, the shape and structure of something as
distinguished from its substance?

Part of the difficulty here is in the translation "forms of the most
immediate reality." What Bakhtin says in Russian is "формы
самой реальной действительности," which might also be
rendered "forms of the most practical (or down-to-earth, or
everyday, common or garden) reality." The meaning of the
phrase when rendered in these terms is quite clear: we experience
the world in all its most common and frequent occasions as *forms*.
Bakhtin is saying that Kant was right to emphasize the central
role of time/space categories in perception, but he was wrong to
locate perception in some transcendent, *general* consciousness.
Time and space do indeed work as Kant said they did, as the
shaping tools by which the potentially infinite variety of the
world is molded into specific forms. But the site at which such
molding occurs is not transcendent. On the contrary, in
dialogism it is most emphatically a site that is *situated*. The
importance of what Bakhtin calls "architectonics," or the forms
that situatedness assumes, will emerge in discussing the need
always to locate any specific chronotope in a particular place
within the spectrum of all its possible uses.

Chronotope and architectonics

Like the utterance, chronotope is not a term that can be invoked
"in general." It must be a chronotope *of* someone *for* someone
about someone. It is ineluctably tied to *someone who is in a situation*.
Our English word "situation" is really already a chronotope that
has had its temporal and spatial components separated into two

distinct usages: on the one hand it means a place or location, as in the expression, "the house was in a good situation." On the other hand, it refers to a particular time, a combination of circumstances at a given moment, as in the expression "the current situation." But notice that situation, even in its spatially delimited usage, is not merely *in* a location of its own, in so far as its site, in order to be located at all, must be situated with reference to *other* factors. For instance, we say a house is "in a good situation" because it commands a good view or is not exposed to the weather. Situation is a site that is defined by its relation to elements *other* than itself in space. Situation as time is also implicated in elements other than itself: "the current situation" has to be understood as a combination of factors that mark a moment not in itself, but as a discrete point in the development of several interrelated factors. Chronotope, like situation, always combines spatial and temporal factors with an evaluation of their significance as judged from a particular point of view.

What marks the necessary presence of a human subject in both is the assumption that time and space are never merely temporal or spatial, but *axiological* as well (i.e. they also have *values* attached to them). As experienced by subjects, time and space are always tied up with judgments about whether a particular time or a particular place is good or bad, in all the infinite shadings those terms can comprehend. Perception is never pure; it is always accomplished in terms of evaluating what is perceived. Dialogism conceives being (*sobytie*, событие) as an event (*sobytie bytiya*, событие бытия) and human being as a project (*zadanie*, задание) or a deed (*akt-postupok*, акт-поступок), the deed of having constantly to make judgments.

It is difficult to untangle all the implications of such an a priori (especially in such early fragments as "Toward a philosophy of the deed"). But one thing is clear: so long as a human being *is*, he or she has no choice but to *act*. As a human being, I have "no alibi" in existence for merely occupying a location in it. On the contrary, I am in a situation, the unique place in the ongoing event of existence that is mine. And since existence is an event, my place in it is best understood not only as a space, but also as a time, as an activity, an act, a deed. Bakhtin was a great reader of Bergson, who shared the assumption (particularly in *Matter and*

Memory, 1896) that in so far as human beings are organisms, they cannot help but *pay attention to life*. Life will not let me be inactive, no matter how dormant I may appear (relatively) to be in the eyes of others. I cannot be passive, even if I choose to be, for passivity will then be the activity of choosing to be passive. My relation to life in all its aspects is one of intense participation, of interested activity; having "no alibi" means I have a stake in everything that comes my way. This in turn means that generalizing categories like "culture" must be understood as a shorthand means of referring to a set of highly specific activities, a collective of actors, each of whom has a unique place in it. Dialogism is a philosophy of the trees as opposed to a philosophy of the forest: it conceives society as a simultaneity of uniqueness.

In his focus on the unique placement of each individual human being, with a consequent emphasis on the need of each to act, Bakhtin manifests clear connections with West European *Lebensphilosophie* of the early twentieth century (as we noted, especially with Bergson). It is perhaps less obvious that he also shares many of the same concerns that dominated two trends in Soviet science of the time. The first of these was the extraordinary importance Russian psychologists (such as Bernstein and Anokhin) assigned to the problem of *attention* in human behavior, the physiological and mental operations involved in concentrating on one set of concerns to the exclusion of others. The second of these was work done by the Leningrad school of physiologists on control mechanisms in the human body: they sought to understand how relations among the body's various different systems (vascular, breathing, sensory, and so on) were ordered. This last connection is important for any attempt to understand Bakhtin's use of the chronotope, since the leader of the Leningrad school was none other than the same Ukhtomsky in whose 1925 lectures Bakhtin first heard the term "chronotope."

Physiology and chronotope

This is not the place to go into Ukhtomsky's work in any detail, but certain aspects of it will help us grasp why Bakhtin found Ukhtomsky's use of chronotope so important. Ukhtomsky was a scientist with a broad philosophical background: before entering medical school he had attended an Orthodox seminary where he wrote his dissertation on differing theories of time, with pride of place assigned to Kant. It was not surprising, then, that in his work on the human nervous system he should have been attracted to the idea that time played a role in efforts made by the individual organism to arrange priorities among the various stimuli competing for its attention. His concern for how time/space categories served to govern relations among sensory and motor nerves was tied to another of his research interests: the quest for a cortical "system of systems," or the "dominant," as he called it: the faculty that was able to select from the many responses a human body *might* make in a particular situation the *one* response that would actually be chosen. The dominant, in other words, was posited as the form taken by the organism's most *responsible* response.

Now, responsibility, or *answerability* had been an obsessive concern of Bakhtin's even before he encountered Ukhtomsky in 1925. The Leningrad physiologist's work had the effect, however, of reinforcing dialogism's assumption that behavior is constituted by actions, and further that these can be known only by the *change* they enact in space and time. Human being is a deed in the sense that our lives are shaped by constant choices, each of which has consequences. Choice is an act in so far as it effects a change between what is and what was, and thus the act is simultaneous with the difference that defines it. From the situation of a subject whose existence is defined by deeds, time and space have the most immediate significance, in so far as they always give a final contour to his or her project. And thus time or space can never occur (or "be") alone, but always constitute an event in which time (or space) exists only when coupled with a value.

We will examine some of the effects produced by the addition of *value* to the co-ordinates of time and space in the chronotope, but a small caveat is first in order. The issue of value requires us to invoke two terms that Post-structuralism has rendered notoriously suspect: "human subject" and "intention." It is important to remember, then, that these terms as used in dialogism are neither monologic nor dialectic: "subject" does not imply a consciousness in itself, for it is always stratified by the other. Nor does "intention" signify a direct correlation between inner plan and outer act directed toward a specific telos: for all deeds are connected to the deeds of others, so their meanings can never be grasped in themselves or from the point of view of a supra-situational end. In dialogism, "subject" and "intention," as we saw in chapter 1, are *positional* or interlocutive terms, which is precisely why chronotope is a necessary component in Bakhtin's project.

Chronotope is a term, then, that brings together not just two concepts, but four: a time, plus its value; and a space, plus its value. Chronotope is not something that Bakhtin "discovered." Rather, chronotope describes something that has always been inherent in experience, even when that experience has sought to generalize itself in "scientific" descriptions of, or "metaphysical" meditations on, the phenomena of time and space. It is a useful term not only because it brings together time, space, and value, but because it insists on their simultaneity and inseparability.

Time as value

It will perhaps help us to appreciate the ineluctability of their appearance together if we remember how powerful their simultaneity has been even in the history of physics, an area often thought to be value-free and in which the most rigorous attempts have been made to define the relation between time and space. At the beginning of western science, as the marine biologist Michael Ghiselin has recently pointed out,[2] Aristotle's descriptions of nature often appear bizarre because they were arranged according to a scheme that is less descriptive than it is *ethical*. Aristotle maintained, for instance, that round eggs produced males, and elongated eggs females, a conclusion that seems absurd until we remember that what he is saying about animals is less a zoology than it is an axiology, a local illustration in the animal kingdom of a global set of values: "round is male, because spheres are more perfect than other forms, and since males are superior to females, the two attributes go together."[3] In his many works on animals Aristotle "devotes much space to discussion on the relative positions of anatomical structures, saying that up is more noble than down, right more noble than left, and anterior more noble than posterior."[4] We might say that the master chronotope organizing Aristotle's work (in politics and metaphysics, as well as in his scientific treatises) is characterized by a pattern in which "right" and "high" are better and "left" and "down" are inferior in space, while "before" is always better than "after" in time.

From a twentieth-century perspective, Aristotle appears naive not because he combines time and space with value, but because he does so uncritically. Einstein's physics differs from Aristotle's not in claiming that time and space are free of value; the difference consists rather in Einstein's self-consciously reasoned argument for (precisely) the *ineluctability* of value. If Einstein's revolution means anything, it refers to the great physicist's overturning of the absolute time and absolute space of Newtonian cosmology: the recognition that there is no absolute, homogeneous time/space that includes everything. After Einstein, the choice of one point of view over another becomes necessary. In Newtonian physics, time and space articulated God's point of view, and you were correct if you perceived what that was and incorrect if you did not. There was no confusion because the standard was absolute. Any event could thus be located in time and space with a certainty that was absolute because it occurred in the same time and the same space as everything else; the criteria for fixing the site of an event were universal and unchanging. They were given by the nature of time and space as it existed *before* the perception of any particular event. There was no need to conceive a definition of when and where something happened, because the site was already given. An event filled a pre-existing niche, as it were, in homogeneous time and in a space that was all-encompassing.

By contrast, in relativity theory, one cannot avoid making a judgment (choosing, making a concept) as to what will serve as criteria in locating any specific event in time and space. And where there is a need for choosing, there is a need for value. Aristotle's assumption that "before" is better than "after," or "high" better than "low," is fallacious only in what might be called its Newtonian aspect: that is, its assumption that the value of time and space is always already determined in an absolute and unambiguous hierarchy. Relativity theory also assumes the simultaneity not only of time and space, but like Aristotelian physics, the simultaneity of these categories *plus value*: there is no more purity of time/space, that is time or space in themselves (without any attendant value) in Einstein's 1905 paper than there is in Aristotle's *Progression of Animals*. We have seen in previous chapters that relativity theory was extremely important for Bakhtin as he sought to think through the very difficult problem of simultaneity, the cornerstone of dialogism. Dialogism may indeed be defined as an epistemology based on the assumption that knowing an entity (a person or a thing) is to put that entity into a relation of simultaneity with something else, where simultaneity is understood as not being a relation of equality or identity.

The interrelation between dialogism and relativity theory is perhaps nowhere clearer, and certainly nowhere more explicit, than in the essay on the chronotope: Bakhtin begins his monograph by assuming that chronotope

> is employed in mathematics and was introduced as part of Einstein's Theory of Relativity. The special meaning it has in relativity theory is not important for our purposes; we are borrowing it for literary criticism almost as a metaphor (almost but not entirely – почти, но не совсем). What counts for us is the fact that it expresses the inseparability of space and time (time as the fourth dimension of space).
>
> ("The chronotope," p. 84)

Before turning to the question of why relativity works "almost, but not *entirely* as a metaphor," we might reasonably ask why relativity theory should suggest itself as a metaphor at all.

The answer, as we have tried to suggest, is this: because dialogue and relativity are both ways to think about relation, each in its own way is an *architectonics*. Stated most crudely, both are theories that seek to explain why it makes sense to recognize entities as distinct from each other, and yet as somehow bound together, in space and time. Dialogism and relativity focus on different entities, of course. Dialogism is an attempt to think through relations between human beings, and between human beings and the world, while relativity is a way to think about relations between physical objects. The relation of relativity theory to dialogism is metaphorical in so far as Bakhtin is seeking to use its *physical* categories as a means to model relations between conscious subjects.

We may note in passing a significant parallel with Marx in the particular way Bakhtin seeks to use relations between things as markers of relations between people. In Bakhtin's philosophical anthropology, to be human is to mean. Human being is the *production* of meaning, where meaning is further understood to come about as the articulation of values. In *Capital*, Marx's dismissal of vulgar economists is based on his argument that they have not perceived the deep structure of social relations among people engaged in production. For Marx, value always shows "a relation between persons expressed as a relation between things."[5] It is at the level of social relations that the true meaning of value and exchange must be sought; this is the level that underlies the surface phenomena of commodities and prices which only *formally* manifest relations between people.

In dialogism, things on the one hand, and persons on the other, will necessitate different conceptions of relation, and we will examine those differences in a moment. However, relations among persons, and relations among physical objects also have a certain number of features in common; these are less obvious than the differences, so we shall consider them first.

The value of relativity theory

While relativity theory concerns itself with things not people, it posits the need for an observer, since an event's occurrence can only be fixed in coordinates established from a particular point of view (what we have called "the law of placement"). Thus relativity is deeply immersed in many of the same questions that (since at least Hume) have preoccupied anyone who sets out to define the identity of subjects.

Hume argued that the idea of identity has its source "in the notion of time, or duration. The notion of identity arises from the propensity of the human mind to attribute invariableness or uninterruptedness to an object while tracing it without a break in the span of attention, through a variation in time."[6] Identity for Hume meant an object was "same with itself," and on that understanding he conceived identity to be a *fiction* (for many of the same reasons Bakhtin argued that the finished-off, static quality which self always assigns to the other is merely a construct). Hume's deduction has played a role in most attempts to define identity since at least the seventeenth century. It is present in the attempts of both dialogism and relativity theory to

understand why the quality of being "same" or "itself" is such a
necessary fiction, that is to understand how identity could be a
fiction, and at the same time be so universally present in the
assumptions most people make about their own status as
individuals, in human social experience, language, and even (for
pre-Einsteinian millennia) scientific speculation.

Einstein's great 1905 paper establishing the special theory of
relativity is centrally concerned with "the Electrodynamics of
Moving Bodies." But it has a kind of philosophical preamble, an
initial section (preceding the mathematical formulae making up
the core of the text) that is devoted to a patently metaphysical
treatment of the problem of simultaneity within a single inertial
system. Einstein's way of thinking the paradox of absolute *identity*
was to repudiate Newton's claims about absolute *simultaneity* (the
identity of two objects' or events' attributes as the same in every
reference system in which the object or event is specified).
Einstein begins his revolution by positing the priority not of
things, but of relations among things: above all, the master
relation of time and space among physical things which insures
they will not merely be static, isolated *objects*, but active,
simultaneous *events*.

In order for any statement about sameness to make sense,
there must be a concept of difference which can serve as a
standard: "now" requires a "then," "earlier" needs a "later."
For this reason relativity theory and dialogism begin by
assuming that time is knowable only in terms of action, that is of
changes in the material world: temporal relations are first
constituted by physical relations that obtain not among static
things but among *events*. The concept of "absolute time" implies
among other things, that the temporal relation between any two
events is always *un*ambiguous. But the priority (the value) of
one or another temporal/spatial category in dialogism, as in
relativity, does *not* give itself unambiguously. There are no
Newtonian absolutes, there is no priority as such. In this sense,
time/space coordinates, too, have "no alibi," and the priority of
any given (*dan,* дан) set of co-ordinates over others must always
be achieved (*zadan,* задан). And this achievement, this deed, is
accomplished through the active relation of a particular set of
coordinates to a particular observer's architectonic responses, to
his/her assignment, of precisely, *relation*.

Einstein's innovation begins in the suspicion that meaningful statements about time/space relations could only be made within the context of specific reference systems. If time and space were in fact always *unambiguous*, we could assume a purely physical basis for absolute simultaneity; in that case, two clocks synchronized at one place, and then separated, would, when brought together again in another place, still be synchronous no matter how different in length the routes by which they arrived at the second point might be. But in one of his most provocative thought experiments, Einstein deduced that this could not be the case.

Let us say that two clocks are synchronized at point A, but that one of the clocks gets to point B by a route longer than that taken by the other travelling at the same speed. Now, even if (as should be possible in Newtonian physics) both clocks were to coincide in their arrival, then it is obvious they will no longer be synchronized even when they once again occupy contiguous space. Or if both clocks took the same route but at different speeds, they would also show different readings at point B. Thus merely looking at two clocks in the same room, each of which appears to be telling the same time, is never sufficient to know that they are in fact simultaneous with each other: both may indicate one o'clock, but one of the clocks might just have been unpacked from the luggage of someone who has arrived from a distant country and be indicating 1 a.m., while the other registers 1 p.m. It is necessary to *choose* one of the two clocks showing different times as the standard for positing simultaneity (or non-simultaneity) between them. It follows that in a world where time/space relations are ambiguous, the perceiving subject must make choices, and thus values come into play.

Travelling clocks provided a means for Einstein to think relations between things. But almost everything he has to say about such a relationship bears as well on the way dialogism conceives relations between conscious subjects (as well as between subjects and things, of course): the dialogic subject is a *travelling clock that thinks*. And the reference system for synchronizing such clock-subjects, as it were, will always be the relation of "I" to "another." It is as if Einstein's clocks were themselves constantly having to calibrate their *own* time/space relations with *other* clocks. In a world without absolute space or time, the dialogic subject is forced to make choices. He or she has a "non-alibi in the event of existence," and thus cannot point to a pre-existing, absolute as a source for value. The dialogic subject manifests its unique place in existence as an event, the deed of choosing, of constantly making judgments about value that are sculpted in the material of time and space in relation to the time/space of other "travelling clocks."

Bakhtin contrasts the ability of post-Einsteinian scientific thought to "orient itself among the complex circumstances of 'the probability of the universe'" with the demand for "primitive definiteness" that still governs much of what happens in the world of art (*Problems of Dostoevsky's Poetics*, p. 272).[7] There are of course exceptions, most notably Dostoevsky, whose novels are organized precisely around the great clashes and fusions that result from his characters' attempts to orient their chronotopes with each other. Thus Bakhtin's lifelong meditation on Dostoevsky will aid us in understanding the deeper meaning of chronotope, in particular as it relates to the project of a historical poetics.

A "Newtonian," or monologic author, even one as great as Goethe, "strives to perceive all existing contradictions as various stages of some unified development" (ibid.). Dostoevsky, by contrast, attempts

> to perceive the very stages themselves in their *simultaneity*, to *juxtapose*, and *counterpose* them . . . and not stretch them out into an evolving sequence . . . to get one's bearings in the world [is] to conceive all its contents as simultaneous, and *to guess at their interrelationships in the cross-section of a single moment*" (ibid., p. 28). The simultaneity of chronotopes in such a novel "is considerably more complex and profound than that of the Newtonian world, it is a unity of a higher order (a qualitatively different unity)."   (ibid., p. 298)

The fundamental difference between Goethe and Dostoevsky (the difference between two represented worlds) could be brought out only in a study that was both *historical* and devoted to *poetics*. Bakhtin opens his revised version of the Dostoevsky volume by stressing that, "The present book is devoted to problems of Dostoevsky's *poetics*, and surveys his work from that viewpoint *only*" (ibid., p. 3). Because monologic and dialogic texts are so different from each other, they require a different kind of study. A dialogic poetics must first of all be able to identify and arrange relations between points of view: it must be adequate to the complex architectonics that shape the viewpoint of the author toward his characters, the characters toward the author, and of all these toward each other.

Before going any further, let us clear up a misunderstanding that can be a major stumbling block in any attempt to grasp the nature of such an architectonics. Point of view is often taken to be a merely "characterological" or "psychological" category. In other words, point of view is frequently taken to be a "viewpoint" whose fixity serves to define a character associated with it. As such, it is a static category, and therefore one that dialogism will avoid (dialogism abhors stasis). Bakhtin is thus careful to observe "the fundamental distinction between character and person" (ibid., p. 297).

As Bakhtin makes very clear in the notebook he kept for himself in the early 1960s as he was preparing his 1929 Dostoevsky book for republication, the difference between "character" and "person" is a specification of the even more fundamental distinction between "I" and "another." Character is a monologic, finished-off, generalized category that is given and determined – all aspects of "anotherness." Person, on the other hand, is a dialogic, still-unfolding, unique event that has the "made-ness" and unpredictability rooted in conditions relating to "self." Thus the viewpoint of a literary protagonist treated as a person (as in Dostoevsky) would seem to fall outside the limits of what is usually considered literary analysis, even before the question of representing such a viewpoint in language is raised (a point to which we shall return in a moment). Moreover, due to Bakhtin's emphasis on the indeterminacy and the uniqueness of such a viewpoint, it most of all would seem to be an improper subject for any study claiming to be a poetics.

A different point of view on point of view

But in a world in which a thing can be seen only from a particular point of view, so must the very concept of point of view itself. That is to say, all points of view are relative to other points of view. Thus, in attempting to employ point of view as a constitutive category in historical poetics, it will help to discriminate between point of view as an object for analysis in one text, or in many, that is in a genre. The problem is clearer in its outlines when treated at the level of genre, so we shall deal with it first, before turning to other aspects of the problem of establishing a point of view.

Bakhtin treats genres as a sub-topic of the larger problem of point of view; a genre is a particular way of looking at the world. For instance, the emergence of the novel is for him an event in not only the history of literature, but the history of *perception*: for those who have experienced novelness, the world will not look the same. But how can we talk about many different texts as having a single point of view? By conceiving, as Bakhtin does, the history of a genre as the history of a species, much as evolutionary theory has come to perceive the life and death of a species as the history of forms adapting to – or failing to adapt to – changing environments.

What permits – indeed, requires – viewpoint to be known through formal analysis is the fact that values can only be articulated by formal (non-subjective) means. A point of view is never complete in itself; it is rather the perception of an event as it is perceived from a particular place, locatable only as opposed to any other place from which the event might be viewed. Values are sculpted out of time and space. It is always necessary that some means be available for marking the difference between this view as opposed to that view of an event. The means by which such distinctions are marked may vary depending on circumstances, but they will in all cases be systematic, extra-individual, and repeatable – in a word, formal. In grammar, the distinction between points of view is formalized through pronouns: all utterances require that they be identified as belonging to "me," "you," "we," "they," or even (as in the case, let us say, of the law) as belonging to "it." In the syntax of spoken speech, or the punctuation of written utterances, there will be, depending on the particular language in question, highly complex rules for setting off my "own" words from the words I quote from others. In a work of fiction, all these devices (and, of course, many others) are at work to distinguish the speech and actions of the various protagonists (including those of the "author') from each other.

Nevertheless, the protagonist who is marked off by these means can still lack the radical specificity, the uniqueness, required to be the kind of complex subject Bakhtin calls a person. Generally available devices for marking the boundaries of meaning, such as grammatical "laws" or the "rules" of punctuation, are not in themselves adequate to render the distinctiveness of a subject who can attain to a point of view.

We here approach the limits of the two kinds of trope used to indicate relative differences in perspective: the metaphor of vision and the metaphor of the voice. We have so far talked about the semantic energies of a text as they might be apportioned between different pairs of eyes, each of which sees things from a different vantage; and of course, "voice," as in expressions such as "to speak in one's own voice," has long been a means for representing the *distinctiveness* of what otherwise is called a "point-of-view." Terms such as "surplus of seeing," "polyphony," and "dialogism" make it clear that metaphors of vision and voice are inescapable elements in any consideration of Bakhtin's thought. What these metaphors seek to render is what we called in the first chapter of this book "the law of placement,"[8] the law that says perception can only be achieved from a unique point in the spectrum of possible perspectives. Returning to a visual metaphor, it could be said that what we see is governed by how we see, and how we see has already been determined by where we see *from*. In other words, Bakhtin's key tropes of sight and voice are attempting to figure something that in its most fundamental expression is neither visual nor vocal. Rather, it is a condition more accurately expressed in terms of time and space, which is why the name "Einstein" can also be invoked as a metaphor ("almost, but not quite") for what is essentially the same condition – and perhaps with less conceptual static than is generated by the ancient and highly implicated tropes of sight and voice. For it is physics, and more recently the burgeoning new science of chronobiology,[9] rather than literary theory, that has most characteristically concerned itself with the question of how to locate a thing.

True to his essentially Kantian (and anti-Hegelian) roots, Bakhtin sought to square his epistemology with the findings of science as well as with the speculations of metaphysics and the deductions of logic. In particular, he sought to apply to the conscious human subject the same set of conditions that would apply in attempts to locate any other entity. Two physical laws in particular – one from classical physics and another from Einsteinian physics – bear directly on dialogism's obsession with placement. The first is that two bodies cannot occupy the same space at the same time; the second is that the time/space of any specific body can only be known relative to a particular reference system appropriate to it. The human subject, before it is anything else, is a body. The implication of the first law is that each subject is a body occupying a unique site in time and space. The funereal formula, "ashes to ashes," is one of the ways we recognize that the decomposition of our physical bodies after death marks the evacuation of the unique time/space we materially occupied in life.

Every human being has, as a body, a very clearly marked beginning and end. But the human subject is not merely a body, of course – it is a conscious body. And here arises a paradox: others may see us born, and they may see us die; however, in my own consciousness "I" did not know the moment of my birth; and in my own consciousness, "I" shall not know my death. Consciousness "for its own self, in terms of its own consciousness . . . can have neither a beginning nor an end." (*Problems of Dostoevsky's Poetics*, p. 291). In thinking through this distinction (the difference between the mode of knowledge others have of my beginning and end, and the way I myself am forced to imagine such limits), the second physical law we mentioned above comes into effect: the necessity that says a particular body can be located only by invoking a reference system appropriate to its particular situation.

Bakhtin is arguing that because consciousness cannot have a (consciously perceived) beginning or end, it is experienced as "infinite, revealing itself only from within, that is, only for consciousness itself. Beginnings and ends lie in the objective (and object-like) world for others, but not for the conscious person himself." (ibid., p. 290). From an external, "objective" perspective, the human subject is unique, but that unique place is always *one among others*. For like all others, its uniqueness can only be located (consummated, finished off) by reference to its finite beginning and end; whereas, from the perspective of the subject as an I-for-itself, consciousness produces the effect of a uniqueness that is utter, one that cannot be immediately calibrated by the standards of material beginnings or ends which serve to locate the place of others. The reality of another's time/ space is different from my own: I can imagine my birth and my death, taking the beginning and end of others as my model for doing so (exercising my "excess of seeing" *vis-à-vis* them, the faculty that lets me view their termini in a manner denied to them, as objective perception of my own are denied to me). But my own beginning and end exist only as potentials in my consciousness, while the birth and death of others appear to me to be irreversibly real.

There is a certain paradox here, so we shall have to proceed very cautiously and make some fine discriminations. The life and death of others seem more objectively real to me than do the termini of my own life as I am aware of them from within the consciousness that is uniquely mine; yet every other aspect of existence seems more real as I perceive it in the relative immediacy of my I-for-itself:

> Mathematical time and space guarantee a possible intellectual unity of possible judgments . . . but my actual involvement with them from my unique place gives flesh and blood, as it were, to their inescapably-necessary reality and the uniqueness of the value assigned to them; from within my involvement and with relation to it, all mathematically possible time and space (a possibly infinite past and future) fleshes itself out in concrete valorizations; it is as if rays emanated from the placement of my own uniqueness, which, passing through time, proclaim the humanity of history [?], penetrate all possible times, temporarily as such itself, with the light of value, for I am actually involved with it.
>
> ("К философии поступка" ["Toward a philosophy of the deed"], p. 126)[10]

Yet as Bakhtin said in 1961, the

> internal uniqueness of consciousness does not contradict materialism. Consciousness comes second, it is born at a specific stage of the development of the material organism [primarily when we as infants begin to acquire language], it is born objectively and it dies (also objectively) together with the material organism (sometimes before it [as in the phenomenon we call "brain death"]).
>
> (*Problems of Dostoevsky's Poetics*, p. 290)

At different levels, then, both the body and consciousness participate in time/space relations, although the perception of the reality those relations articulate is different in each.

The role of language in value formation

Bakhtin's assumption is that the body becomes a consciousness when its aboriginal signals are enriched by the signs we acquire in language: "consciousness could have developed only by having at its disposal material that was pliable and expressible by bodily means." (*Marxism and the Philosophy of Language*, p. 14)[11]. Bakhtin, of course, is not alone in positing a subject produced by language. However, his insistence on the *responsibility* entailed by subjectivity of this kind sets him apart from most other twentieth-century figures who, like Lacan, have also assumed a language-centered (and thus language-*de*centered) ego. When we are invaded by language (or, as we might more hopefully say, when we enter language – both descriptions being accurate under different conditions) it is not *Language* as such that invades us, or which we enter. Rather, each of us makes an entrance into a matrix of highly distinctive economic, political, and historical forces – a unique and unrepeatable combination of ideologies, each speaking its own language, the heteroglot conglomerate of which will constitute the world in which we act. It is only in that highly specific, indeed unique placement that the world may address us: in a very real sense it is our "address" in existence, an address expressed not in numbers, but by our proper name. It is only from that site that we can speak. Bakhtin concludes from this that we cannot be excused from being in the place that heteroglossia assigns us, and which only we will ever occupy. The subjectivity whose placement is determined by the structure of addressivity requires us then to be answerable for that site, if only in the sense that the subject occupying that particular place (who *is* that place) will be the source of whatever response is called forth from it by the physical forces of nature and the discursive energy of society. What the self is answerable *to* is the environment; what it is responsible *for* is authorship of its responses: "it is not the content of a commitment that obliges me, but my signature beneath it." (Toward a philosophy of the deed").

It is largely the way I use language that lets me sign my name, in this responsible sense. We have seen how I, as a subject, differ from others in the way time and space work in my perception, as opposed to the way they operate to shape others as I see them. The subject operates as if its environment were open, unfinished (*nezavershen*, незавершен), existing in an "absolute future" so long as it is conscious, whereas the other is perceived by me as if consummated, completed (*zavershen*, завершен) in so far as he or she can already be known as he or she already is. Consciousness is organized by language, and the assumption is that this fundamental coupling of open/closed in perception is a function of the duality of the sign itself: as Karcevskij pointed out long ago,

> In a "complete" sign (a word as opposed to a morpheme) there are two centers of semiotic functions, one for formal values, the other for semantic values. The formal values of a word (gender, number, case, aspect, tense) represent aspects of signification known to every speaking subject which are more or less safe from any subjective interpretation on the part of interlocutors; they are assumed to remain identical to themselves in all situations. The semantic part of a word, in contrast, is a residue resistant to any attempt to decompose it into elements as "objective' as formal values.[12]

Karcevskij is arguing that the apparently unitary sign is in fact "both static [formal] and dynamic [semantic] at the same time."[13] This dual aspect of the sign, the necessary simultaneity of its formal closedness its semantic openness, is reflected in inner, as well as outer speech. Bakhtin (and Karcevskij) are not alone in recognizing the effects on perception of the geological fault line dividing the formal from semantic properties of the linguistic sign. While much of Structuralist theory has been toppled by the various schools nominated as Post-structuralist, this fundamentally Structuralist principle continues to be affirmed. Lacan, for instance, in speaking of the subject's relation to the simultaneous stasis and dynamism of the sign says:

> The signifier, producing itself in the field of the Other, makes manifest the subject of its signification. But it functions as a signifier only to . . . petrify the subject in the same moment in which it calls the subject to function, so to speak, as subject.[14]

The master distinction of self/other is the mechanism which language drives through ceaseless slippage from static to dynamic, formal to semantic, to produce the subject. And just as the self's time, the activity of the dynamic aspect of language, is never exhausted by the present "now," the space of the self's placement, in his or her own subjectivity like that of the constantly sliding aspect of the sign, is never completely "here." It must be transgredient and not completely coincidental with *this* environment if it is to have the wider perspective needed to do its work in the ceaseless dialogue with the static and formal elements of language, a condition modeled in the subject's drive to constitute a finished whole out of the other and his or her placement. Others are seen by me as completely here in so far as I equate their subjectivity, body, and environment as a unified totality – in so far as I architectonically complete them.

The site to which language assigns us as subjects is unique, but never ours alone. The subject determined by language is never singular: like language itself, it is divided between dynamic and static aspects of its activity. Language has a canonical *langue* aspect that is the more comprehensive expression of the individual sign's formal properties. Simultaneously, it has a freer, performative or *parole* aspect, that globally manifests the individual sign's semantic tendencies. In much the same way, the individual subject is organized by both an abstract, normative category – the other – and a specific, more open category – the self.

It has always been recognized that language can work only if it exists between subjects, only if it belongs to more than one speaker. But this has usually reflected itself in little more than a mere subject/object distinction, as reflected in the gross features of most grammars which deploy nominative, accusative, and dative cases as if one speaker were an active sender and the other no more than a passive receiver. Bakhtin goes further: he insists that language can work only if it belongs to more than one aspect of self *within* the subject. By making language the framing condition for Kant's a prioris of perception, Bakhtin was impelled to double the forms of intuition: there is one time/space organizing perception of the subject by the subject; and there is another time/space that shapes the subject's perception of others. Bakhtin calls this model of intuition an "architectonics of responsibility," because it is the algorithm that structures responses made from the site where subjectivity is addressed.

There is always something of a contradiction in any attempt of the kind we have been making to generalize about specificity. It will once again help things along, perhaps, if we spend some time with a single text that illustrates at least some of the principles we have been discussing in this chapter. *The Great Gatsby* has been chosen for this purpose because it is a work particularly concerned to lay bare its own architectonics by dramatizing the complexities of point of view.

The Great Gatsby

Before examining the relation between the novel's formal aspects and some of their functions, it will be useful to keep in mind its narrative features. *The Great Gatsby* offers itself as a memoir, written down in 1924 in the American Midwest by Nick Carraway, as he seeks to make sense of events that unfolded two years earlier. At that time, Nick's neighbor on Long Island, Jay Gatsby, was murdered by a crazed mechanic who held him responsible for the death of his wife in a hit-and-run accident. Although Gatsby was in the car, it had actually been driven by the great love of his life, Daisy. After Gatsby's death, Daisy returns to her husband, and Nick to his birthplace in the Midwest, where, after an interval, he writes "a history of that summer." While the main body of the narrative is compressed in time to a few months in 1922, and in space to a small area of the east coast, this time/space is complicated both by its own pastness and thereness relative to the moment of its being put into writing by Nick, and by the pastness and thereness of the major characters prior to the events of 1922. In each case the relation of here and now to then and there is enacted as an incongruity, a discordance modeled in the constant inadequacy and break-down of stereotypes that result from contradictions of perspective in the major characters' points of view.

There are so very many of these, and they are of such a variety, that it may be said that the text is governed by the trope of oxymoron. It is first of all the most characteristic feature of Nick's narrative voice; the novel contains page after page of locutions such as "that most limited of all specialists, the well-rounded man," "the rock of the world was founded securely on a fairy's wing"; the First World War is a "delayed Teutonic migration"; ceilings have "Presbyterian nymphs" on them, and characters eat their food with "ferocious delicacy." But the oxymoronic nature of the narrator's epigrams and descriptions is not merely a feature of style. A dramatized incongruity characterizes virtually every aspect of the text. The title of *The Great Gatsby* is itself an oxymoron, an eponymous gap between its honorific adjective and the proper name of the sentimental gangster. Incongruity is at work in the novel's most obvious and superficial thematic level, the gap between Gatsby's image – his stereotype – of Daisy, and Daisy as she is outside Gatsby's "riotous dream" of her as quest object.

Incompatibility legislates the novel's basic narrative pattern, which is articulated as a rupture between events as they unfolded in 1922, and Nick's act of chronicling the "same" events two years later. This break between event and representation disfigures all attempts in the novel to make past and present cohere, as in the gap between the moment in 1917 in Louisville when Gatsby and Daisy first meet, and the struggle each undertakes to continue that moment when they encounter each other on Long Island five years later. A grotesque incommensurability dominates all the incidental features of the narrative: for example a vagrant whose name is Rockefeller sells stray dogs on the streets of Manhattan. This incommensurability is particularly bizarre in its mapping of America: when asked what part of the Midwest he is from, a character replies, "San Francisco." Another character has been assigned the task of finding "a small town," and when queried on his choice, answers "Detroit."

The narrative voice keeps insisting on its "honesty": "Every one suspects himself of at least one of the cardinal virtues, and this is mine: I am one of the few honest people that I have ever known." But the particular form this "cardinal virtue" assumes is a "Midwestern" plainness (for all Nick's habit of turning fancy metaphors), as opposed to "eastern" corruption and excess. This is just one of the ways chronotopic complexities of geography and social force are reduced by the narrator to stereotype, raising questions that put his claims to accuracy in doubt. On the one hand, Nick is a tireless chronicler of the different identities rumor assigns Gatsby (that he is related to Hindenburg, that he is a

German spy, that his house is really a boat that detaches itself from the shoreline to cruise as a rum runner, that he is related to Kaiser Wilhelm II, that he has killed a man – all associations that stress his exotic otherness). In addition, he is aware of the difference between Gatsby's account of himself (Oxford graduate, scion of inherited wealth, etc.), and Gatsby's activity as a bootlegger and dealer in stolen securities. But Nick's whole activity as narrator is directed toward consummating a unified image of Gatsby.

Not knowing his birth, his "I" creates an origin for itself. It is not by chance that the image he constructs is one almost precisely the opposite of that he manufactures for his own persona: Nick comes from a large, old, closely knit family, whereas Gatsby has no family in the most radical sense that he gives birth to himself (when he transforms himself from James Gatz to Jay Gatsby); Nick values solidity and the value of being a *careful* driver (which is a recurring figure in the text), while Gatsby is absolutely reckless, and is as much killed by the careless driving of his great love as the victim she actually runs over. Nick works at the Probity Trust where he deals in "securities," whereas Gatsby specializes in stealing bonds.

The meaning of oxymoron

The oppositions are too obvious to dwell on. More often than not in the critical literature they have been treated at a char-acterological or psychologistic level, as strategies that obscure the implications of such programmatically precise binarization for the process of subject formation – subject formation not just for this or that individual actor in the novel, but at the non-trivial level where it is a problem in representation of the specific kind that language will permit. At that level, the differences begin to appear less capable of articulating a uniqueness for any of the individual characters, least of all those that are deployed by Nick to set himself off from Gatsby. The same extrapersonal force speaks through them in their representation of each other and in their representation of their selves to themselves. That force is the necessity that requires perception to be accomplished through the simultaneous interaction of stasis and flux, the *ukaz* that language imposes on producing subjects. From the point of view of our topic (point of view), the most important consequence is that not only do Nick and Gatsby perceive each other as stereotypes, but each is guilty of perceiving aspects of himself as stereotypical as well.

That is to say, each operates from a site in addressivity that is assumed to be not only unique, but identical with itself. As such, it can globalize the meaning of the other. Invoking parallels with Neo-platonism, we may say that the subject's assumption of his fixed identity is similar to the claim God makes when He intones "I am that I am." And like a god-figure, the subject assumes he can, with respect to the other, see all and know all, completely exhausting the other's capacity to elude the subject's categories – if, as is the case in Fitzgerald's novel, the self of others is ignored. Thus Nick, who is the teller of this tale, makes explicit his desire to have a panoptic point of view: looking out of a tall New York building, he says,

> high over the city our line of yellow windows must have contributed their share of human secrecy to the casual watcher in the darkening streets, and I was with him too, looking up and wondering. I was within and without, simultaneously enchanted and repelled by the inexhaustible variety of life.[15]

But his vaunted honesty is based not on the enchantment of variety. Rather, on the contrary, it is based on a truth that is guaranteed by its stability, its unity. Thus, after his initial doubts about Gatsby's account of his past at Oxford, Nick is easily convinced when a photograph is produced showing a group of young men in blazers "loafing in an archway through which were visible a host of spires."

As if this were not enough to establish the degree to which his sense of truth is based on clichés (a form of stereotyping), Nick adds, "There was Gatsby, looking a little, not much, younger – with a cricket bat in his hand. Then it was all true."[16] I emphasize not only the photograph's ability to serve as a metaphor for Nick's willingness to regard fixity as a condition of truth, but the mindbending banality of the stereotypes (blazers, cricket bats, spires) he is prepared to accept.

Gatsby's self-stereotyping is caught in one of the least remarked formal features of the text, its punctuation. I have in mind the place in the text where the name Jay Gatsby is printed in quotation marks. On the night that Daisy runs over Myrtle Wilson, and after she has returned to her husband Tom, Gatsby tells Nick the story of his past, particularly about that point when he ceased being just James Gatz and told Dan Cody, the millionaire yachtsman who adopts him, that he is Jay Gatsby. Nick writes: "It was that night he told me the strange story of his youth with Dan Cody – told it to me because 'Jay Gatsby' had broken up like glass against Tom's hard malice, and the long secret extravaganza was played out."[17]

"Jay Gatsby" is James Gatz's attempt to fix a meaning for the subjectivity nominated by that name. The quotation marks frame the stereotype in which Gatz/Gatsby has sought to inscribe himself, and at the same time they ironize the fixity of such an identity. Before looking at the specific instance of these quotation marks, and the central Bakhtinian question they raise about who is talking and who is being quoted, we should remember the peculiar textualizing role that punctuation plays in general.

Punctuation is an appropriate vehicle for dramatizing stability, for it belongs to the formal, static pole of language activity. It is (in its dictionary definition) "the use of standard marks and signs in writing and printing in order to clarify meaning." Like that most rigid of all linguistic phenomena – grammar – punctuation is, then, a formal means that seeks to contain the volatility of semiotic operations. It is thus not merely an appropriate way to enact the fixity of identities, but an ironic one as well, for of course no matter how florid or complex, punctuation becomes, it is never completely able to harden a single meaning in the words it diacritically seeks to govern.

Of all punctuation marks, none is more radical than those that fix the borders between speakers, for in doing so they double the function of pronouns: they assign responsibility for words. Thus, when the site of Gatsby's place in the structure of addressivity is put into quotation marks, what is foregrounded is the degree to which he has shaped that site in his own image: he is, as it were, quoting himself, in so far as he is responsible for the identity that "Jay Gatsby" names, just as he is responsible for other words ascribed to him by quotation marks that establish that it is he who is speaking.

It is here that the crucial role of narrative in the process of subject formation makes itself felt: "Jay Gatsby," for all its author's attempts to make it so, is less a name than it is a story. In so far as it is a name for a story, "Jay Gatsby" is structurally similar to mythic names, in so far as Hercules cannot be thought of without his labors, or Odysseus without his voyages. "Jay Gatsby," as a name that is a story, dramatizes the central role of stereotyping in formation of the individual subject on the one hand, and on the other, the role of stereotyping as a dynamic in social and historical formation. Gatsby is the story of his career; in it we can see how history uses stereotypes, the formulaic categories of what might be called a poetics of the social, to form the subject as a link in the discursive chain.

In order to do this in more detail, it will be helpful to keep in mind the bases of the argument so far. These may be stated as a number of theses: the nature of the linguistic sign is synergistic, a constant struggle and co-operation between the necessity to be static and repeatable, and the opposed but no less imperative necessity of the same material to be open to constantly new and changing circumstances; the individual subject is constituted by his entrance into the world of signs, therefore the asymmetric dualism of the sign governs the perceptual activity of subjects in so far as they must process experience through the "open" category of the self, and the "closed" category of the other; this universal condition is reflected in our inability to eradicate stereotypes, since they are a function of the nature of the sign itself and precede any particular subject or experience; but this general condition is specified into particular stereotypes in different times and places. In other words, the universality of stereotypes is imposed by language; their specificity derives from history. It is this set of conditions that make a historical poetics a factor in the history of literature, and also the history of perception.

Since we are pointing to the narrative shape of Gatsby's career as evidence for this view, let us remember that career's gross outlines. A boy named Jimmy Gatz is born to a family of unsuccessful farmers in the Midwest, "but his imagination had never accepted them as his parents at all." He leaves home early to wander the shores of the Great Lakes, changing his name to Jay Gatsby when he encounters a wealthy miner whose

travelling companion he then becomes. The First World War
sees him in training outside Louisville, where he meets Daisy.
They fall in love, Daisy assuming Gatsby is as wealthy as she;
before the deception can be discovered, Gatsby is sent to France.
After some time, Daisy is persuaded to marry the Chicago
millionaire Tom Buchanan, and they move to his estate on Long
Island. Gatsby has in the meantime had a spectacular war, and
has been decorated by several governments. After the armistice,
he is permitted to enroll in a special program for American army
officers in Oxford, where he spends five months before returning
to the States. On his return, he becomes associated with the
underworld boss Meyer Wolfsheim. He makes immense amounts
of money selling bootleg liquor and stolen securities, and buys a
mansion across the bay from Daisy and Tom. All his labors have
been in the service of recapturing Daisy; they meet again, Daisy
is involved in a hit-and-run accident, and in a case of mistaken
revenge Gatsby is shot by the victim's husband.

Quest romance as quest for self

The poverty of this account obscures the overwhelming degree to
which *The Great Gatsby* is a quest romance. At the level of work, it
is the quest of Gatsby for his dream of Daisy, a dream that is
specified in terms that clearly show that it is also the distinctively
American dream of going from rags to riches, for beautiful as
Daisy may be, it is her voice that sings the siren song to Gatsby,
the voice that is not only full of promise, but "full of money," as
Gatsby himself once says (it is the *only* memorable thing he says).
Gatsby is first perceived as he stands on his shore, reaching out in
the night to a green light shining across the bay, the green light
that is at the end of the pier belonging to Tom Buchanan's estate.

The quest has more to do with Horatio Alger than it does with
Chrétien de Troyes. It is further elaborated with associations of
frontier: Gatsby's first patron, whose name evokes Buffalo Bill,
and he is "a product of the Nevada silver fields, of the Yukon, of
every rush for metal since seventy-five . . . [a] pioneer debauchee
who during one phase of American life brought back to the
Eastern seaboard the savage violence of the frontier brothel and
saloon." The association of violence with money that is so much a
part of the dream of rapidly acquired wealth is maintained by

Gatsby's second patron, Meyer Wolfsheim, who fixed the World Series of 1919, wears human teeth for cufflinks, is associated with several murders, and says of his relation to Gatsby that he not only started him off in business, but that he "made him." Gatsby is a composite figure, then, who incorporates a number of key American stereotypes that extend to his childhood bible: a cowboy novel about Hopalong Cassidy. Inside this book, the young Gatz writes rules that savor of Benjamin Franklin, a reminder that "the west" was once a frontier in "the east." The rules ("No wasting time . . . Bath every day, Study electricity [a reference to the untutored genius not only of Franklin and his kite, but Edison and his light bulb])" are those of *self*-improvement, and point to the degree to which Gatsby seeks to make his self.

Unlike Jimmy Gatz, the self that chance has assigned him and which is prey to every contingency, "Jay Gatsby" – the self he lusts to produce for himself – is one that will be improved in the sense that it will be liberated from chance, free of intervention from the other, characterized by the absolute stasis of identity that guarantees the higher reality of a god. In this, as I tried to suggest earlier, he is simply manifesting the pattern of subject formation that language-produced subjects are condemned to, given the nature of the linguistic sign. What is particular about the way Gatsby goes about this task is determined by American history, not only in the apparent features of frontier, dreams of success, and technical innovation, but by the very *temporality* that governs all its major moves, which is recognizably a New World variant of Neoplatonism.

If dialogism is correct about the nature of stereotyping, then the mode of its activity must be understood as being Neoplatonic. A major reason why *The Great Gatsby* is so paradigmatic a text for any attempt to understand the relation of perception and subject formation to history is that it works out not only the surface features of stereotyping as they are particularized in a specific history, but also the more basic level of temporality. Gatsby is someone who is seeking to erect his own selfhood, an identity that is whole, immaculate, and lasting; from a Bakhtinian point of view, he, like everyone else, must consummate the fluidity of his self in the more stable contours of the other. Gatsby is an extreme case of this general pattern, because what he seeks in particular is a biography that will be free of changes, thus a *narrative without time*. This is, like the sign or the stereotype, an absurd condition, one that is literally oxymoronic, which is why, at the level of text, the oxymoron dominates *The Great Gatsby*.

The chronotope of American Neoplatonism

The Americanness of Gatsby's dilemma is caught in the general term for what he seeks to become: a self-made man. Thus, like Henry Ford, he must believe that "history is bunk." America is the sort of place where you can get a "jazz history of the world" with no discrepancy felt between the improvisatory nature of jazz and the linear nature of history – the irony being compounded by the composer's name – "Tostoff." The chronotope of "self-made" men is one that must be split-level: it requires change, and radical change, very *rapid* change, to move from the contingent space of rags into which such men are thrust by the accident of birth to the absolute space of riches that they *intend* to inhabit, and which must be free of contingency and change. Thus they *need* time at one stage, and must *deny* it at another stage. This double bind determines the dual asymmetry organizing the narrative shape of biographies appropriate to self-made men. In order to emphasize the American peculiarities of such a life narrative, I will quickly pass over the parallels between such a temporal asymmetry in the lives of a Horatio Alger, Henry Ford, or Thomas Edison and the very similar temporal asymmetry in the lives of Christian saints who, like St Augustine, are born again in conversion experiences.

In light of this, it should come as no surprise that Gatsby has great trouble with time, especially time as it relates to Daisy, the icon of his individual appropriation of the American dream. As he is about to meet her for the first time after his return from the army and her marriage, he becomes anxious, and says to Nick, who is hosting the meeting, "It's too late!" But Nick points out that it is in fact early for the meeting: "It's just two minutes to four." He is out of sync with the time of his dream, a point reinforced when he almost knocks over the clock on Nick's mantelpiece. Even at this first meeting, there are hints of a rupture between Gatsby's stereotype of Daisy, and Daisy's capacity to be adequate to the stereotype, a problem expressed in temporal terms: "He had been full of the idea so long, dreamed it right through to the end, waited with his teeth set, so to speak, at an inconceivable pitch of intensity. Now, in the reaction, he was running down like an overwound clock."[18]

Gatsby has trouble with clocks because of his need to deny time. When Nick tells him "you cannot repeat the past," Gatsby, as a good American Neoplatonist, is outraged: "'Can't repeat the past?' he cried incredulously. 'Of course you can!'"[19] Of course, as someone who gave birth to himself in the past, he must take such a position. It is the American version of stereotyping that is captured as well in the careers of other self-made men, such as the brewer who originally built the great mansion Gatsby has bought. It is a monument to the proposition that you *can* repeat the past, at least architecturally: it "was a colossal affair by any standard – it was a factual imitation of some Hotel de Ville in Normandy." But it is an eclectic repetition of the past: it has "Marie Antoinette music rooms and Restoration salons," and its books are kept in "the Merton college Library," a locution that the text gives in quotation marks, as it does Gatsby's name. But such radical attempts to repeat the past, to make time stop, have consequences for the future. The brewer who built Gatsby's house had wanted to imitate the past so badly that he had "agreed to pay five years' taxes on all the neighboring cottages if the owners would have their roofs thatched with straw."[20] But men who spring from themselves, who resist continuity, pay the price in their own genealogies: the brewer goes into decline and "his children sold the house with the black wreath still on the door." Stereotyping history, relating to the past as if it could be packaged and bought, and then rearranged not in time but in the fixed space of "period rooms," has the effect of catapulting Americans back into flux and change so rapid that "historical" houses are sold "with the black wreath on the door." The symbol of ultimate stasis, death, is transformed by such haste into a sign of change and movement: new owners come, as Gatsby does, to repeat the dream of fashioning history with a fixed identity, only to fall back into a transience beyond the power of human categories to arrest.

The house in which Gatsby's corpse lies at the end of the novel is his true home in so far as it is an architectural monument to the architectonics of his place in existence, the place at which he has been addressed by the conflicting but equally binding mandates of language: on the one hand, a demand for global fixity; and on the other, a requirement that local meanings should not be identical. The oxymoron that fuels all the others in Fitzgerald's novel is this double bind inherent in language itself: the simultaneous but opposed requirements for stasis (enabling a general structure that can be shared) and change (enabling the possibility of unique meanings in particular utterances). In Fitzgerald's version of the American dream, this linguistic double bind has been figured in its temporal dimension. The novel embodies a *difference* that is at the same time recognizable as "the same" as the conflict between global patterns of history and the local demands of biography. It is the situation in which American history has been stereotyped into biographically localized versions of the American dream: a situation in which history's ability to mean is produced in the particularity of individual lives, but a situation as well in which biographically unique selves must constantly confront the otherness of a generalized history. No one has put it better than Fitzgerald in the great last lines of the novel, where what we have been calling otherness is nominated as "the past"

> Gatsby believed in the green light, the orgiastic future that year by year recedes before us. It eluded us then, but that's no matter – tomorrow we will run faster, stretch out our arms farther. . . . And one fine morning – And so we beat on, boats against the current, borne back ceaselessly into the past.[21]

Instead of an envoi

The elegiac quality of *The Great Gatsby* derives from its meditation on the darker implications of being situated in time. On the one hand, Jay Gatz seeks to make himself up; all his work, from the rules he sets out for himself as a child to his last quixotic sacrifice, is directed toward the future Gatsby whose name shall indeed be great. He is the poet of openness, the future, the green light. On the other hand, his most profound profession of faith is that the past can "of course" be repeated; he is a prophet of stasis. It is this dilemma at the heart of the book that makes it a useful exemplar of the novel as a genre and of dialogism as a way of conceiving the world. Jay Gatz lives toward the future of a "new" persona that is constructed from shards of an all-too-familiar past that constantly erupts into the situatedness of his present. And the novel, when it does the work of novelness, is energized by forces set in motion by the give-and-take between stasis and change, the fixity of language vs. the flux of utterance, all of which animate the dialogue between self and other.

The darker vision of the dialogue we get in *Gatsby* may serve as well to remind us that the emphasis on an "orgiastic future" which has been so much a feature of Bakhtin's reception in the west, is only part of the story. Much as the more disturbing aspects of Freud were converted into the optimistic philosophy of "ego psychology" in the United States, so Bakhtin's clear-eyed insistence on the more disturbing implications of being *fated* to the condition of dialogue have frequently been ignored in the service of establishing a mindless pluralism or a toothless "carnivalism."

If there were only one message in this book (recognizing that it is in the nature of its subject that so monoglot a message is quite impossible), I would hope that it would be simply this: dialogism is dialogic. This apparent tautology has many implications, but none more important than this: dialogue always implies the simultaneous existence of manifold possibilities, a smaller number of values, and the need for choice. At all the possible levels of conflict between stasis and change, there is always a situated subject whose specific place is defined precisely by its in-between-ness. To be responsible for the site we occupy in the space of nature and the time of history is a mandate we cannot avoid – in the ongoing and open event of existence we have no alibi.

The version of futurity and openness that we get in *The Great Gatsby* has a dark, elegiac resonance. It is therefore not an inappropriate way to close a book about dialogism. The reception of Bakhtin in the west (including my own complicity in that reception) has tended to emphasize the joyful, hopeful, and open features of dialogism. These are undoubtedly to be found in Bakhtin's work, as we have seen. However, as the carnivalization of Bakhtin's concept of carnival has made all too evident, such an emphasis has obscured other and arguably more important aspects of dialogism.

Notes

1 Bakhtin's life

1   For a fuller account of Bakhtin's life, see: Katerina Clark and Michael Holquist, *Mikhail Bakhtin* (Cambridge, MA: Harvard University Press, 1984).

2   See Katerina Clark and Michael Holquist, "The influence of Kant in the early work of M. M. Bakhtin," in Joseph P. Strelka (ed.) *Literary Theory and Criticism* (Festschrift for René Wellek) (Bern: Peter Lang, 1984), pp. 299–313.

3   Paul Natorp and Ernst Cassirer are the other leading members of the school, although it could be argued that Cassirer's work after the 1920s sets him apart in significant ways from basic "Marburgian" tenets. But he never abandoned the Marburgian concern for squaring metaphysics with the latest work being done in the precise sciences of physics and mathematics.

4   В. И. Ленин, "Материализм и эмпириокритицизм," in *Полное собрание сочинений*, (Москва: Наука, 1947), том 18, pp. 326–7 (V.I. Lenin, "Materialism and Empirio-criticism" (Moscow: Progress Publishers, 1964), pp. 264–6).

5   Cf. his *Logik der reinen Erkenntnis* (Berlin, 1902).

6   The dates given in this chapter are of first publication in Russian. Full details of these and of English translations are given in the Select bibliography.

7   For the latest, but predictably not the last, exchange of opinions on this topic, see the round table forum in *Slavic and East European Journal* 30 (1) (spring, 1986): 81–102.

2 Existence as dialogue

1 М. М. Бахтин, "Проблема текста в лингвистике, филологии, и других гуманитарных науках. Опыт философского анализа," *Естетика словесного творчества* (Москва: Искусство, 1979), p. 281. Cited in the text as *Estetika*.
2 Émile Benveniste, *Problems in General Linguistics*, trans. Mary Elizabeth Meek (Coral Gables: University of Miami Press, 1971), p. 219.
3 Sergi Karcevskij, "The asymmetric dualism of the linguistic sign," in Peter Steiner (ed.) *The Prague School: Selected Writings 1929–1946* (Austin: The University of Texas Press, 1982), p. 50.
4 ibid., p. 51.
5 ibid., p. 50.
6 M. M. Bakhtin, *Speech Genres and Other Late Essays*, ed. Caryl Emerson and Michael Holquist, trans. Vern McGee (Austin: University of Texas Press, 1986).
7 For a fascinating account of self-authorship by a contemporary philosopher of cognitive science, see Daniel C. Dennet, "Self-invention," *The Times Literary Supplement*, September 16–22, 1988, pp. 1016, 1028–9.
8 This formulation is frequently encountered in Bakhtin's early writings, but for a particularly interesting connection of how the lack of an alibi relates to authorship, see *Estetika*, p.179.
9 See Ernst Robert Curtius, "The book as symbol," *European Literature and the Latin Middle Ages*, trans. Willard R. Trask (Princeton, NJ: Princeton University Press, 1953).
10 Henri Bergson, *Matter and Memory*, trans. Nancy Margaret Paul and W. Scott Palmer (London: George Allen & Unwin, 1911), p. 5.
11 Ferdinand de Saussure, *Course in General Linguistics*, trans. Wade Baskin (New York: McGraw-Hill, 1966), p. 120.
12 ibid., p. 111.
13 ibid., p. 117.
14 The term is especially important in Kant's third critique (of judgment), which of all his works was the one that most preoccupied Bakhtin.

3 Language as dialogue

1 Ferdinand de Saussure, *Course in General Linguistics*, trans. Wade Baskin (New York: McGraw-Hill, 1966), p. 81.
2 ibid., p. 81.
3 ibid., p. 9.
4 ibid.
5 Roman Jakobson, "Retrospect," *Selected Writings* (The Hague: Mouton, 1971), vol. II, p. 721.
6 Sergei Karcevskij, "The Asymmetric dualism of the linguistic sign,"

184   Dialogism

in Peter Steiner (ed.) *The Prague School: Selected Writings, 1929–1946*, (Austin: University of Texas Press, 1982), p. 49.

7 V. N. Voloshinov, *Marxism and the Philosophy of Language*, trans. Ladislaw Matejka and I. R. Titunik (Cambridge, MA: Harvard University Press).

8 Charles Sanders Peirce, *Collected Papers* (Cambridge, MA: Harvard University Press, 1931–58), vol. IV, p. 127.

9 V. N. Voloshinov, *Freudianism: A Marxist Critique*, trans. I. R. Titunik (New York: Academic Press, 1976).

10 Sigmund Freud, *Group Psychology and the Analysis of the Ego*, trans. James Strachey (New York: Bantam Books, 1960), p. 52.

11 ibid., p. 61.

12 Another important figure in this movement was the sociologist Charles Horton Cooley (1864–1929), author of *Human Nature and the Social Order* (1902).

13 George Herbert Mead, "Social psychology as counterpart to physiological psychology," in Andrew J. Reck (ed.) *Selected Writings* (Chicago: University of Chicago Press, 1964), p. 103.

14 ibid., pp. 101–2; italics added.

15 George Herbert Mead, "The objective reality of perspectives," in Reck, *Selected Writings*, pp. 312–14.

16 Largely because he was still conceiving language as defined in the pre-Saussurian terms used by W. Wundt in his *Völkerpsychologie*, 2 vols (Leipzig, 1904).

17 Roman Jakobson, "Two aspects of language and two types of aphasic disturbances," in Roman Jakobson and Morris Halle, *Fundamentals of Language* (The Hague: Mouton, 1956), p. 74.

18 Лев Якубинский, "О диалогической речи," *Русская речь* (Петроград, 1923), I, p. 132.

19 ibid., p. 139.

20 Largely, I suspect, because he had a rather limited conception of how the formal elements of language related to the process of communication; it was Yakubinsky, after all, who had in 1916 formulated the Formalist doctrine that there is a distinction between practical and literary language on the basis that the former communicates information while the latter does not.

21 Jan Mukarovsky, "Monologue and dialogue," in John Burbank and Peter Steiner (eds and trans.) *The Word in Verbal Art* (New Haven: Yale University Press, 1977), p. 85.

22 ibid, p. 102.

23 ibid.

24 V. N. Voloshinov, "Discourse in life and discourse in art (concerning sociological poetics)," in *Freudianism: A Marxist Critique*, pp. 93–116.

25 Cf. footnote 1, Chapter 2.

Notes 185

4 Novelness as dialogue: The novel of education and the education of the novel

1 Specifically included in the following discussion are Bakhtin's books on Dostoevsky (1929, 1963), Goethe (fragment dating from 1939–41), Rabelais (1965), and general novel theory (1975). Quotations are taken from the following editions: *Problems of Dostoevsky's Poetics*, ed and trans. Caryl Emerson (Minneapolis: University of Minnesota Press, 1984); *Rabelais and his World*, trans. Hélène Iswolsky (Bloomington: Indiana University Press, 1984); "Discourse in the novel," in *The Dialogic Imagination*, ed Michael Holquist, trans. Caryl Emerson and Michael Holquist (Austin: University of Texas Press, 1981); "Epic and Novel," in *The Dialogic Imagination*; *Marxism and the Philosophy of Language*, trans. Ladislaw Matejka and I. R. Titunik (Cambridge, MA: Harvard University Press, 1986); "Author and hero in aesthetic activity," *Art and Answerability: Early Philosophical Works by M. M. Bakhtin*, ed. Michael Holquist and Vadim Liapanov, trans. Vadim Liapunov (Austin: University of Texas Press, 1990).

2 Georg Lukács, *The Theory of the Novel*, trans. Anna Bostock (Cambridge, MA: MIT Press, 1971), p. 41.

3 ibid., p. 80.

4 ibid., p. 80.

5 M. M. Bakhtin, "From the prehistory of novelistic discourse," in *The Dialogic Imagination*, p. 68.

6 Jean Piaget, *The Language and Thought of the Child* (London: Routledge & Kegan Paul, 1959).

7 Howard Gardner, *The Quest for Mind* (New York: Alfred A. Knopf, 1973), p. 94.

8 See Lev Semyonovich Vygotsky, *Thought and Language*, ed and trans. Eugenia Hanfmann and Gertrude Vakar (Cambridge, MA: MIT Press, 1962), especially chapter 6, "The development of scientific concepts in childhood." This is only a partial version of Vygotsky's treatise that might more correctly be translated as "Thinking and speech" (*Myshlenie i rech*). A new translation including all the material excluded in the first version is about to be published. In the meantime, several books by James Wertsch, or edited by him, should be consulted. See especially *Culture, Communication, and Cognition: Vygotskian Perspectives* (Cambridge: Cambridge University Press, 1985); and *Vygotsky and the Social Formation of the Mind* (Cambridge, MA: Harvard University Press, 1985). Michael Cole has been of the greatest importance in introducing the ideas of Vygotsky and his brilliant co-worker and disciple Luria to western scholars. See especially *Mind in Society: The Development of Higher*

Psychological Processes (Cambridge, MA: Harvard University Press, 1978), which he and others edited; Peg Griffin and Michael Cole, "Current activity for the future: the zo-ped," in *Children's Learning in the "Zone of Proximal Development,"*, New Directions for Child Development, no. 23 (San Francisco: Jossey-Bass, 1984), pp. 45–64.

9   Л. С. Выготский, *Избранные психологические исследования* (Москва: Издательство Академии Педагогических Наук, 1956), p. 87. Vygotsky knew the work of Pierre Janet, in which inner speech (and consequently the priority of social, over individual factors of development) plays an important role. See Alex Kozulin, "The concept of activity in Soviet psychology," *American Psychologist* 41 (3) (March, 1986): 264–74.

10   Vygotsky, *Thought and Language*, p. 20. It should be added in all candor that Vygotsky himself did not perceive what he was doing as anti-Hegelian; the use of his ideas to oppose dialectic is very much an interpretation.

11   For a thoughtful presentation of the views of both Bakhtin and Vygotsky on the subject of inner speech, see Caryl Emerson, "The outer word and inner speech: Bakhtin, Vygotsky and the internalization of language," *Critical Inquiry* 10 (2) (December 1983): 245–64. For more detail on the Vygotsky side, see Wertsch, *Vygotsky and the Social Formation of Mind*, especially pp. 224–9.

12   See, for instance, Aidan Macfarlane, *The Psychology of Childbirth* (Cambridge, MA: Harvard University Press, 1977).

13   See his "Introduction," in Catherine Snow and Charles Ferguson (eds) *Talking to Children: Language Input and Acquisition* (Cambridge: Cambridge University Press, 1977).

14   Jerome Bruner, *Actual Minds, Possible Worlds* (Cambridge, MA: Harvard University Press, 1986), p. 77.

15   The obvious parallel with Bakhtin's concept of the other's "surplus of seeing" should not be overlooked here.

16   Iu. M. Lotman, "Reduction and unfolding of sign systems," in Henryk Baran (ed.) *Semiotics and Structuralism: Texts from the Soviet Union* (White Plains, NY: International Arts and Sciences Press, Inc., 1976), p. 302.

17   Both phrases are taken from Bruner, *Actual Minds, Possible Worlds*, pp. 75–6.

18   Vygotsky, *Mind in Society*, pp. 86, 88, 89.

19   Boris Gasparov, "Introduction," in Alexander D. Nakhimovsky and Alice Stone Nakhimovsky (eds) *The Semiotics of Russian Cultural History* (Syracuse: Cornell University Press, 1985), p. 15.

20   ibid., p.15.

21   Wilhelm Windelband, *Logic*, trans. B. E. Meyer (London:

Macmillan, 1913); Wilhelm Dilthey, *Meaning in History: Dilthey's Thought on History and Society*, trans. and ed. H. P. Rickmann (New York: Basic Books, 1962); Emile Durkheim, *The Rules of Sociological Method*, trans. S. A. Solovay and J. H. Mueller (Chicago: University of Chicago Press, 1938).

22 Durkheim, *The Rules of Sociological Method*, p. 103.
23 And his co-author, Janet Woollacott. See their *Bond and Beyond: The Political Career of a Popular Hero* (London: Macmillan, 1987), pp. 45–6.
24 Mary Shelley, *Frankenstein or the Modern Prometheus* (New York: New American Library Signet Classic Edition, 1965), p. 210.
25 ibid., p. 139.
26 ibid., p. 53.
27 ibid., p. 51.
28 ibid., p. 51.
29 ibid., pp. 115–16.
30 ibid., pp. 56, 57.
31 ibid., pp. 140–1.
32 ibid., p. 160.
33 ibid., p. 38.
34 ibid., p. 160.
35 ibid., p. 195.
36 ibid., pp. 140–1.
37 ibid., p. 123.
38 ibid., p. 124.
39 ibid., p. 188.
40 ibid., p. 56.
41 ibid., pp. 98–9.
42 ibid., p. 209.
43 Cited in Arthur Quinn, *Figures of Speech* (Salt Lake City, Utah: Gibbs M. Smith, 1982), p. 93.
44 Ovid, *Metamorphoses*, trans. Frank Justus Miller (Cambridge, MA: Harvard University Pres, 1977), vol. 1, p. 291.
45 Shelley, *Frankenstein*, p. 158.
46 Jorge Luis Borges, "Tlön, Uqbar, Orbis Tertius," in *Ficciones*, trans. Anthony Kerrigan (New York: Grove Books, 1962), p. 17.
47 Shelley, *Frankenstein*, p. 39.
48 ibid, p. 51.
49 ibid, p. 40.
50 ibid, p. 41.
51 ibid, p. 211.
52 ibid.

5   The dialogue of history and poetics

1   "Forms of time and of the chronotope in the novel," in *The Dialogic Imagination*, ed Michael Holquist, trans. Caryl Emerson and Michael Holquist (Austin: University of Texas Press, 1981); cited in the text as "The chronotope."

2   "Искусство и ответственность," *Естетика словесного творчества.* (Москва: Искусство, 1979); cited in the text as *Estetika*.

3   Виктор Шкловский, *О теории прозы* (Москва, 1929), p. 204.

4   ibid., p. 186.

5   Umberto Eco, "The myth of superman," *The Role of the Reader: Explorations in the Semiotics of Texts* (Bloomington: Indiana University Press, 1979), pp. 111, 114.

6   Bakhtin himself identifies Isocrates' encomium of Socrates as the "first biography of ancient times" (*The Dialogic Imagination*, p. 131), but the features he adduces in making such a claim are equally, or even more, present in Xenophon's *Agesilaius*.

7   Nikolai Gogol, *Diary of a Madman and Other Stories*, trans. Ronald Wilks (Harmondsworth: Penguin Books, 1972).

8   M. M. Bakhtin, *Problems of Dostoevsky's Poetics*, ed. and trans. Caryl Emerson (Minneapolis: University of Minnesota Press, 1984).

9   Cf. Peter Steiner's chapter on the organic metaphor as it was used by Zhirmunsky, Skaftymov, and Propp in *Formalism: A Metapoetics* (Ithaca: Cornell University Press, 1984), pp. 68–98.

10   See, for instance, Hendrik Birus' scathing review of a German anthology containing excerpts from Bakhtin's Rabelais book in *Germanistik* 15, especially p. 300.

11   Stephen Jay Gould, "The problem of perfection, or how can a fish mount a clam on its rear end?", in *Ever Since Darwin: Reflections on Natural History*, (Harmondsworth: Penguin Books, 1980), p. 104.

12   ibid., p. 107.

13   ibid., p. 108.

14   ibid.

15   This extract from "The overcoat" is this author's translation of "Шинель," in *Сочинения в двух томах*, ред. Г. Колосова: Художественная Литература, 1968), том 1, p. 537. Another translation can be found in Gogol, *Diary of a Madman and Other Stories*, pp. 72–3.

16   Gogol, *Diary of a Madman*, pp. 33–4.

17   See Ernst Kantorowicz, *The King's Two Bodies: A study in medieval political theology* (Princeton: Princeton University Press, 1957).

18   Gogol, *Diary of a Madman*, p. 41.

19   Edward Sapir, "The status of linguistics as a science," in *Language*, vol. 5 (1929), p. 209.

20   *Marxism and the Philosophy of Language*, trans. Ladislaw Matejka and I. R. Titunik (Cambridge, MA: Harvard University Press, 1986).

6 Authoring as dialogue

1 Mikhail Bakhtin, "Forms of time and of the chronotope in the novel," *The Dialogic Imagination: Four Essays by M. M. Bakhtin*, ed. Michael Holquist, trans. Caryl Emerson and Michael Holquist (Austin: University of Texas Press, 1981); hereafter cited in the text as "The chronotope."

2 Michael Ghiselin, "The individual in the Darwinian revolution," *New Literary History* III (1) (Autumn, 1971), pp. 113–34.

3 ibid., p. 118.

4 ibid., p. 119.

5 Karl Marx, *Capital* (Chicago: Charles H. Kerr & Co., 1919), vol. I, p. 85.

6 Avrum Stroll, "Identity," *The Encyclopedia of Philosophy* (New York: Macmillan and Co., 1967), vol. IV, p. 122.

7 *Problems of Dostoevsky's Poetics*, ed. and trans. Caryl Emerson (Minneapolis: University of Minneapolis Press, 1984).

8 See also Katerina Clark and Michael Holquist, *Mikhail Bakhtin* Cambridge, MA: Harvard University Press, 1984), pp. 69–72.

9 See the magisterial survey of new findings on biological clocks in Jeremy Campbell, *Winston Churchill's Afternoon Nap* (New York: Simon & Schuster, 1986).

10 "К философии поступка," *Философия и социология науки и техники* (ежегодник, 1984–1985) (Москва: Наука, 1986).

11 *Marxism and the Philosophy of Language*, trans. Ladislaw Matejka and I. R. Titunik (Cambridge, MA: Harvard University Press, 1986).

12 Sergei Karcevskij, "The asymmetric dualism of the linguistic sign," in Peter Steiner (ed.) *The Prague School: Selected Writings, 1929–1946*, trans. Wendy Steiner (Austin: University of Texas Press, 1982), p. 52.

13 ibid., p. 50.

14 Jacques Lacan, *The Four Fundamental Concepts of Psychoanalysis*, trans. Alan Sheridan (Harmondsworth: Penguin Books, 1979), p. 207.

15 F. Scott Fitgerald, *The Great Gatsby* (New York: Charles Scribner's Sons, 1961), p. 36. (First published 1925.)

16 ibid., p. 67.

17 ibid., p. 148.

18 ibid., p. 96.

19 ibid., p. 111.

20 ibid., p. 89.

21 ibid., p. 228.

Select bibliography

There are now available several bibliographies devoted to Bakhtin scholarship. The most important of these are the lists included in the (unfortunately difficult to obtain) *Bakhtin Newsletter*, two issues of which have appeared. Both were produced by Clive Thomson in the French Studies Department of Queen's University, Kingston, Ontario, Canada, K7L 3N6. The first issue (1983) contains an analytical bibliography of criticism on the Bakhtin circle in languages other than Slavic, as well as a list of translations by the circle; the second issue (1986) is particularly helpful, containing separate lists for all members of the Bakhtin circle, plus critical articles and reviews in Russian and other Slavic languages, plus an update on translations of the circle.

Annotation in the following list has been kept to what I hope is a sensible minimum; if an essay's subject is obvious from its title, I have not added a further note. I have concentrated on works in English, or translations into English; items in other languages have been included only where they are unusually helpful.

Major works by Bakhtin

The textology of Bakhtin's works is an area of great complexity; listed below are the only the first complete appearances of Bakhtin's texts in print in Russian, followed by their most recent English translations. For a more complete bibliography of Bakhtin's works consult Katerina Clark and Michael Holquist, *Mikhail Bakhtin*, (Cambridge, MA: Harvard University Press, 1984).

1919

"Искусство и ответственность," [Art and answerability] in *День искусства*, Nevel (September 3, 1919), pp. 3–4.
"Art and answerability," in M. M. Bakhtin, *Art and Answerability: Early Philosophical Works by M. M. Bakhtin*, ed. Michael Holquist and Vadim Liapunov, trans. Vadim Liapunov (appendix translated by Kenneth R. Brostrom), (Austin, TX: University of Texas Press, 1990).

c.1920–1924

"Автор и герой в естетической деятельности" [Author and hero in aesthetic activity]. *Естетика словесного творчества*. ред-ы, С. Г. Бочаров, А. А. Аверинцев (Москва: Искусство, 1979), pp. 7–180. (Cited in the text as *Estetika*.)
"Author and hero in aesthetic activity," in M. M. Bakhtin, *Art and Answerability: Early Philosophical Works by M. M. Bakhtin*, ed. Michael Holquist and Vadim Liapunov, trans. Vadim Liapunov (appendix translated by Kenneth R. Brostrom), (Austin, TX: University of Texas Press,1990). (Another fragment of this work, probably from an earlier portion of the MS., was published (under the subtitle "Автор и герой в естетической деятельности") in *Философия и социология науки и техники: ежегодник 1984/1985* (Москва: Наука, 1986), pp. 138–60. This fragment is included as part of "Author and hero in aesthetic activity," in M. M. Bakhtin, *Art and Answerability: Early Philosophical Works*.)
"К философии поступка   [Toward a philosophy of the deed]. *Философия и социология науки и техники: ежегодник 1984/1985* (Москва: Наука, 1986), pp. 80–138.
    A translation of this work will appear in the fourth volume of the University of Texas Press series of Bakhtin translations.

1924

"Проблема содержания, материала, и формы в словесном художественном творчестве" (The problem of content, material, and form in verbal art), *Вопросы литературы и естетики*, ред-ы, С. Г. Бочаров (Москва: Художественная литература, 1975).
"The problem of content, material, and form in verbal art," trans. Kenneth R. Brostrom in M. M. Bakhtin, *Art and Answer- ability: Early Philosophical Works by M. M. Bakhtin*, ed. Michael Holquist and Vadim Liapunov (Austin, TX: University of Texas Press, 1990).

1929

Проблемы творчества Достоевского. [Problems in the work of Dostoevsky]. (Ленинград: Прибой).

This is the first version of Bakhtin's Dostoevsky book, only portions of which are available in English in Caryl Emerson's translation of the second edition.

1934–1935

"Слово в романе," [Discourse in the novel], *Вопросы литературы и естетики* (Москва: Художественная литература, 1975), pp. 72–233.

"Discourse in the Novel," in *The Dialogic Imagination: Four Essays by M. M. Bakhtin*, ed. Michael Holquist, trans. Caryl Emerson and Michael Holquist (Austin, TX: University of Texas Press, 1981).

1937–1938

"Формы времени и хронотопа в романе" [Forms of time and of the chronotope in the novel], in *Вопросы литературы и естетики*, pp. 234–407.

"Forms of time and of the chronotope in the novel," in *The Dialogic Imagination: Four Essays by M. M. Bakhtin*, ed. Michael Holquist, trans. Caryl Emerson and Michael Holquist (Austin, TX: University of Texas Press, 1981).

1940

"Из предистории романного слова," [From the prehistory of novelistic discourse], in *Вопросы литературы и естетики*, pp. 408–46.

"From the prehistory of novelistic discourse," in *The Dialogic Imagination: Four Essays by M. M. Bakhtin*, ed. Michael Holquist, trans. Caryl Emerson and Michael Holquist (Austin, TX: University of Texas Press, 1981).

1941

"Епос и роман (к методологии исследования романа) [Epic and novel (toward a methodology for the study of the novel)], in *Вопросы литературы и естетики*, pp. 447–83.

"Epic and novel: toward a methodology for the study of the novel," in *The Dialogic Imagination: Four Essays by M. M. Bakhtin*, ed. Michael Holquist, trans. Caryl Emerson and Michael Holquist (Austin, TX: University of Texas Press, 1981).

1952–1953

"Проблема речевых жанров" [The problem of speech genres], in *Естетика словесного творчества*, pp. 237–80.
"The problem of speech genres," in *Speech Genres and Other Late Essays*, ed. Caryl Emerson and Michael Holquist, trans. Vern McGee, (Austin, TX: University of Texas Press, 1986), pp. 60–102.

1963

Проблемы поетики Достоевского [Problems of Dostoevsky's poetics] (Москва: Советский писатель).
Problems of Dostoevsky's Poetics, ed. and trans. Caryl Emerson (Minneapolis: University of Minneapolis Press, 1984).

1965

Творчество Франсуа Рабле и народная культура средневековья [The work of François Rabelais and popular culture of the Middle Ages] (Москва: Художественная литература).
Rabelais and his World, trans. Hélène Iswolsky (Bloomington: Midland Books (Indiana University Press), 1984).

1975

Вопросы литературы и естетики. See under "1924" for details.)

1979

Естетика словесного творчества. (See under "c.1920–1924" for details.)

1986

Литературно-критические статьи [Articles in literary criticism], ред-ы, С. Г. Бочаров, В. В. Кожинов (Москва: Художественная литература).

II. Select works published under the names of others, but attributed by some to Bakhtin

For a complete list of disputed works, see Clark and Holquist, *Mikhail Bakhtin*. There is much disagreement about whether certain works published by the Bakhtin circle of the 1920s were written by the men under whose names they appeared in print, or whether they were written by Bakhtin. An extensive literature has developed on this topic, which is still highly fraught. For statements on various positions, see *Disputed texts* below.

by I. I. Kanaev

"Современный витализм" [Contemporary vitalism], *Человек и природа* 1(1926): 33–42; 2: 9–23.

by P. N. Medvedev

1925
"Формальный (морфологический) метод, или ученый сальеризм" [The formal (morphological) method, or scholarly Salieri-ism], *Звезда* 3: 264–76.
"The formal (morphological) method or scholarly Salieri-ism," trans. Ann Shukman, in *Bakhtin School Papers* (*Russian Poetics in Translation*, vol. 10), pp. 51–66.

1928
Формальный метод в литературоведении: критическое введение в социологическую поэтику [The formal method in literary study: a critical introduction to sociological poetics] (Ленинград: Прибой).
The Formal Method in Literary Scholarship: A Critical Introduction to Sociological Poetics, trans. Albert J. Wehrle (Cambridge, MA: Harvard University Press, 1985).

by V. N. Voloshinov

1926
"Слово в жизни и слово в искусстве" [Discourse in life and in art], *Звезда* 6: 244–67.
"Discourse in life and discourse in poetry," trans. John Richmond, in *Bakhtin School Papers*, pp. 5–30.

1927
Фрейдизм: критический очерк. [Freudianism: a critical sketch] (Москва–Ленинград: Госиздат).
Freudianism: A Marxist Critique, trans. I. R. Titunik (New York: Academic Press, 1976) and *Freudianism: A Critical Sketch*, trans. I. R. Titunik (Bloomington: Indiana University Press, 1987).

1928
"Новейшие течения лингвистической мысли на западе" [The latest trends in linguistic thought in the west], *Литература и марксизм* 5: 115–49.

"The latest trends in linguistic thought in the west," trans. Noel Cowen, in *Bakhtin School Papers* (*Russian Poetics in Translation*, vol. 10).

1929
Марксизм и философия языка [Marxism and the philosophy of language] (Ленинград: Прибой).
Marxism and the Philosophy of Language, trans. Ladislaw Matejka and I. R. Titunik (Cambridge, MA: Harvard University Press, 1986).

III. Select list of books about Bakhtin

Bakhtin is one of the three names most mentioned in manuscripts submitted to *PMLA*, one indication of how frequently he is now cited. A full bibliography would be a small book in its own right. What follows is only a a careful selection of a small fraction of works available.

Bibliographies

Two issues of a *Bakhtin Newsletter* with extensive bibliographies have been published in 1983 and 1986 by Clive Thomson of Queen's University in Canada. A special issue of *The University of Ottawa Quarterly* (53(1) January–March, 1983) edited by Clive Thomson also contains lists of works in English, Russian, and French by and about Bakhtin. The *International MLA Bibliography*, published annually by the Modern Language Association of America, is an invaluable resource.

Books or special editions of journals devoted to Bakhtin

Belleau, André (ed.), "Bakhtine mode d'emploi," *Études françaises* 20 (1) (printemps, 1984).
Berrong, Richard, *Rabelais and Bakhtin: Popular Culture in "Gargantua" and "Pantagruel"* (Lincoln: University of Nebraska Press, 1986).
Clark, Katerina, and Holquist, Michael, *Mikhail Bakhtin* (Cambridge, MA: Harvard University Press, 1984).
Corona, Franco (ed.), *Bachtin, Teorico del Dialogo* (Milan: Franco Angeli Libri, 1986).
Lachmann, Renate (ed.), *Diologizität* (Munich: Wilhelm Fink Verlag, 1982).
Morson, Gary Saul (ed.), *Bakhtin, Essays and Dialogues on His Work* (Chicago: University of Chicago Press, 1986).
——, "Bakhtin forum," *Critical Inquiry* 10 (2) (December, 1983).
Morson, Gary Saul, and Emerson, Caryl (eds), *Rethinking Bakhtin: Extensions and Challenges* (Evanston: Northwestern University Press, 1989).

This anthology, with several interesting essays and a polemical introduction by its editors (two of Bakhtin's ablest interpreters) appeared just as this book was going to press.

Bialostosky, Don H., Duifhuyzen, Bernard, Pearce, Richard, Spilka, Mark, and Torgovnick, Marianna. "Still towards a humanist poetics? A largely positive panel," *Novel* 18 (3) Spring, 1985: 199–226.

Perlina, Nina, *Varieties of Poetic Utterance: Quotation in The Brothers Karamazov*. (Lanham, MD: University Press of America, 1985).

Ponzio, Augusto, *Michail Bachtin: alle origini della semiotica sovietica* (Bari: Dedalo Libri, 1980).

——, *Segni e contraddizioni: fra Marx e Bachtin* (Verona: Bertani Editore, 1981).

Thomson, Clive (ed.), "Bakhtin special issue," *Studies in 20th Century Literature* 9 (1) (Fall, 1984).

——, Bakhtin Forum, *The University of Ottawa Quarterly*, 53 (1) (January–March, 1983).

Todorov, Tzvetan, *Mikhail Bakhtin: The Dialogical Principle*, trans. Wlad Godzich (Minneapolis: University of Minnesota Press, 1984).

IV. Articles on particular topics

Carnival

Berrong, Richard, "The presence and exclusion of popular culture in *Pantagruel* and *Gargantua*, or, Bakhtin's *Rabelais* revisited," *Etudes Rabelaisiennes* 18 (1985): 19–56.

Hall, Jonathon. "Falstaff, Sancho Panza, and Azdak: Carnival and history," *Comparative Criticism. A Yearbook* 7 (1985): 127–45.

Herman-Sekulic, Maja, "Towards a New Understanding of Parody," *European Studies Journal*. 2 (2) (1985): 7–13.

Howells, R. J., "'Cette boucherie héroïque': *Candide* as carnival," *Modern Language Review* 80 (2) (April, 1985): 293–303.

Wilson, Robert R., "Play, transgression and carnival: Bakhtin and Derrida on *scriptor ludens*," *Mosaic* 19 (1) (Winter, 1986): 73–89.

Novel theory

Jefferson, Ann, "Realism reconsidered: Bakhtin's dialogism and the 'will to reference'," *Australian Journal of French Studies* 23 (2) May–August, 1986: 169–84.

Jha, Prabhakara, "Lukács, Bakhtin and the sociology of the novel," *Diogenes* 129 Spring 1985: 63–90.

Kristeva, Julia, "Word, dialogue, and novel," in *Desire in Language: A Semiotic Approach to Literature and Art*, trans. Leon S. Roudiez, (New York: Columbia University Press, 1980).

——, "The ruin of a poetics," in Stephen Bann, and John Bowlt, (eds), *Russian Formalism* (Edinburgh: Scottish University Press, 1973).

Malcuzynski, M.-Pierette. "Polyphony, polydetermination, and narratological alienation since 1960," in Anna Balakian, *et al.* (eds), *Proceedings of the Xth Congress of the International Comparative Literature Association* (New York: Garland, 1985).

Patterson, David, "Mikhail Bakhtin and the dialogical discussion of the novel," *Journal of Aesthetics and Art Criticism* 44 (2) (Winter, 1985): 131–8.

Segre, Cesare and Morse, Elise, trans. "What Bakhtin left unsaid: The case of the medieval romance," in Kevin Brownlee and Marina Scordilis Brownlee (eds), *Romance: Generic Transformation from Chrétien de Troyes to Cervantes* (Hanover: University Presses of New England, 1985).

Dostoevsky (polyphony)

Emerson, Caryl, "The Tolstoy connection in Bakhtin," *PMLA* 100 (1) January, 1985: 68–80.

Wellek, René, "Bakhtin's view of Dostoevsky: 'Polyphony' and 'Carnivalesque'," in Robert Louis Jackson, and Stephen Rudy (eds), *Russian Formalism: A Retrospective Glance* (New Haven: Yale Center for International and Area Studies, 1985).

Language

Danow, David K., "M. M. Bakhtin's concept of the word," *American Journal of Semiotics* 3 (1) (1984): 79–97.

Emerson, Caryl, "The outer word and inner speech: Bakhtin, Vygotsky, and the internalization of language," in Gary Saul Morson, (ed.), *Bakhtin, Essays and Dialogues on His Work* (Chicago: University of Chicago Press, 1986).

Holquist, Michael. "The politics of representation," in Stephen J. Greenblatt (ed.), *Allegory and Representation* (Selected Papers from the English Institute, 1979–80) (Baltimore: The Johns Hopkins University Press, 1981).

——, "Answering as authoring: Mikhail Bakhtin's trans-linguistics," *Critical Inquiry*, 10 (2) (December): 307–20.

McHale, Brian, "Free indirect discourse: A survey of recent accounts," *PTL: A Journal for Descriptive Poetics and Theory of Literature* 3 (1978): 249–87.

Schuster, Charles I., "Mikhail Bakhtin as rhetorical theorist," *College English* 47 (6), October: 594–607.

Stewart, Susan, "Shouts on the street: Mikhail Bakhtin's anti-linguistics," in Gary Saul Morson (ed.), *Bakhtin, Essays and Dialogues on His Work* (Chicago: University of Chicago Press, 1986).

Todorov, Tzvetan, "Dialogisme et schizophrénie," in Benjamin A. Stolz, I. R. Titunik, and Lubomir Dolozel, (eds), *Language and Literary Theory* (Ann Arbor: University of Michigan Press, 1984).

Worldview, self/other

Averintsev, Sergei, untitled article, *Soviet Literature*. I (1977): 145–51. An important statement by a leading Russian philosopher who was close to Bakhtin, and has helped to edit some of his more important texts. A clear statement of the anti-dialectical, Aristotelian strain in dialogism.

Clark, Katerina, and Holquist, Michael, "The influence of Kant in the early work of M. M. Bakhtin," in Joseph P. Strelka (ed.) *Literary Theory and Criticism (Festschrift* for René Wellek) (Bern: Peter Lang, 1984).

DeJean, Joan, "Bakhtin and/in history," in Benjamin A. Stolz, I. R. Titunik, and Lubomir Dolozel, (eds), *Language and Literary Theory* (Ann Arbor: University of Michigan Press, 1984).

Geppert, Hans Vilmar, "Peirce und Bakhtin: Zur Ästetik der Prosa," *Semiosis* 11 (2) (1986): 23–45.

Holquist, Michael, "Inner speech as social rhetoric," *Dieciocho* 10 (1) (Spring, 1987): 41–52.

Hirschkop, Ken, "The domestication of M. M. Bakhtin," *Essays in Poetics: The Journal of the British Neo-Formalist School* 11 (1) April, 1986: 76–87.

Ivanov, Viacheslav Vs., "The significance of M. M. Bakhtin's ideas on sign, utterance and dialogue for modern semiotics," *Soviet Studies in Literature* (Spring–Summer, 1975): 186–243

Ponzio, Augusto, "Altérité et écriture d'après Bakhtine," *Littérature* 57 February, 1985: 119–27.

Todorov, Tzvetan. "Vers une tradition dialogique: Entretien avec Tzvetan Todorov," *Esprit* 7–8 (July–August, 1984) 99–103.

Zepp, Evelyn H., "Self and other: Identity as dialogical confrontation in Camus' *La Chute*," *Perspectives on Contemporary Literature* 12 (1986): 51–6.

Feminism

Berrong, Richard M., "Finding antifeminism in Rabelais, or, a response to Wayne Booth's call for an ethical criticism," *Critical Inquiry*, 11 (4) (June, 1985): 687–701.

Select bibliography 199

Freccero, Carla, "Damning haughty dame: Panurge and the Haulte Dame de Paris," *Journal of Medieval and Renaissance Studies* 15 (1) (Spring, 1985): 57–67.

Disputed texts

Bennett-Matteo, Susan, "Bakhtin: The disputed texts," 124–9 in R. Kirk Belknap and Dilworth B. Parkinson, (eds), *Deseret Language and Linguistic Society: Selected Papers from the Proceedings* (Provo: Brigham Young University, 1986).

Clark, Katerina, and Holquist, Michael, "A continuing dialogue," *Slavic and East European Journal* 30 (1) (Spring, 1986): pp. 96–102.

Morson, G. S. and Emerson, Caryl, "Introduction," *Rethinking Bakhtin: Extensions and Challenges* (Evanston: Northwestern University Press, 1969). (This is an important text that became available to the author only when this book was in press.)

Perlina, Nina, "Bakhtin-Medvedev-Voloshinov: An apple of discourse," *The University of Ottawa Quarterly* 53 (1) January-March: 33–50.

——, "Funny things are happening on the way to the Bakhtin Forum," *Kennan Institute Occasional Papers* 231 (1989).

Dialogism as a method in literary interpretation

Bennett, Tony, "Bakhtin's historical poetics," in *Formalism and Marxism* (London: Methuen, 1978).

Bialostosky, Don H., "Dialogics as an art of discourse in literary criticism," *PMLA* 101 (5) (October, 1986): 788–97.

Donoghue, Denis, "Reading Bakhtin" *Raritan* 5 (2) (Fall 1985): 107–19.

Hansen-Löve, Aage A., *Der Russische Formalismus: Methodologische Rekonstruktion seiner Entwicklung aus dem Prinzip der Verfremdung* (Vienna: Verlag der Österreichischen Akadamie der Wissenschaften, 1978).

Hirschkop, Ken and Shepard, David (eds) *Bakhtin and Cultural Theory* (Manchester: University of Manchester Press, 1989). (This is an important text that became available to the author only when this book was in press.)

Smith, John H., "Dialogic midwifery in Kleist's *Marquise von O* and the hermeneutics of telling the untold in Kant and Plato," *PMLA* 100 (2) (March, 1985): 203–19.

Liao, Ping Hui, "Intersection and juxtaposition of wor(l)ds," *Tamkang Review: A Quarterly of Comparative Studies Between Chinese and Foreign Literatures* 14 (1–4) (Autumn–Summer, 1983–4): 395–415.

Pechey, Graham, "Bakhtin, Marxism, and post-structuralism," in Francis Barker, *et al.* (eds.), *Literature, Politics, and Theory: Papers from the Essex Conference, 1976–1984* (London, Methuen, 1986).
——, "On the borders of Bakhtin: Dialogization, decolonization," *Oxford Literary Review* 9 (1–2) (1987): 59–84.
Thomson, Clive, "Bakhtinian methodologies," *Semiotic Inquiry/Recherches Sémiotiques*, 4 (3) September–December, 1984: 372–87.

Index